MONSIGNOR WILLIAM BARRY MEMORIAL LIBRARY
BARRY UNIVERSITY
E181.S55 S5
Smith, Cornelius Cole, 19   010101 000
Don't settle for second : life

0 2210 0109945 8

D0992020

E
181   210860
.S55
S5

Msgr. Wm. Barry Memorial Library
Barry University
Miami, FL 33161

SMITH

DON'T SETTLE FOR...

Don't Settle for Second

Second Lieutenant Cornelius C. Smith, Fort Wingate, New Mexico, February 1893. (Photo from personal files)

CORNELIUS C. SMITH, JR.

Don't Settle for Second

Life and Times of Cornelius C. Smith

with
ILLUSTRATIONS BY THE AUTHOR

PRESIDIO PRESS
SAN RAFAEL · CALIFORNIA

Barry University Library
Miami, FL 33161

DON'T SETTLE FOR SECOND

by Cornelius C. Smith, Jr.

Copyright © 1977

PRESIDIO PRESS
1114 Irwin Street
San Rafael, California

Library of Congress Number 76-52040

ISBN 0-89141-007-4

Printed in the United States of America

E
181
.S55
S5

210860

FOR MY MOTHER

The perfect wife for a soldier.

Foreword

Anytime someone attempts to write about his own family, the old accusation of being "biased" toward the subject is raised against the author. Yet, it is oftentimes this very bias which lends a certain air of authority to the biography. For, who is better equipped than a son to describe what his father really was? Cornelius Smith has given us a rare insight into the life and times of a professional soldier who truly believed in the motto "Duty, Honor, Country." Having been born in Tucson, Arizona, and having spent a large part of his military career in my home state, the senior Colonel Smith's career spanned a significant period of Arizona's history. From the raw frontier of territorial days to the coming of statehood, Arizona was greatly influenced by the military and men such as Colonel Smith. Because the military was such a small group, however, Colonel Smith was destined to lead an active career in many parts of the globe including the Far East and Latin America as well as in the United States.

Having begun my own military career at Fort Huachuca as a young Second Lieutenant in the old 25th Infantry Regiment, I experienced a certain amount of nostalgia as I read about the days of the 10th Cavalry at that historic post. For those of us lucky enough to remember the old Horse Cavalry, it was sights and sounds which never fade from our memories.

For those who missed these things, I heartily recommend this book for the glimpse it gives of an era which can never return. Although this book is ostensibly a biography by a son of his soldier-father, nonetheless, it adds to our knowledge and understanding of the historic events which helped to shape our nation's destiny.

Barry Goldwater
Washington, D.C.

Preface

How does one approach the task of writing about one's father? If the parent was a despot, the prose is bound to bristle with indignation, even hatred. If, on the other hand, the sire was respected and just, his son's story may be overprotective, even fatuous. Regardless of that pitfall, I feel that the subject is worthy of praise. To equivocate with prim denials of the man would be to treat him unfairly. Whatever I relate about my father will be misconstrued by some. Recognition of this fact gives me sufficient latitude to write his story exactly as I see it—no more, no less.

The following story is that of an unusual human being. Cornelius Cole Smith could normally be found wherever there was action; not on the fringes, but in the thick of things, exerting himself fully to do the right as he saw it. He was spirited, enthusiastic and motivated by the old-time virtues of honor, self-reliance and love of country. A born leader and pure soldier, he volunteered for the difficult and dangerous assignments. He was a firm disciplinarian, expecting his men to behave according to a strict interpretation of the Army Code. Although he served well in his diplomatic posts, he was by nature forthright, and always employed candor in lieu of subterfuge and diplomatic jargon. Double-talk was not his idiom. Often he spoke when silence might have served him better. Moral issues were clear cut; there was no middle ground.

In addition to his soldierly approach to life, Cornelius Smith often displayed other sides of his robust personality. He was full of good humor and consideration for others, never turning away those in need or dealing peremptorily with those of lower station.

Scrupulously honest in his dealings with people, he was forever puzzled by those who shortchanged or hoodwinked him. I have seen him reprimand a butcher for giving short-weight on the scale and berate a garage mechanic who padded a bill. At the time, these confrontations were terribly embarrassing to me and to other members of the family. Now, with the passing of years, I can appreciate the motivation behind his behavior. Childlike in money matters, he often said too much and offered too much and, as a consequence, paid too much. He never accumulated money because money was not his god. In our house there never seemed to be enough money to stretch from one payday to the next but, somehow, there was.

Although Cornelius C. Smith had little formal education, he was a scholarly man, reading avidly on a variety of subjects. Among these were history, government, philosophy, religion, literature, poetry and music. He spoke several languages, and some rather esoteric ones at that: Navajo, Apache, Papago, Visayan, Maguindano, Tagalog and one or two other Filipino dialects. He also wrote scores of articles for historical journals spanning the country. In particular, he could not abide the contemporary school of writers which took every opportunity to censure the army. He "answered" all such experts with acerbic and pithy letters to "put the record straight."

In sum, my father lived a full, rich and rewarding life, serving his country well and providing a good and happy home for his family. What more could any man ask?

A word is needed here concerning footnotes, or the lack of them. Originally, each chapter contained some twenty or thirty notes. This scholastic exercise certainly tended to prove statements, but it also impeded reading by directing almost as much attention to notes as to text. Since the bulk of source material comes from the subject's personal dairies, observations and field reports, it was decided to eliminate notes in the interest of narrative flow. A list of these sources appears in the bibliography.

Acknowledgments

First among those who have made this study possible is the subject, Cornelius Cole Smith. A notable army officer skilled in his craft, he was also a first-class administrator and chronicler of events. His files burgeoned with documents of all kinds: official reports, diaries, letters, telegrams and a number of handwritten, unpublished manuscripts bearing upon his long career. As expected, the gaps within these voluminous papers needed augmentation from other sources but my father's writings are the chief source from which his story is told. For these files and for passing on to me an avid enthusiasm for the army and its role in national affairs, a grateful son acknowledges a historian's appreciation.

I am also indebted to other members of my family. My mother recounted her happy reminiscences of the Philippines, Naco, Hauchuca, and other way stations along the army line. My brothers, Gilbert and Graham, served as "walking encyclopedias" of army lore, with built-in computers for names, places and dates. Marge Smith, my sister-in-law, supplied several important documents and a fine selection of old photographs. Finally, my nephew, Jay G. Smith, of Seattle, provided some missing data of the 1908-09 era.

Among the many individuals who so generously offered their knowledge and time, several deserve special recognition. Mrs. John Healy provided spirited tales of my father's Fort Huachuca days. Her husband, the late Lt. Col. John Healy, served with my father then and wrote several anecdotes about him in subsequent years. Miss Judith Acre of the *Denver Post* supplied numerous back issues of the paper which pertained to the Southern Colorado Coal Strike of April-May, 1914. The late Orville Cochran, long-time curator of the post museum at Fort Huachuca, Arizona, made significant items available to me.

I am indebted also to several fine libraries for research facilities pertaining to specific information on army units, civil disorders, and general historical background of foreign lands in which my father served. Included in this list are the libraries at the University of Arizona, the Arizona Historical Society, the Gordon Cox Company in Tucson, and the city libraries in Los Angeles and Riverside, California, and Tucson and Nogales, Arizona.

Finally, a special offer of thanks to my wife Grace for typing this manuscript in its final form.

Cornelius C. Smith
Fort Huachuca, Arizona
September 11, 1974

Contents

Illustrations

Chronology

1869	7 April	Born in Tucson, Arizona.
1876	May	Family journeys from Fort Union, New Mexico, to Fort Grant, Arizona.
1889	22 May	Enlists in Montana National Guard.
1890	9 April	Enlists in Regular Army, Missoula, Montana.
1891	1 January	Fights Sioux Indians near White River, South Dakota.
	4 February	Awarded Medal of Honor.
1892	23 November	Commissioned Second Lieutenant.
1895	April-May	Rides 1,000 miles from Fort Wingate, New Mexico, to Fort Sam Houston, Texas.
1896	22 December	Marries Frances Agnes Graham (Fanny) in Fort Leavenworth, Kansas.
1897	1 November	Birth of his son Gilbert Cole at Fort Riley, Kansas.
1899	February	Transferred to Cuba with 2nd Cavalry, variously stationed at Santa Clara, Matanzas, Trinidad and Havana.
	26 December	Promoted to First Lieutenant.
1900	27 September	Birth of his son James Graham in Leavenworth, Kansas.
1901	3 April	Promoted to Captain.
1903	5 September	Sails for Philippines with 14th Cavalry.
1904	May - June	Undertakes jungle expeditions into uncharted country, Mindanao, P.I.
	9 August	Receives orders to take field against Datu Ali.
	September onwards	Conducts raids on Moro villages.
1905	10 February	Provisional Troop deactivated. All units return to home stations.
	October	Datu Ali and his sons tracked down and killed at Malala by Captain Frank McCoy.
	October	Assigned to recruiting duty at Jefferson Barracks, St. Louis, Missouri.
1907	June	Assigned to Presidio, San Francisco.

1908	July-August	Assigned duty as Superintendent of Sequoia and General Grant Parks.
1909	27 February	Frances Graham Smith dies at Letterman Hospital, Presidio, San Francisco.
	June	Resumes Superintendency of Parks.
	September	Detailed as Major of Philippine Scouts with detached duty in Manila.
	30 October	Marries Kathleen Crowley of Lockport, New York, in Old Walled City, Manila.
	November	Takes honeymoon vacation in China, Japan and Philippines.
1910	October	Assumes duties as Governor of District of Lanao, Moro Province of Mindanao.
1912	August	Transferred to 5th U.S. Cavalry, Fort Huachuca, Arizona.
	October	Ordered to duty on Mexican border and meets Colonel Emilio Kosterlitzky, Chief of Sonoran Rurales in Nogales.
1913	13 March	Kosterlitzky defeated by Obregon at Nogales and surrenders 209 officers and men to Captain Cornelius C. Smith at Nogales, Arizona.
	18 July	Birth of his son Cornelius Cole at Fort Huachuca, Arizona.
	December	Leaves Huachuca for Fort Leavenworth, Kansas.
1914	April	Leads the Second Squadron of the 5th U.S. Cavalry Regiment to Southern Colorado Coal Fields, Walsenburg, Colorado, scene of conflict between mine owners and employees.
	September	Assigned to duty with 10th U.S. Cavalry, Fort Huachuca, Arizona.
	November	On duty on Mexican border, Naco, Arizona.
1915	April	Ordered to Bogotá, Colombia, as Military Attaché, U.S. Legation.
1916	April	Ordered to Caracas, Venezuela, as Military Attaché, U.S. Legation.

	1 July	Promoted to Major.
	16 July	Birth of daughter Alice Crowley.
1917	23 June	Promoted to Lieutenant Colonel.
	August	Assigned to temporary duty in Office of the Chief of Staff in Washington, D.C.
	5 August	Promoted to Colonel.
	September	Assumes command of 341st Infantry, Camp Grant, Rockford, Illinois.
1918	April	Assumes command of 314th Cavalry. Selects derelict Camp Owen Beirne as campsite.
	October	Assumes command of 10th U.S. Cavalry, Fort Huachuca, and is post commandant. Recommended for promotion to Brigadier General by General DeRosey C. Cabell.
1919	February	Ordered to recruiting duty in St. Louis, Missouri.
	July	Teaches Military Science and Tactics at University of Arizona, Tucson.
1922	June	Moves family to Durango, Mexico, for Kathleen's recuperation following her tragic accident.
1926	June	Employed by motion picture studios as technical director for military motion pictures in Hollywood, California.
1928	10 July	Assumes position as president of Electoral Board of Granada, Nicaragua.
1932		Engages in sharp literary exchanges with journalists while residing in Riverside, California.
1935	1 July	Suffers a stroke.
1936	10 January	Dies in Riverside, California.

CHAPTER ONE

A Wild Country

WHEN ONE CONSIDERS the life of any man, whether he be tinker, tailor, soldier or sailor, that man's life can be summarized by three short statements: he was born, he lived, and he died. In the specific case of a soldier, the three-sentence summary can be modified to read: he was born, he served, and he died. Each man's life – each soldier's life – is a collage of his personal experiences. Some are quite commonplace, others unusual; a few are truly distinctive. Years after that man has gone to whatever reward awaited him, his experiences are normally forgotten. In rare instances, however, the man recorded what he saw and what he did during his lifetime. Fortunately, one man who rewarded posterity with a mirror of his existence was Cornelius Cole Smith, Colonel, United States Army. Because Smith was an astute observer and an above average diarist, his writings provide a keen insight into military life at the end of the nineteenth century and the beginning of the twentieth. His life, viewed through his own eyes and recorded in his letters and diaries, can be considered typical of the life of any soldier of that period. And like any other soldier or any other man, his life began with his birth . . . .

Early on Tuesday morning, April 7, 1869, a son was born to Gilbert and Lola Smith in the windswept village of Tucson, Arizona Territory. He was named Cornelius Cole Smith after his father's illustrious uncle, Cornelius Cole, a Sacramento lawyer and later United States senator from California. The patrician ring of the youngster's given name quickly resolved into "Corney." Except on formal occasions and in signing documents, Cornelius was seldom used.

Two weeks after his birth the baby accompanied his parents on a brief wagon trip to the San Xavier del Bac Mission. Amid the crude but colorful decorations adorning the walls, he was christened in the presence of several Papago Indians. It happened to be the anniversary of the founding of San Xavier and, although the pertinent church records were destroyed by fire in 1925, family lore maintained that Cornelius Cole Smith was the first Anglo child to be baptized in the Mission. This frontier environment also provided Corney his chief characteristics: resolution, courage and a straightforward manner which frequently proved as much a drawback as an advantage. Such traits, however, were necessary for a young man growing up in the wild, undisciplined Tucson of the eighteen seventies and eighties.

Although destined to be a large and attractive city in the mid-twentieth century, Tucson did not favorably impress its early visitors. In 1868, John C. Cremony, an interpreter for the Bartlett Boundary Commission of 1850, recorded: "Tucson is cursed by the presence of the most infamous scoundrels it is possible to conceive. Innocent and unoffending men were shot down or Bowie-knifed merely for the pleasure of witnessing their death agonies."

The year after Corney's birth, John G. Bourke noted: "Tucson has no streets or pavements, lamps are unheard of, and drainage is not deemed necessary." J. Ross Browne provided a similar scathing assessment: "Tucson is a place for speculators, gamblers, horse thieves, murderers and vagrant politicians. If the world were searched over, there could not be found so degraded a set of villains as form the principal society there . . . . The best view one gets of Tucson is leaving it."

Unfortunately, Corney Smith was in no position to take Browne's advice. His father, Captain Gilbert Smith, served as the

Army's Chief of Commissary of Subsistence for the entire military district. This responsibility led to short tours at the numerous posts in the area: Fort Lowell in Tucson, Fort Union, Fort Grant and others. Some of Corney Smith's fondest memories were of his father's tours at Fort Lowell.

His position as Quartermaster enabled Captain Smith to pass on to his son stories about memorable characters or unusual events. The Captain frequently hired civilian drovers and roustabouts of questionable character simply because he could not afford to be too choosy in selecting employees. Among these was a young man named William Bonney who had worked satisfactorily for several weeks and who seemed an amiable and quiet sort. Smith put him in charge of a team which was cutting logs on Mount Graham for transfer to Fort Grant. One day he loaded up a wagon and drove it off in the direction of Tucson intending to sell logs, team and wagon, and then disappear. Smith, on hearing of Bonney's absence, took out after him with two troopers. Seeing his pursuers from a distance, the young thief abandoned the wagon and rode off on the lead mule. Smith caught him near Tres Alamos, returned him to Fort Grant in manacles and threw him in the guardhouse.

Several nights later Smith was entertaining guests in his quarters when two shots rang out. In moments, the Officer of the Day reported that Bonney had burst out of the guardhouse and disappeared into the night. Sentries saw the escape and fired at the fugitive. Before Sheriff Pat Garrett shot him at Fort Sumner, New Mexico, on the night of July 14, 1881, William Bonney, "Billy the Kid," reportedly killed twenty-one men.

In addition to stories about the notorious figures of the day, Corney gathered a colorful collection of personal vignettes. One of his earliest recollections was a trip taken in 1876. His account written in later years revealed a surprising amount of detail about the journey.

In 1876, when I had just passed my seventh birthday, my father was ordered from Fort Union, New Mexico, to Fort Grant, Arizona. Despite my tender years I remember that overland journey pretty well. There were no railroads in the area then, and so we made the trip by army ambulance, drawn by six strapping mules. In addition, my father brought along a couple of six-mule, jerk-line teams for baggage, mess gear and general camp equipment. Riding along with our plodding train was a small detachment of the Eighth Cavalry. These troops were sent along to protect us from Apaches, whose tribal members had waylaid such caravans for years and had been on the warpath intermittently since the Cochise-Bascom incident of 1861.

At Santa Fe, Captain Lafferty of the Eighth Cavalry put us up for the night. He and my father had known each other in California in the days before the Civil War and were both appointed to the regular army from the famous "California Column." It was here that Father Lamy lived. During my father's tour at Union the Bishop had frequently come to the post to hold mass for Catholics on that station. He was a frequent visitor in our home and upon occasion had held mass right in our house.

On that night we spent at Santa Fe (Fort Marcy) our ambulance driver got himself in trouble. He was a Swede named Leffler and a big man. He went in to Santa Fe to do the town and almost got done in, sustaining a pretty thorough working over by a band of burly ruffians. In the morning he was still groggy as he took his driver's seat and his head was wrapped in bandages. My father observed: "Too much Santa Fe for Leffler."

From Fort Marcy we went on down to Albuquerque, passing Camp Vigilance, but making no stop there. We followed the Rio Grande south on down to Mesilla before heading west. We passed a number of forts en route, among them Craig, McRae, Thorne, Selden and Fillmore. We made short stops at Craig and Fillmore. It had been only fourteen years since the fight at Valverde, and I recall that when we arrived at Craig my father told us about Canby's fight there with Baylor and Sibley, and about the death of Captain George Bascom whose intemperate action at Apache Pass had triggered the Apache Wars. It was Bascom along with Isaiah Moore of the First Dragoons who had strung up six Apaches in retaliation for Anglos and Mexicans killed by Cochise's band. My father had no unkind words for Bascom, even though his actions had been the subject of controversy in both military and civilian circles in Arizona for several years. He was not so generous with Major Lynde, though, who had given up Fillmore to Baylor without a struggle.

From Mesilla we headed west for Fort Cummings and then on to Apache Pass in Arizona. I looked around for the Apaches hung by Bascom and Moore but could find no sign of them. My father had told us of seeing one over on the Gila which had hung on a mesquite tree for several years. It is small wonder I could not see those of the Apache Pass incident; it had been fifteen years. My great-aunt, Mina Sanders Oury, had seen them though, in 1865, just four years after the sorry affair.

It was west of Fort Cummings that we nearly suffered a tragedy. One of our baggage wagons, driven by a greenhorn, went astray. Taking a short cut to catch up with the leading wagons he drove off into waterless country and became thoroughly lost. We were held up for several days while searching parties scoured the countryside for this unfortunate man. I remember that when he was brought in he was crazy looking and raving. He did pull out of it, but it took several days.

We continued on to Tucson without further incident and stayed a few days with my grandparents. Before taking up his duties at Fort Grant, my father had to go to San Francisco to confer with the Commander of the Division of the Pacific, General [John] Schofield. My mother and I went along. Father was taken sick there and had to turn in to the hospital for several weeks. General Schofield thought that a sea-voyage might put father right again. Consequently we sailed away from the Golden Gate down the California Coast and into the Gulf of California. At the mouth of the Colorado we transferred to a smaller vessel and steamed up to Fort Yuma and from there proceeded to Fort Grant by ambulance. Grant was then the headquarters of the Sixth Cavalry, a fine outfit in which I would serve some fourteen years after arriving at Grant on that day in 1876.

That trip took place a long time ago, but in my mind's eye I can still see the rumps of those mules swaying under the traces and hear the groaning of the wheels as we crawled slowly over the grasslands of New Mexico and Arizona. I should add that during our three-year stay in Fort Union my father had a brief tour at Fort Ringgold, Texas, down on the Rio Grande not far from Brownsville. Mother and I did not make the trip.

We were lucky on that wagon trip; we saw not a single Apache although crossing over the very heart of Apache Country. It is probable that our escort made the difference. Three years later my friend Emory Madden was killed by Apaches near Fort Cummings. Emory was the son of Captain Dan Madden of the Sixth Cavalry, stationed at Grant. Returning to the post from his studies in the east he was ambushed just outside Cummings and killed. A part of our trip was made over the famous Jornada del Muerte stretch of desert in New Mexico. I remember the stretch around San Marcial and the lava beds to be particularly arid and forbidding.

From 1876 until 1884 Corney attended the Catholic school in Tucson, with the exception of the year 1880 when his parents sent him to Brewer's Academy in San Mateo, California. In the summer he returned to his father's station but during the school term lived with William and Inez Oury on Calle Real. During these years Corney formed a strong attachment for Tucson. Some years later he affectionately recalled his boyhood when the Tully and Ochoa fuel trains passed through town — wagons drawn by yokes of oxen and driven by Mexican and Negro drovers. "Whenever they used the lash," he wrote, "it sounded like a rifle shot." These memories of the frontier often included more ghastly incidents:

I saw more than one man breathe his last from shoot-outs and free-for-alls. Once, when I was about fourteen, I saw a man come staggering out of a saloon. He was trying desperately to free his pistol from its holster but couldn't do it. A second man ran out after him and the two began trading shots. The first man went down mortally wounded and his assailant went back into the saloon to resume his drinking. I peeked over the shoulders of the crowd and saw the poor man die, right before my eyes.

Though too young to enter the lurid palaces of sin, Corney recalled Charley Brown's Congress Hall, Hand and Foster's Saloon, and the bawdy houses run by "Apache Luisa" and "Big Carmel." A number of these houses of easy virtue stretched along Calle de la India Triste and Gay Alley, a short street running south from Ochoa, one block east of Meyer. A seemingly endless array of miners, cattlemen, soldiers and townspeople milled about these establishments.

In his brief reminiscences, Corney described the town and some of its inhabitants:

> I remember Tucson as a place where it behooved the greenhorn to keep under cover. The streets were dangerous to walk in since firearms were always prevalent and used at the slightest provocation. The cowboy, miner, prospector, gambler, horse thief, soldier, cattle rustler and prostitute mingled with townspeople on the noisy streets, and it seemed to me that there was always talk of some shooting, knifing or hell raising of one kind or another. It was an exciting place to be in, no doubt about it.

Corney also remembered the infamous Clanton boys, Ike and Billy:

> As I recall it, they came to Tucson from the South, Georgia, I think, and settled on the San Pedro in about 1875. Old man Clanton feared nothing; neither did his sons. In 1877 they came to Tucson to attend school. I was younger than they but attended classes with both. This was at the school run by Catholic priests, one of whom, Father Jouvenceau, was a favorite of all of us. It was not until after the opening of the mines in Tombstone that Ike and Billy got into trouble. Billy was killed by Wyatt Earp, his brothers and "Doc" Holliday in the famous shoot-out on Fremont Street on October 26, 1881. I never knew what became of Ike.

His memories of Fort Lowell reflected a happy and idyllic boyhood. Moreover, because of his father's assignment, Corney Smith knew a host of prominent citizens. He wrote of many of his acquaintances:

> As a boy, and later, I knew and remember well the old timers of Tucson and Southern Arizona. These included Governor A.P.K. Safford, Pete Brady, Jimmy Lee and Solomon Warner. I remember too Mr. E.N. Fish, a government contractor

and miller, Sam Drachman, Theodore Welisch and Bill Zeckendorf. Then there was Bob Leatherwood, a peppery Southerner who ran a stable, Bob Paul, Sheriff of Pima County, and Riordan, Soto and Tully — all teachers in the parochial school I attended. In my father's house these men were entertained many, many times: E.A. Carr, Leonard Wood, M.P. Maus, E.C. Hentig, J.B. Kerr, George Crook, Samuel P. Heintzelman, A.V. Kautz and many others.

I remember Teofilo Burruel, a Mexican scout employed by my father at Fort Lowell in 1881. A large man of great courage and physical strength, he had been a captive of the Apaches as a boy. I remember Merijildo Grijalva too. He too had been a captive of the Apaches and because of this was frequently able to beat them at their own game. My father employed him as a scout and said that he could smell an Indian camp over a mile away. Once when they were riding together from Fort Crittenden to Tucson, Grijalva caught the bridle on my father's horse and held him up. Some hundreds of yards away, in an arroyo, a band of Apaches were roasting meat. The two men skirted the camp and went on in safety. When Grijalva escaped from the Apaches who held him he did so by binding sheepskin around his feet, wool-side out, leaving no trail.

Chato was an Apache scout, also employed by my father in the 1880's. An ugly man, he got his name because of his flat nose. He served in Lt. Tony Rucker's company of the 6th Cavalry out of Fort Grant. It was said that Chato brought in his own brother's head to authorities at Grant. The episode became the incentive for a painting by Frederic Remington dramatizing the event. I remember Chato at Grant, along about 1879 or 1880.

I also remember Al Sieber, H.W. Daly and Dan Ming, great scouts all, but perhaps one of the most colorful of the lot was Candido Martinez. He was a scout employed by my father in 1877 at Fort Grant. In those days there were many antelope about the post and Martinez had his own way of hunting them. He fashioned an antelope head of wood covered with antelope hide from which trailed a complete skin, capelike over the body. Thus camouflaged he would get down on hands and knees and cavort about, attracting curious antelope with his peculiar antics. At the proper moment he would whip out his rifle and drop a buck before it could dart away. Once he let me try on his antelope suit.

I also recall "Pata de Oso" ["bear -foot" because a misshapen clubfoot forced him to shuffle along like a bear] clumping along on the streets of Tucson, an eccentric, but a man of intelligence and learning. Also, there was D.W. "Shotgun" Smith, still a celebrity in the eighties as the result of mowing down some half-dozen Apaches with a single blast of his double-barreled "cannon" at Pantano Wash during the Civil War. These are but a few of the names and faces responding to memory's call. All are gone now, over the hills into the blue shadows of eternity.

Although his reminiscences were written many years later, Corney recalled clearly and in vivid detail his youth in adventurous and colorful Tucson. His youthful days in the Territory were nearing an end; he would not return to Arizona until 1912 as a captain with the 5th U.S. Cavalry at Fort Huachuca.

Two Strike's Camp, Pine Ridge Agency, South Dakota, fifteen days before fight with K Troop, 6th U.S. Cavalry. (Photo courtesy National Archives)

CHAPTER TWO

The Corporal Wins a Medal

GILBERT SMITH LEFT ARIZONA in December 1882 for his new station at Vancouver Barracks, Washington Territory, just across the Columbia River from Portland. During brief stops en route, at Fort Yuma and San Diego, Gilbert regaled his son with stories of previous adventures. Corney toured the grim desert prison cut into the riverbanks of the Colorado at Yuma and enjoyed a leisurely look at the fine old Spanish adobes in the Old Town section of San Diego. He admired the clean, washed skies and the emerald green look of the Portland countryside but wrote years later that he preferred the deserts of Arizona.

In 1883 Corney was sent to live with relatives in Louisiana, Missouri, a sleepy, little town on the Mississippi River just above Hannibal. To a boy from the austere, sunbaked deserts of Arizona, the lyrical quality of Louisiana was a distinct change. He fished for catfish in the summer and skated over the thick river ice in winter. To earn his keep, he worked in his great-uncle's grocery store. Though pleasant, in Corney's eyes the small Missouri town was no match for the land of piñon, ocotillo and saguaro.

The Smith family moved again in May 1884, this time to

Baltimore, Maryland. Corney and his brother Gil enrolled in a military school in Washington, D.C. The school's main distinction was its baseball team which fielded four sets of brothers and one odd man. Corney was the squad's third baseman and Gil the center fielder. The youngsters were a tough lot. Once, when playing a game against Harpers Ferry, the catcher forgot to bring along his gear and had to catch the game bare-handed. Why the opposing team was unwilling to lend him a glove, mask, chest protector and shin guards was never made clear. In any case, Washington won and a bruised catcher went home to soak his swollen hands in hot water.

Few records exist to reveal Corney's activities in this period. One exception is his father's booklet entitled "Memos, June-November 1888." On June 27 he wrote: "Letter from Corney today calling for money to go to Harpers Ferry. I sent him five dollars, maybe as a little extra gift since it was my birthday." A July 2 entry reads: "Went down to Washington today arriving on the ten-fifteen, Corney being at depot to meet me. Bought some fireworks for Billy before going home." Two days later he wrote: "Went down to Alexandria today, met Corney and we visited the old church where Washington used to worship. Had the honor of sitting in his pew. Corney sat in that once used by R.E. Lee. After church we went to river to watch a regatta, passing the old slave pens on the way. Saw first boat race but it was not closely enough contested to make it interesting."

On Friday, July 27, Gilbert Smith penned these words: "Took a walk today to the old stone fortifications at Maryland Heights used during the war. Corney found some old bars of lead by the path, probably some of the stuff used by John Brown. Nearby we found great quantities of blackberries which we ate to satiety." After a brief transfer from school in Washington to Baltimore City College, Corney joined the family on the train for Montana.

September of 1888 saw the Smith family at the old mining community of Helena. By then Corney was old enough to strike out on his own and to no one's surprise decided to go into the army. On September 16 he wrote a letter to the Secretary of War requesting an appointment to West Point. Despite his father's fine record, Corney was unsuccessful. On May 22, 1889, he enlisted in the Montana National Guard. Here advancing to the rank of sergeant, he so earned the respect of his superiors that all, including the Territorial Governor, Joseph K. Toole, provided laudatory recommendations for his transfer into the Regular Army. He was discharged from the Guard on April 3, 1890, and enlisted in the 6th U.S. Cavalry six days later.

Gilbert Smith's old friend, Captain John B. Kerr, then commanding K Troop of the 6th at Fort Wingate, New Mexico, had written to the Adjutant General in Washington requesting that Cornelius C. Smith be permitted to enlist at Fort Missoula for immediate transfer to Wingate. "This man is personally known to me," he wrote, "reliable, and would make a very desirable soldier. He is presently a Sergeant in the Montana State Militia at Helena and is desired by me for a noncommissioned officer."

From this beginning, it took more than a simple request to effect a transfer. Two weeks after Kerr's letter, the Adjutant General replied that Smith's enlistment at Missoula was approved, but that "he will be assigned to your troop provided he passes a satisfactory examination. If enlisted, Smith will be sent to Fort Wingate." This official correspondence took a circuitous course, receiving endorsements from Headquarters, Division of the Pacific in San Francisco, and Headquarters, Department of Arizona, then located in Los Angeles, California, before reaching Captain Kerr. Even a New York Congressman, J.B. Hendersen, undertook Corney's cause by writing to Major General Schofield in Washington requesting that the enlistment be expedited. Thereafter, Corney made the short trip from Helena to Missoula and, two days after his twenty-first birthday, was sworn into the U.S. Army on April 9, 1890.

While Corney was serving with the 6th Cavalry at Wingate in the fall of 1890, the Sioux began ghost dancing in Dakota. The great medicine man Sitting Bull foretold an Indian messiah who would soon appear and drive the hated white man from the land. The Indians were assured that bullets fired by the soldiers would harmlessly glance off warrior bodies. Soon his people were dancing day and night exhorting the Great Spirit, finally sinking to the ground exhausted from emotion and physical stress. Excited to a frenzy, all of the Sioux tribes — Mineconjou, Oglala, Brulé, Sans Arc and Hunkpapa — prepared to drive the hated paleface into oblivion.

Because these ghost dances increased tension among settlers, pressure mounted on Congress to authorize a showdown with the Sioux. Early in November 1890 the 6th Cavalry was ordered from its several stations in the Southwest to South Dakota. Corney Smith left Fort Wingate with K Troop of the Regiment for the rendezvous.

All of the Regiment's troops were assembled in Rapid City by late November. The men first drew special clothing for a winter campaign including: warm buffalo skin overcoats, muskrat caps and gauntlets, heavy socks and arctic overshoes. As temperatures on the plains frequently dipped to minus forty degrees or lower, the campaign ahead caused a number of Corney's "bunkies" to suffer severe frostbite. Corney himself had his chin and cheeks frozen — almost destroying the exposed tissue. In later years he recalled the fiery pain of "thawing out" by rubbing great handsful of icy snow on the affected areas. The Sioux referred to the month of December and its bitter cold as the "Moon of the Popping Trees," an apt description.

As troops arrived in Dakota, the Division Commander, Major General Nelson A. Miles, directed elements to strategic points. The 6th Cavalry under Colonel Eugene A. Carr was sent to scout the Belle Fourche and Cheyenne Rivers north of Rapid City. It then doubled back on the South Fork of the Cheyenne and screened the Badlands.

On the afternoon of December 24, while the Regiment scoured the South Fork of the Cheyenne, a courier came into camp reporting that a large band of Indians had left the reservation and was heading for the Badlands. "Boots and Saddles" was sounded immediately and the Regiment moved out at a trot. Corney wrote: "We marched until nightfall, and then, on Christmas Eve, bivouacked in the hills some distance from the river. Though bitterly cold, no fires were allowed."

The fleeing Indian column soon divided, one part under Chief Red Cloud returning to the agency, while another under Two Strike, a Brulé Sioux, went on to Little Grass Creek near its junction with the White River. On the twenty-sixth, K Troop, under Captain Kerr, was detached and ordered back to Rapid City to escort General Miles to the Pine Ridge Agency. Arriving in Rapid City and learning that Miles had gone ahead, Kerr swung the column about to rejoin the Regiment but very nearly failed.

About midnight on December 30, two of Kerr's Indian scouts reported that Two Strike and a band of about 180 warriors were camped nearby and would attack in the morning. Kerr's force numbered forty-seven men and officers. Huddled around a few small fires in a thirty-degree-below-zero temperature, the small force spent an unhappy night.

"Bright and early on New Year's Day," wrote Corney, "we broke camp and started on our march." Kerr's plan was to rejoin Carr's column before Two Strike's force could attack. Actually, Two Strike, splendidly armed, mounted and spoiling for a fight, was between the two cavalry groups. The Sioux planned to hit Kerr, kill his entire command, and make off before Carr could arrive. Corney remembered, "We had gone scarcely a mile from camp when we saw small patrols of hostiles in our front, on our flanks, and in our rear."

Seeing that he was outnumbered almost four to one, Kerr determined to keep moving until he could find ground offering cover and tactical advantage. It was rough going. Fresh snow covered the ground and the horses plodded slowly ahead. Luck was with the Captain for, almost as he despaired of reaching good ground, he came upon a small rise in the angle formed by the junction of Little Grass Creek and White River.

Immediately the Troop dismounted and a ground picket line established for the horses in a coulee near the hill's crest. "The wagons were corralled on the highest ground attainable and preparations made to receive an attack." Bedrolls were taken from the wagons and put into a line some 100 yards long. Each roll was from twelve to eighteen inches high, permitting troopers in prone position to use them for cover. Obscured by the snow, they offered fairly effective concealment. Kerr's report to the Regimental Adjutant described the action:

> The Indians came in from the south, mounted, until about seventy appeared in sight and circled our position. They opened fire on us at a range of about 800 yards. The troop was ordered not to return their fire at such a long range. They soon came within about 200 yards, however, and we began to return their fire.

Next came a diversionary tactic employing two columns of

mounted braves, about twenty-five in each line. The columns zig-zagged between the two partially frozen streams. One column would ride in full tilt from the direction of the river, whooping, yelling and firing. Simultaneously the second column rode in from Grass Creek. Passing, the two lines would then execute the same tactic from the new position. Corney noted in his account:

> They rode fast, letting out shrill war whoops, all to draw our fire and take our attention, while the main body, dismounted, were snaking their way towards our line. The riders were pretty far out but I saw two fall from their horses, which immediately bolted. As we were using the old Springfield carbine these two men must have been badly hurt, as a lead ball from a weapon of this calibre has terrific hitting power.

By noon this tactic ended and the Indian mounts were tethered in a small clump of trees on the south bank of the river. The braves then began inching toward the beleaguered troopers, coming in on hands and knees, bellies, and at a crouch from all sides. Shortly after the fight had begun, at about 8:00 in the morning, Kerr dispatched a scout and one trooper to find Colonel Carr and bring in reinforcements. The fighting had been going on for over four hours but no relief was in sight.

About this time Corney Smith made a move which helped win time for the sorely pressed troopers. He had taken position on the extreme left of the firing line. Just a few yards farther on, to the northeast, a small stream emptied into the river. The stream had bluffs or cutbanks some eight feet high. From his location Corney could see Indians grouping under the bluffs for a surprise flank attack on the thin line of troopers.

Nudging Sergeant Fred Myers and tapping three other men on his immediate right, he apprised them quietly of the situation. The five men snaked their way to the edge of the bluff and jumped headlong on top of six or seven braves. Within moments the air filled with yells and shrieks, flailing arms and legs and swinging gun butts. Several Indians fell under blows from the carbines and others crumpled from well-applied fists and knees. The remainder fled with Corney Smith and Fred Myers after them. Kerr reported in an official letter: "Sergeant Myers and Corporal Smith pursued a detachment of Indians a great distance. They did not rejoin the command until after dark.''

At the height of this wild melee Carr's reinforcements arrived at the very end of the line where the free-for-all continued. The Indians began to retreat across the river to their horses. Pursuit proved impossible because the ice on the river was too thin to support the animals.

After the fight, conjecture began as to what might have happened had not Smith jumped the Indians. An attacking party in force could certainly have turned the line, but not for long. Carr arrived shortly after the fracas began with the equalizer. Of the contending forces Smith wrote:

> It has always been my opinion that had the Indians attacked any time before we reached our defensive position they might have won, and there would have been a repetition of the Custer Massacre on a smaller scale. These Indians were determined fighters and their tactics showed military skills. No doubt many of them had fought Custer and Miles in previous engagements as an interval of only fourteen years had passed between Little Bighorn and Little Grass Creek. I hold this opinion because there were no defensive positions between our camp of the night before and the place selected by Captain Kerr for defense, all of the country up to this point being dead level and thus favorable to the Indians.

By his own count, Two Strike had nine men killed and several wounded. Kerr suffered no casualties.

Meanwhile, the entire command proceeded to Colonel Carr's camp, arriving about dark. Corney Smith and Fred Myers straggled in shortly thereafter weary from several hours' chase after the "ones who got away." In Carr's camp, the command learned of the tragic affair at Wounded Knee.

On the day following the fight at Little Grass Creek, Captain Kerr described the decisive incident stating:

> I wish to mention Sergeant Fred Myers and Corporal C.C. Smith of my troop for distinguished service in action. Corporal Smith with four men drove a detachment of some six or seven Indians away from a prominence within easy range of our line and held the same against repeated efforts of the Indians

to regain it. Myers and Smith pursued a detachment of Indians a great distance. They did not rejoin the command until after dark. I recommend that Medals of Honor for distinguished and conspicuous bravery in action be given these men.

That same day Colonel Carr endorsed Kerr's report. Within forty-eight hours Brigadier General John R. Brooke made a similar endorsement at Headquarters, Department of the Platte; and, nine days later, General Miles added his approval from Headquarters, Division of the Missouri in the field (Pine Ridge Agency).

Kerr forwarded a similar letter to Washington on January 2, dealing solely with Smith's action and carrying a recommendation for the Medal of Honor. It carried endorsements by Carr, Brooke and Miles approving the recommendation. The War Department forwarded certificates to Smith and Myers about one month later. Finally, on December 17, 1891, Corporal Cornelius C. Smith (then the Troop's first sergeant) was officially awarded the nation's most coveted award, the Medal of Honor.

About a year later Corney's Regiment served at old Fort Fetterman in Wyoming. Chief Red Cloud and a band of his people were camped nearby and Corney went out to see him.

> I went over and had a talk with the old chief and asked what he knew about the fight Two Strike had with a troop of cavalry about a year ago. He said that he had tried to get Two Strike to go into the agency and surrender with him, but could not convince him. He also said that he had surrendered some 400 men and that had these gone with Two Strike, the 40 or 50 troopers on the Grass Creek fight would have been killed to a man. Looking back on the affair, I was glad of Red Cloud's persuasive powers with his own men.

The Roman playwright Terence observed "Fortune helps the brave." Although Corney Smith's resolute action at Little Grass Creek helped to turn the tide of battle, it also was a matter of good fortune for him. By fall of the following year he would be a commissioned officer in the U.S. Army.

CHAPTER THREE

Fort Wingate

CORNEY ARDENTLY PURSUED his quest for a commission in the Regular Army. Within weeks after the Little Grass Creek Fight he wrote letters to prominent people and enlisted others to do the same in his behalf. From Helena, Montana, Colonel John R. Miller wrote:

> Smith was a sergeant in my troop in the Montana National Guard for about two years. He won his appointment in a competitive drill at which a regular army officer acted as judge. He is a sober, obedient and intelligent individual. As he has always been a fine soldier, I believe he could prove an excellent officer.

Montana's Governor, Joseph K. Toole, wrote to the Secretary of War: "I am personally acquainted with Smith's family and know that he is a young man of gentle blood and good breeding, whose ambition since a youth has been to 'rise from the ranks.' I believe that he is a natural soldier, worthy of appointment to commissioned status, and who would appreciate honorable recognition."

Perhaps the most telling of all the endorsements was written on May 26, 1891, by two majors, three captains, seven first lieutenants and two second lieutenants:

> We the undersigned officers of the Sixth U.S. Cavalry serving at Fort Niobrara, Nebraska, certify that 1st Sergeant C.C. Smith, 6th Cavalry, has served in garrison and field in the same commands with us, and that he is a man of intelligence, gentlemanly characteristics, proficient in the discharge of his duties and of excellent character. We believe that he possesses the necessary qualifications for a commissioned officer and cheerfully recommend him for an appointment as Second Lieutenant.

Captain Kerr wrote a long letter to the Adjutant General in Smith's behalf on June 2, 1891, recommending "that he be brought before a board as a meritorious noncommissioned officer as early as practicable.... Sergeant Smith is an exceptionally fine soldier. I believe it will be in the interest of the service for him to be advanced now."

If Smith and his commanding officer were eager for the commission, the higher echelon in Washington was not. The letter writing continued for another six months but Smith remained an enlisted man. On December 22 Kerr wrote again, this time outlining Corney Smith's entire service record and the circumstances surrounding his meritorious conduct in the Sioux campaign. Both Colonel Eugene A. Carr, the regimental commander, and Brigadier General John R. Brooke added endorsements without success. Carr reasoned that, "Expense and labor will be saved by making this appointment now, in the evidence of character and ability here presented. I have known this man for twelve years and certify that he is entirely capable. I would be glad to have him in my regiment."

In the months that followed Corney Smith served in the field, in and out of Fort Fetterman, Wyoming, chasing cattle rustlers and other frontier desperadoes. Finally, on April 19, 1892, he was ordered from Fort Niobrara to Fort Omaha on May 2 to be examined by a board of officers for a commission.

He was ready. For months he had been boning up on cavalry tactics, troop administration, logistics and supply matters, U.S. history and the particulars of the U.S. Constitution. In fact,

Captain Kerr, while admiring Corney's tenacity, warned him against studying too long into the night. Corney replied, "I don't feel as though I am doing right by you and my friends unless I do." Of the several departmental candidates taking the exam in Omaha, Corney Smith finished in first place. Then, in the final examination at Fort Leavenworth, Kansas, in competition with scores of candidates from all over the country, he placed fifth. Consequently, he was discharged from the Army some six months later, and commissioned on the following day, November 23, 1892.

Corney's next two and one-half years were spent at Fort Wingate, New Mexico, a post which he dearly loved and where he would serve two separate tours of duty. One month after being commissioned he was reassigned to the 2nd U.S. Cavalry at Wingate. He hated to leave the 6th but would become accustomed to leaving old friends to serve in new commands.

Life at Wingate resembled that of most frontier establishments, with the welcome exceptions of an invigorating climate, beautiful scenery and an engaging social life. The area around Wingate was known by the Navajo as Shash B'toh, "Bear Spring." The tribe had been using Bear Spring and other cold mountain streams as watering places long before the arrival of the Spanish Conquistadores.

The independent and warlike Navajo also contested the intrusion of the white men. "Long Knives," or U.S. Cavalry, reached Santa Fe in 1846 and were soon taking the field against the marauding Navajo who were raiding the surrounding Pueblo tribes. In 1860, Fort Fauntleroy was established at Bear Spring. The garrison relocated the following year to Old Fort Wingate, some sixty miles to the east at San Rafael. From this new location, Kit Carson journeyed in 1863 to round up the Navajo for the infamous "long walk" to imprisonment at Fort Sumner. Decimated by disease, starvation and homesickness, the tribe was permitted to return to its home five years later.

Corney's new post was "new" Fort Wingate, established in 1868 and named for Captain Benjamin Wingate, 10th U.S. Infantry, who had died from wounds received in the battle at Valverde in February 1862. The post resembled the usual frontier-post square, with barracks, officers' quarters, a hospital, guardhouse, storehouse, repair sheds, corrals and stables and the inevitable sutler's store. The daily routine also reflected life on the frontier. First call for reveille sounded at 5:20 A.M. with reveille following in ten minutes. In the winter, troopers formed in the dark, mumbling and cursing, and perhaps wondering why they had not taken up the law in Cincinnati or storekeeping in Atlanta. Breakfast, served at 5:40 A.M., generally consisted of hash or fresh pork or bacon, eggs, pancakes, molasses and coffee.

Drill followed until about 8:30 A.M. when Guard Mount took place. This formation was one of the most important parts of the soldiers' day. Companies formed in front of barracks for inspection. At second call, all details marched to a central point on the parade ground to be inspected by the Post Adjutant. As the band played, the detail marched to the guardhouse to relieve the old sentries. With jingling spurs, nickering horses and pennants snapping in the wind, Guard Mount provided a stirring spectacle. At sunset, retreat was even more impressive as troopers stood at solemn attention as the flag was lowered. Tattoo, or call to quarters, usually sounded at 9:00 P.M., its sweet notes hanging in the clear mountain air, and then taps, a haunting melody played slowly as the bright stars pierced the velvety dark of New Mexican skies.

The soldiers' diet proved simple but adequate. Beef, potatoes, onions and beans were staples. Coffee was always available and generally taken black. Sweets were limited, consisting mainly of stewed apples and prunes, bread puddings, honey, molasses and maple syrup. It was possible, however, to augment the monotony of the army diet. The green mountains around Wingate abounded in game. Frequently Corney led small hunting parties to bring in venison and wild turkeys. The cold streams provided abundant trout. Clumps of wild blackberries, currants and blueberries covered the hills. Food was not a problem. Although recreation was limited for the rank and file, Wingate was a gay place to its officers and their ladies. Post dances were frequent affairs attended not only by military personnel but by civilians from Gallup, Thoreau and sometimes even Santa Fe and Albuquerque. If limited in repertoire, band music at these functions was gay and spirited. Abundant liquor was available, and participants generally enjoyed a high old time.

For enlisted men, social gatherings were ordinarily limited to one another's company, in quarters or in the sutler's store. Boredom and monotony caused overindulgence, rowdy behavior and brawls. After payday the guardhouse was often filled with troopers sleeping off drunks. Enlisted men were by no means the only offenders in this matter — overindulgence and hell raising by officers, although not serious at Wingate, did happen on occasion. On some of the plains posts like Fetterman, Casper, Phil Kearny, Rice, Reno and others, the sheer monotony of army life made officer drunkenness a real problem which some posts countered by forming temperance unions. At Fort Sully, in 1881, the surgeon reported that seventy soldiers had taken a pledge of abstinence and were getting along without spirits entirely.

Theatricals and minstrel shows were occasionally staged by post personnel or professional troupes augmented by the post band, some of whose members were fine musicians. In addition to these entertaining diversions, competitive athletics played an important part in the soldier's life. Almost all were excellent horsemen, and on special days such as the Fourth of July, men competed in gymkhanas or rodeos for prize money from a regimental general fund. Events included bareback riding, bronco busting, bulldogging, calf roping, Roman riding and similar trick handling of mounts. Frequently cowhands from surrounding ranches were invited to compete. In these meets the soldier-riders came off very well indeed.

Lieutenant Corney Smith had a few wrinkles of his own to add to these affairs. On the dusty streets of Tucson, he had learned the trade of the horseman the hard way, taking his knocks as a teenager from the bulls, mustangs and cow ponies of the old pueblo. He could ride a horse bareback at full gallop and crawl under the horse's belly using only the animal's mane as a handhold. Also at full gallop, he could pick up a playing card, vault from side to side, swinging his feet in a high arc above the horse's withers. In the betting he usually "cleaned up." After a while, no one would ride against him for money. Later, at Fort Riley, Kansas, he put on a riding exhibition for Secretary of War Elihu Root, who commented, "Sir, you are the champion rider of the United States Army."

Track-and-field events also enlivened special holidays. These were almost wholly limited to footraces, although jumping events were scheduled from time to time. Corney Smith was a sprinter. Although never clocked in the 100- or 220-yard dashes, he was seldom beaten by soldiers or Indians in the short distances. Indians proved natural gamblers willing to risk anything. Once, some Zunis came up from the reservation and asked to enter the races. The course was marked off on the parade ground and bets taken. A blanket laid by the finish line held money and Zuni jewelry. At the gun, Corney got a late start but finished several yards ahead of his nearest rival.

Neither Corney nor any of the soldiers, however, would face the Indians in long-distance runs. "Nobody can beat them," he said, "they can go all day." Frequently, on scouting trips in the mountains around Wingate and Gallup, he had seen breechclouted Zuni runners jogging along easily and endlessly, disappearing finally over a rise or behind a stand of trees.

In the winter of 1894, Corney played the role of truant officer to some Hopi Indians who refused to send their children to school. Somehow, the Indian agent at Keam's Canyon had offended the elders of the tribe who retaliated by keeping the children home. An innocuous revenge certainly, but one calculated to nettle white authorities. Captain Constant Williams of the 10th U.S. Infantry was ordered from Fort Marcy to Keam's Canyon to look into things.

Passing through Fort Wingate with only an Indian guide for company, Williams called upon the commander, Colonel G.G. Hunt, for a detachment of troops to accompany him to the scene of trouble. Hunt ordered Troops G and H under Lieutenant D.L. Brainard and Captain Frank U. Robinson to accompany Williams. Their mission was to take into custody the ringleaders who, going beyond the truancy stage, had threatened nearby settlers. Corney Smith, nominally in Robinson's Troop, was on detached duty with Williams, commanding a Hotchkiss gun unit of eight men, four each from Troops G and H. Years later in a letter to the *New York Times*, Corney described the affair:

> In due course we arrived at Keam's Canyon near First Mesa, on which was located the villages of Walpi, Hano and Sichomovi. Walpi was the seat of trouble. Captain Robinson camped us at the foot of the mesa in the late afternoon, planning to climb the hill in the morning and make the necessary arrests.
>
> While we were thus encamped hundreds of Indians

appeared on the mesa-rim, howling and cat-calling at us. Captain Robinson then ordered me to select a target about 1,000 yards off and fire several rounds at it. I directed my chief gunner, Sgt. Henry Heuser, to blast a rock some 1,000 yards away. He knocked the top from it with the first round. The jeering Hopis fell silent.

We found a good climbing place on the eastern side of Walpi and went on up. Robinson put me and my gun in the center of his line. When we were within about 200 yards of the cluster of houses comprising Walpi we halted. Robinson told me he would go in with an interpreter and demand surrender. Should he fire a shot, both troops would advance immediately, and I would direct gunfire point-blank into the houses.

Nothing happened. So stunning was the effect of our Hotchkiss in the demonstration with it that no resistance of any kind was made. Robinson came out with 21 men; one had gone over the steep sides of the precipice and escaped. The 21 men were taken to Fort Wingate where they were clapped into the guardhouse. Several days later they were sent to prison on Alcatraz Island in San Francisco Bay and imprisoned for some months. Ultimately, they were returned to Walpi.

In the spring of 1895, Corney Smith made his "long ride," from Fort Wingate to Fort Sam Houston, Texas. The ride resulted from a conversation in the officers' mess at Wingate when Corney boasted that he could ride his horse, Blue, to Fort Sam Houston in thirty days, "easy." Several officers wagered he could not. Corney had several reasons for accepting the bet. First, he had a good horse. Second, his father was stationed at Fort Sam Houston as Chief Quartermaster of the Department of Texas, and, finally, his sister Inez was to be married on the post within several weeks and had written to invite him to the wedding.

Corney had purchased Blue from Lieutenant Bruce Wallace of the 2nd Cavalry. Wallace had used the animal to run down Eskebenedel, the "Apache Kid," in Arizona and was convinced of its general fitness and stamina. Corney agreed:

Blue was not of proud lineage, just a good-sized horse bred in the Maxwell Ranch in New Mexico. He was a slate roan, known to Mexicans as "grullo," and was full-barreled, deep-chested, with a black stripe on his back and across the withers, and zebralike stripes on his legs from knees and hocks down. He was a gelding about fifteen hands high and weighed 998 pounds on the quartermaster's scale on the morning we left. He was 12 years old, docile, intelligent, and for stamina I never saw his equal, before or after.

Prior to the ride, the animal ate the daily government ration of oats and hay with some bran mash once a week. On the ride, however, Blue would have to shift for himself, subsisting on whatever prairie fodder Corney could find. Since it was spring, very little clothing or bedding was needed. Blue's load was limited to extra underclothes, a few toilet articles, a currycomb and brush. Corney indulged himself by adding a packet of crackers and several cans of sardines. For bedding he carried a saddle blanket and a light raincoat rolled on the cantle of the saddle. A rifle, canteen and rider brought Blue's baggage to about 185 pounds. Of Blue's training, Corney wrote:

> I have always thought myself fortunate to belong to an organization whose Captain believed in making camp early in the day. To do so, he trotted the horses, perhaps three-quarters the length of any march we ever made. This allowed men and horses to rest comfortably in camp, a rest they could not attain by loafing along the road all day. I patterned after this, and indeed did so during my entire career in the cavalry. Of the thousand miles of my ride to Texas, I trotted Blue for about 700 miles. I did not gallop him one step.

Corney's trip was no secret. George R. Mitchell observed in an El Paso newspaper that:

> Army circles everywhere are taking a spirited interest in the movements of Lieutenant Cornelius C. Smith, Second Cavalry, who yesterday started on a long ride from Fort Wingate to Fort Sam Houston. He intends to make the 1,000 miles on a single horse, alone, and will carry neither rations nor forage, depending solely on the country through which he passes. His intended route is wild and barren. Old teamsters who know the country doubt that he will make it.

Corney started early on the morning of April 10, 1895. Jogging leisurely, he soon crossed the Continental Divide and headed for Bluewater where the post trader from Wingate, W.F. McLaughlin, was building a dam for some Mormon settlers. In his overland journey, Corney alternately lived off the land and bought or was given food in towns, settlements or ranches. On this first night "Mac" put him up and saw to Blue's comfort.

The following day, midway between Bluewater and Cubero, a blinding, stinging sandstorm enveloped horse and rider forcing them to take cover for several hours beneath a railroad bridge. That night, Corney slept near a Mexican ranch whose owner sold him some eggs, tasajo (jerked beef), frijoles and tortillas. At Cubero, Corney bought a nose bag and some oats for Blue. The two dined royally.

Corney reached Belen, a small town on the Rio Grande on the sixth day. He rested overnight in the home of a German store-keeper named Becker. They would meet again years later in Springerville, Arizona. By then Corney would be a captain in the 14th Cavalry and Becker a prominent local merchant.

Spring freshets were emptying their waters into the Rio Grande turning the river into a tumultuous cascade of roaring water and tumbling logs and tree branches. Becker mentioned a ford near Casa Blanca but doubted that Corney could cross it. Corney visualized his bet being swept away but rode to Casa Blanca for a look. He found the river just as hazardous but narrower. Fortunately, a Mexican on the western bank had a light skiff. Corney persuaded the man to ferry him across the raging waters for a five dollar bill. Corney stripped down to skivvies for swimming should the frail craft capsize. Blue swam the turbulent waters with only a lariat as a towline. Corney marvelled:

How well the old fellow did it, a truly fine animal. . . . My next objective was the Socorro-Fort Stanton Stage Station, beyond the ABO Mountains and about 83 miles southeast of Belen. Despite our swim, Blue was in good shape, so I decided to make the ride in one day. It was the longest single day's ride on our entire journey. When I arrived at the station and told the old agent about starting out from Casa Blanca that morning he said, "The hell you say!" It was near midnight, but the agent's wife rustled up a great supper of bacon, eggs, hot biscuits, jam and coffee. Outside, the old man was treating Blue like a blue ribbon winner. I figured 83 miles by map, a government geological survey chart; the old man said, "Nope, 95 miles."

The next day I rode into Fort Stanton, a pretty little post garrisoned by one troop of the 1st Cavalry under Captain Peter S. Bomus. . . . His lieutenants were E. S. Wright and "Hoss" Yates, the latter a messmate of mine in the 14th Cavalry a little later on. These officers and the men of the garrison expressed interest in my ride. On the following morning, Yates rode out with me for about fifteen miles until we came to the edge of the Mescalero Reservation. A couple of days later I was in the little burg of Eddy on the Pecos River.

In Eddy I met a man named Tansil who told me he lived year-round in New York City but was spending some time at his ranch. He asked me to take the noon meal with him there on the following day, and I accepted. His ranch turned out to be a model stock farm where he bred fancy stock of all kinds with scientific precision. His hogs were scrubbed and brushed daily with special brushes, and fed with grain and milk from his prize cows.

Mr. Tansil was a wealthy man, having made his money on "Tansil's five-cent cigar," a popular smoke throughout the country and advertised in journals everywhere. After leaving my genial host I crossed the Pecos, here a deep, narrow stream with cut-banks, and headed for Midland. On this portion of the trip, some four days, I saw not a single soul, but did see a lot of stock which came to drink at community windmills along my route.

I made several camps at these reservoirs, always on the inside of the fence so as to be out of the way of cattle coming in at night. Some of these range animals were so dry when they got to the tanks that I could see their flanks swell from the great draughts of water they took in.

While on the plains between the Pecos and Midland I saw some antelope and quite a few rattlesnakes. One morning as I awoke at sunrise, two insolent lobos stood watching me from about one hundred yards out. A pistol shot sent them packing. Another day I saw a lone tree with a hawk's nest in it, so low in the branches that I could look into it by standing on Blue's back behind the saddle. Two hawks sailed around the tree overhead, whistling. I peeked into the nest. There were no eggs or fledglings, only some ten or twelve prairie dog heads.

At San Angelo the mayor took great interest in me and Blue. That night he took me to a dance where I met some good-looking Texas girls. On leaving San Angelo and crossing the Concho River I rode through old Fort Concho. The houses were in good repair and a few were occupied. The post had been established in 1867 by Col. Edward Hatch of the Ninth Cavalry. As I rode through it in 1895 it was abandoned as a military establishment.

Within several days I was at Fort McKavett on the San Saba and from there on in to San Antonio the country was beautiful and interesting. McKavett was established in 1852 and had been on the Overland Mail route between San Antonio and El Paso.

I rode into Fort Sam Houston at about 4 P.M. on May 8th, just twenty-eight days and ten hours out of Wingate. The ride was completed as I dismounted in front of my father's quarters. The ride had been generally pleasant all along the way — little rain, no broiling sun, no encounters with troublesome people, no accidents. Both Blue and I had been on short rations at times, particularly on the stretch between Eddy and Midland, on the "staked plains" (noted for trail markers driven by Spanish explorers), but all things considered we made out quite well. I weighed Blue on the very day I arrived at Fort Sam Houston. He weighed in at exactly 948 pounds, having lost 50 pounds on the trip. I had his shoes removed and turned him into pasture for a rest.

So ended Corney's "long ride." He furloughed in San Antonio for several weeks, saw his sister married, and returned to Wingate by train. From his stall in an animal car, Blue had an easier trip, happily munching on oats as the cars whizzed by the waving prairie grasses.

While serving at Fort Wingate, Corney met some of the interesting personalities of the area. "I knew Don Lorenzo Hubbell well, and more than once was the recipient of his kind and generous hospitality." Hubbell was a famous Indian trader among the Navajo and a prominent and respected citizen of Arizona and New Mexico. "When he died in 1930," wrote Corney, "Indians came into Ganado from all parts of the reservations to mourn their friend and attend his funeral."

Another friend of Corney's in the 1890s was Chee Dodge, a power among his own people as the owner of thousands of head of livestock. As a Navajo tribal judge, his word was far more important than that of the Indian Agent at Fort Defiance. A good and just man, the rancher's decisions were respected by Navajo and Bilikana (white man) alike. Corney wrote of his friend Dodge:

> I remember that he made periodic visits to Wingate to trade and to see our Commanding Officer. He was always superbly mounted, with heavy silver ornaments on his bridle and saddle. He was a picture in his broad-brimmed Stetson, black velvet clothing and his fine top-boots. When I knew him he was in his mid-forties. Had there been motion pictures in those days, Dodge would have been a star. He could ride like Tom Mix, shoot like Buffalo Bill, and he had a physique and noble countenance that no present-day movie favorite could emulate.

Corney also described Manuelito, the great War Chief of the Navajo:

> This grand old man was about 70 when I knew him in 1892. When he was younger he had been herded with hundreds of his people to the Bosque Redondo near Fort Sumner in New Mexico. These unhappy Navajo were kept there from 1864 until 1868, when they were permitted to return to their home grounds in and around the Carrizo Mountains.
> Manuelito in fact profited from the dreadful experience in the Bosque Redondo, bending all of his energies toward a permanent peace with the whites whose numbers made them invincible. He was a silent, reserved man, but in the presence of an attentive audience would speak eloquently of the old days. His declining years were spent on a little ranch on the reservation about midway between Wingate and the San Juan River.

He was frequently used by our troops as a scout or guide. Old as he was, he could stay in the saddle as long as the best of us.

I was with him on a campaign in the Spring of '93 and spent much time listening to his tales of the past. He was especially kind to me because I could speak a little Navajo. He told me that once, many years ago (about 1848), he led a raid into Comanche country in Texas. The Comanches followed Manuelito back into the Carrizos and he then told his warriors: "I do not want one Comanche left in our country. I want them hunted as rabbits are hunted — in every gulch, cave, gully and hollow tree; on every hill, mountain and crag. We got them all — all."

Another acquaintance was "Old Washie," an ancient squaw who had saved Fort Fauntleroy from massacre in 1864. Corney remembered her as a white-haired old woman at Wingate in 1892. She lived by begging but was looked upon as a sort of pet in fond remembrance of her great service to the troopers at Fauntleroy.

Ben Wittick was an ex-soldier who had served at Wingate in the 13th Infantry. When discharged he established a post photo gallery and recorded the people and activities of the era. A "Buffalo Bill-like" character with long, white silken hair, goatee and flashing blue eyes, he was a favorite of all who knew him. A genial companion and avid storyteller, he became one of Corney's favorites. Ben's pictures of Indian life were so outstanding that well-known photographers from New York, Chicago, Denver and San Francisco came to observe his techniques and methods. Years later, Corney noted: "I was thrilled and surprised to see Ben's exhibition of Pueblo Indian life in the National Museum in Tokyo."

Wittick often loaded his photographic gear into a light Studebaker wagon drawn by two mustangs and headed for the remote parts of the reservation. He spoke Navajo, Moqui and Zuni, and was a welcome guest in the hogans and pueblos of these peoples. In August 1903, he was bitten by a rattlesnake and died in the post hospital.

Corney's friends included Miguel Otero and his brother Page. Miguel later became Governor of the Territory; Page was New Mexico's first game warden. He won that post after eloquently arguing his case for conservation in repeated appearances before the Territorial Legislature. It was not easy. Many old trappers and hunters resented him and referred to him as the "fish, coyote and skunk man."

Corney left Wingate in August 1895 to go to the Cavalry School at Fort Leavenworth, Kansas. Some months after his arrival, he met Frances Graham, daughter of a prominent businessman in the community, James Graham. Throughout the winter and spring of 1896, Corney courted Frances, taking her to "hops" on the post and on picnics along the tree-shaded Missouri. In August 1896, the romance was temporarily interrupted when the officer was sent to Fort Riley where he remained until November.

When new orders to report for duty with the Arizona National Guard arrived, however, Corney immediately asked for a leave of absence. On December 22, 1896, Corney and Frances were married at the Episcopal Church in Leavenworth. The longtime bachelor quickly became a devoted husband, and, in time, father. The Smiths were blessed with two sons, Gilbert Cole on November 1, 1897, and James Graham on September 27, 1900. Frontier garrison duty gained a new dimension for the professional soldier.

In April 1901, Corney returned to Fort Wingate and took "Fanny" and the boys with him. During this second tour, Corney left his mark on a rock just north of Prewitt, New Mexico. Incredibly, below the *C. C. Smith, 2d Lieut., 2d Cav'y., 2/23/95,* crossed sabres show blades and scabbards curving in the wrong direction! As Corney was an absolute stickler in such matters, the drawing presumably represents the artistic touch of some later visitor. In another of his numerous patrols in the area, Corney tried to clarify a segment of local history. Near the Pueblo of Zuni, El Morro, or "Inscription Rock," rises from the desert floor like a great battleship. It bears the carved initials or comments of hundreds of passersby over the centuries. The oldest inscription, dated 1606, is barely legible. The oldest one in decipherable condition was left by Don Diego de Vargas in 1692. In 1902, Corney made his own translation: "General Don Diego de Vargas was here, conquering for our holy faith and for the royal crown, all of New Mexico, at his own expense, year of 1692."

In the spring, 1902, Corney stopped at Cooley's Ranch in New Mexico. Cooley was an ex-army officer whose ranch provided a way station for travelers in the area. His guest books were filled with signatures and comments of hundreds of people.

Several months later Corney led Troop G of the 14th Cavalry on a long practice march to Arizona. They spent the first four days traveling to St. John's, an Arizona mountain town of 2,500 people. In his official report to the Post Adjutant, Corney noted that the road between Wingate and St. John's was generally fair for wagon travel but that there were some places where sections of road had to be cut for passage. "At Zuni village," he wrote, "water is poor, grazing bad, and wood must be hauled for about eight miles."

The Troop then went on to Tule Springs, a splendid spring in the middle of a 300-foot crater. Residents of St. John's told the troopers that no bottom had ever been found to this well. On the seventh day, the van arrived in Springerville, a Mormon settlement slightly smaller than St. John's. "Here we were joined by Mr. Hill, Treasurer of Apache County, and Ike Barth. They came to guide us to a good camping place and did — to about as fine a spot as might be found in the White Mountains."

The air was clean and cool and the fishing excellent. Grazing for the horses was plentiful and everything was idyllic until the rains came. From the eighth through the nineteenth it rained day and night, making a soggy mess of camp. The driving rain often turned to sleet or hail, and the nights were bitter cold. "Fortunately," reported Corney, "not a man, horse, mule or pony came down sick, either in this miserable period or at any other time on the march."

On the return trip the Troop came upon Salt Lake, a crater some one thousand yards in diameter. Two volcanic cones rose about 200 feet high on the southern edge of the lake. Both cones had deep pools measuring forty to sixty yards wide. Troopers bathing in the pools found it impossible to sink in the concentrated saline water. Corney indicated that eight or ten Mexican families lived in shacks along the shores of the lake earning a precarious living by selling salt.

Corney noted that although the waters of the big lake and the two craters were on the same level, the crater water was much clearer. "It would seem from this that the small craters are fed by a spring whose waters travel in underground passages to reach the larger body outside." Corney concluded his report stating that the citizens in St. John's and Springerville told him that his troops were the most orderly and well behaved who had ever come into these towns.

Barry University Library

Miami, FL 33161

First Lieutenant Cornelius C. Smith and fellow officers in camp in Tampa prior to embarking for Cuba. (Photo from personal files)

First Lieutenant Cornelius C. Smith, Commanding E Troop, 2nd U.S. Cavalry, Santa Clara, Cuba, 1899. (Photo from personal files)

CHAPTER FOUR

Cuba

SUPPORTED BY CONGRESSIONAL authorization and a jingoistic press, President William McKinley, in April 1898, propelled the United States into a whole new phase of national behavior, waging war with Spain essentially over a Cuban insurrection against Spanish authority. The United States emerged victorious on both land and sea, but the actions in these areas were not comparable. At sea it was a textbook war with overwhelming victories and ridiculously low casualties. On land, however, a mixture of regular units and volunteer conglomerations finally surmounted administrative confusion to defeat a poorly led enemy. Regulars like those in Corney Smith's 2nd Cavalry looked askance at the posturing of the volunteer outfits. Forced to admit that the "Rough Riders" had performed well at San Juan Hill, Corney added: "Just the same, that loudmouthed outfit got too damned much credit!" His plaudits went to the regulars in the 1st Cavalry and the members of the Negro 9th and 10th Regiments which stormed the hill alongside Teddy Roosevelt's volunteers.

Corney's Regiment, although a part of General Joseph Wheeler's Cavalry Division, was not a participant in the two major battles of the war. Corney had accompanied his Regiment to Chickamauga Park, Georgia, then on to Mobile, Alabama, and finally to Tampa. When the battles of El Caney and San Juan Hill were taking place, Corney Smith was flat on his back with malaria in Tampa. His bout with that debilitating disease was so severe that he took sick leave from July to November 1898, and did not arrive in Cuba until February of the following year.

By the time Corney arrived, the fighting in Cuba was over and garrison duty was the order of the day. Training was conducted amid a challenging and interesting landscape. Although he spent most of his time in Santa Clara and Matanzas, on the northern shore, he also held typical field exercises in several parts of the country. With E Troop, 2nd Cavalry, Corney conducted such an exercise in December 1899. His report begins:

> At 8:10 A.M. on December 12th, I left Santa Clara with sixty men and two of the hospital corps, all mounted, taking along ten days' rations and five days' forage for horses, a necessary precaution since much of the country we would negotiate would provide no fodder. The forage was carried by a string of packmules.

Coming to a fork in the road outside Santa Clara, Corney sent a detachment of nine men towards Ranchuelos with orders to rejoin the column at San Juan de las Yeras. Throughout the march Corney dispatched small bodies of seven to ten men to scout alternate trails and to submit written reports.

Arriving at San Juan he found a community of some 1,500 people, mainly tobacco or sugarcane field hands living in thatched huts (Bohios). These farmers obviously had suffered from the effects of war. Most of the draft animals had been appropriated by the Spanish or Cuban guerrillas, leaving families only chickens and hogs. Fluent in Spanish, Corney engaged villagers in conversation and quickly drew a crowd. People willingly posed for pictures. Before long, cane workers, oxcart drivers and naked children were waiting patiently to be photographed.

The column broke camp at 7:00 A.M. on the next day and headed for La Teresa, a small cluster of houses nearly hidden in a vast sea of sugarcane. As on the previous day, Corney split his force sending a detail to Potrerillo and Lomas Grandes, with orders to rejoin the Troop at Ojo de Agua.

The main body proceeded to Camarones on the Caunao River, finding a settlement resembling San Juan with its naked urchins, flea-bitten dogs and scrawny chickens. The scouting party found Lomas Grandes deserted and Potrerillo nothing more than a grouping of six or seven huts and a single store selling candles, staples and a few tinned sardines. The two columns met at Ojo de Agua on schedule and continued on through a vast sea of high grass so thick "we had to cut a path with machetes. This place has about 300 people and is so situated between mountains and sea that it has suffered the ravages of war from both Spaniards and rebels."

On the fourteenth, Corney detached Sergeant Jorriman with seven men to Cuao, San Antonio, and Arimao, with instructions to rejoin the Troop at La Sierra. Corney's group headed for Cumanayagua, a village of about 1,000, a few tiny stores and a military post consisting of a corporal and eight men. Its redeeming feature was its position astride the road between Cienfuegos and Mainicaragua thus facilitating deployment in either town.

Leaving Cumanayagua the Troop proceeded due south, passing the Seibabo River and an abandoned sugar mill at El Negrito. At Ojo Padilla River, the good water and plenty of firewood and fodder made the site so attractive that camp was made early in the day. A man rode ahead to notify Jorriman of the delay. The Sergeant found Cuao to be an attractive hamlet with narrow but clean streets and smiling people. San Antonio, however, was dirty, impoverished and the inhabitants sullen.

The Troop proceeded to the abandoned town of Gabilancito at the junction of the Cienfuegos and Trinidad roads. Here an old Spanish blockhouse of indeterminate age, apparently centuries old, had jungle creepers running over its stones and lizards scampering over the walls. The Troop crossed the San Juan River in midmorning on the sixteenth and made camp at the base of some steep, jungle-covered hills. Lieutenant Smith held a tactical exercise because of the peculiar formation of the terrain: "The defensive value of this place cannot be overestimated, since it is a pass between the sea and all but impassable mountains. A handful of men could hold it against a superior force."

In a "walk-through" exercise, the main body watched from a hilltop rather than take its normal position a mile to the rear. A reserve line of skirmishers was placed in high grass just west of camp. A second reserve unit on its right flank extended the line to the military crest of a hill across the river. A support group was posted in front, about 400 yards east of camp.

Receiving fire from the "enemy" coming in from the west, support-line skirmishers separated, some going to a picket post on a nearby hill to the north, the remainder to another picket post on a similar conical hill to the south. This created a funnel through which any enemy column would have to pass, unless he chose to dissipate his forces in a goatlike scramble up sheer cliffs or go into the sea. A critique analyzed the use of cover and concealment, employment of fire, and general conduct. Thoroughly bushed and caked with sweat, the troopers took a dip in the river before lighting the supper fires.

Later that afternoon, the Troop crossed Bauila swamp, a pestilent place filled with great clouds of mosquitoes. At Yaguanbo River the gorge was so narrow that soldiers had to dismount and lead horses and pack mules through the swift waters. Exhausted, they reached Trinidad at about 4:00 P.M. after crossing the Rio Hondo, Cabagan and Guanayara Rivers.

Corney found Trinidad to be an intriguing place. Established in 1514, the second oldest city in Cuba had a population of about 9,000, clean cobblestone streets, huge shade trees, colorful flowers and interesting old colonial buildings. A seaport, Casilda, was three miles away. The Troop rested except for the more adventurous souls who wandered into town for a fling at the fleshpots.

The column left Trinidad the next day and headed due north for Sabanilla, Magua and Rio Cayahaca where the men built a causeway over the streams as a practical exercise in field engineering. The twenty-five-yard-wide causeway consisted of saplings and grass rope cut and woven for the occasion and filled with rocks. It was demolished the next morning to prevent its forming a dam and changing the river's course. The troopers' reaction to this bit of military "make-work" remains uncertain; certainly they could not have been wildly enthusiastic.

The column moved on over steep and slippery mountain trails towards the Seibabo River. The pack mules were the most sure-footed on the rain-slick paths. Occasionally a horse and its rider floundered, thrashing through the wet undergrowth; but the quiet, steady mules kept up the pace. On the other side of the mountain the Troop made camp at Rio Mabujina.

The column soon came to Mainicaragua, a community of about 800 in a tobacco farming region. Characteristically, the town had a small military guard, in this case a lieutenant and ten ill-equipped and ragged men. Outside the town the cavalry came to the Arimao River, a meandering stream which they had to cross eight times before finally putting it behind them.

The final camp was made at Seibabo River. The Troop made the last leg of the great circle into Santa Clara the following morning. Corney reported that all men, horses and mules finished the exercise in good shape, except one horse which was traded for another mount and some money in Trinidad. Despite the rough country, the Troop blacksmith had to change only twenty horseshoes during the entire exercise. The Troop had travelled 128 miles, averaging about thirteen miles daily through dense jungle growth, steep mountain trails and over many rivers and streams. The training proved useful for within two years, Corney would be in the Philippines with the 14th Cavalry, chasing Moros in the mountains of Luzon, Mindanao and Mindoro.

When not in the field, Corney's life in Santa Clara was idyllic. Fanny and Gilbert were with him, and the couple had made a number of friends. Although Fanny knew very little Spanish, Corney was an able interpreter and they enjoyed the hospitality of Santa Clara's leading families. Different from the spartan quarters of Army posts, these cool, thick-walled old mansions frequently covered an entire city block, their great high-ceilinged rooms and patios filled with fruit trees and cages of singing birds. Furniture was usually ornate and heavy, carved from solid pieces of mahogany, and the chandeliers and crystals were imported from Italy and Spain.

In contrast, however, the exterior was not so luxurious. More often than not the carriage sent to transport them was met at the patron's door by beggars and naked children. Walking in the streets of Santa Clara, Havana, or Cienfuegos, Corney would see the seamier side of Cuban life: desperately poor people living in crowded narrow little alleys, fly-covered market stalls, and hordes of skinny sad-eyed little urchins. In fetid backwaters of the town, dogs competed with pigs for rubbish, and frequently people would drive away the dogs and pigs. Defecation in the streets was not unusual. Corney later saw this terrible disparity between poverty and wealth again and again — in the Philippines, South America, China, Macao. He never ceased to marvel at the complacence of the wealthy and the submission of the poor.

Corney's photographs of Cuba are a small history in themselves: pictures of ox-drawn sugarcane sleds; water vendors; "carteneros" (the ubiquitous breakfast peddlers in all large Cuban towns); rural school children beside their prim, wasp-waisted schoolmarms; and cockfights attended by the usual bunch of loafers and sports seeking easy money. Saddest of all, perhaps, are those showing the funerals of the poor, pitiful processions of six or eight people, and frequently a father carrying a tiny coffin alone, with only the grieving mother behind.

He also took pictures of the stacks of the battleship *Maine*, jutting from the placid waters of Havana Harbor, the transport *McPherson* beached at Matanzas, the U.S.S. *Nashville*, and the steamers *Yucatan* and *Orizaba* riding at anchor at Cienfuegos. Photographs given him included some of Cuba's prominent citizens.

Typical of the sentiments expressed on these photos is a letter written to Corney in April 1899 by the Mayor of Trinidad:

Dear Lieutenant Smith:

I have the honor to convey the regrets of our city council on your completion of duty as Military Commander of this district. In the short while that we have had the pleasure of having you as our commander, we have seen and appreciated your efficient manner of managing difficult duties. This is doubly so because of the uncertain conditions of affairs on this island. We are genuinely sorry to see you go.

Wishing you and yours great future happiness, I remain your obedient servant,

Carlos Yznaga
Mayor

All things considered, it had been a happy two years in Cuba; but it was time to move on once again. On September 24, 1900, the Smith family boarded the passenger ship *Sedgwick* at Havana, and four days later arrived in New York harbor.

CHAPTER FIVE

A Far Corner of the World

CORNEY SMITH'S NEXT STATION, the Philippine Islands, provided him the most hectic and turbulent field service of his entire career. He served three separate tours in the Philippines, a total of nearly six years. His first tour extended from September 1903 until October 1905; the second from October 1906 until June 1907; and the final one from October 1909 until July 1912.

As Corney prepared to depart in the fall of 1903, the Philippines seethed with unrest and rebellion. The United States in 1898 inherited from the Spanish a legacy of implacable hatred between Moslem (Moros) and Christian Filipinos. Islam had come to the islands first and its tenacious followers waged a relentless if intermittent war against the encroaching and Christianizing Spaniards. The establishment of strategic garrisons could not bridge dissimilar dialects or divergent cultures, habits and beliefs. Religious hostility fostered the turbulent conditions following the Spanish-American War.

The Filipinos, understandably vexed at not gaining their freedom after the Spanish defeat, rebelled against their new overlords. The natives, especially the Moslem Moros living in the southern islands of the archipelago, turned to guerrilla warfare and raided small U.S. Army garrisons and villages inhabited by Christian Filipinos who supported American rule.

Initially pacification attempts were made but the Moros proved intransigent. American planners confidently expected that all dissident elements would be brought quickly under control. Unfortunately they misjudged the enemy and the terrain. The ensuing struggle lasted more than a decade; and even then, small pockets of guerrillas held out in the green hell of rain, mud, vegetation and steep mountains.

Corney Smith, however, was not aware of the dangers awaiting him. On September 5, 1903, his Regiment sailed from the Embarcadero in San Francisco amid joyous noise and confusion. The band played regimental airs and patriotic songs while friends, well-wishers and loved ones waved tearful good-byes from shore. The *San Francisco Chronicle* reported that:

> Among the officers and men who sailed on the transport *Logan* for the Philippines on Saturday was Captain Cornelius C. Smith, 14th U.S. Cavalry. Captain Smith is admitted by all experts and officers to be the finest cavalry officer and expert in that branch in the United States Army if not in the world. He is typical Cavalry, lithe, easy of carriage and bronzed by the sun.

The laudatory prose accompanied a drawing of Corney's head and shoulders over crossed sabers and an olive wreath. Looking at it in wonder and some embarrassment he could only say, "Well, I'll be damned!" Aboard ship, the soldiers wondered about their new station. Reaching Manila, Corney wrote:

> About dark on the twenty-fourth day out of San Francisco the big transport dropped anchor in Manila Bay. All was commotion on board since we were in a strange land and were wondering where the several squadrons would be sent.

The men had not long to wait to find out. About ten minutes after anchoring, word circulated that the First Squadron was slated for Camp Vicars, the Second for Camp Overton at Iligan on the Island of Mindanao, and the Third for Jolo on Jolo Island. The squadrons soon embarked on interisland steamers for their new stations. Corney's Second Squadron drew the *Ingalls* but the ship was too small to take all hands. Troops E and F and the regimental band made the first run to Mindanao; G and H, the second. While waiting at Pasay Cavalry Barracks in Manila for the second shuttle to Overton, Corney remarked, "It was great. Fanny and I had a chance to look Manila over, ride along the Lunetta in a carriage, and relax for a few days."

The vacation, however, did not last long as Corney later wrote:

On October 11, the *Ingalls* carried troops G and H to Iligan Bay. We arrived after dark, but our Colonel was there to give us a hearty welcome. I had immediate work to do though; Lt. Ross and D Troop were to return to Manila on the *Ingalls* so the two of us set about inventorying and checking property right away. We worked until almost daylight in a driving rain.

A few days later Colonel T.C. Lebo, the regimental commander, gave the new troop leaders written instructions pertaining to garrison and field duty. According to Corney:

The orders were so liberal that I had practically an independent command. Within a week we had put up in our area a canteen, billiard room, reading room and small gymnasium in addition to renovating barracks, hospital, stables, saddle rooms and offices. It was little enough for the men. The duty was hard, privates drawing guard duty several times weekly and noncoms pulling one night in two.

Saturdays were market days and brought the Moros out of the hills in great numbers. Soon Corney and his men would be taking the trail against these fierce mountaineers but for now both were satisfied simply to "size each other up." Frequently from 300 to 400 Moros would be milling around the market square in Iligan. Corney quickly discovered that Moro customs and appearance were disconcerting for the newly arrived Americans:

Moro cooking is rudimentary, consisting of rice, fish and a sort of sweetmeat made of sugar-cane and coconut meat. They have no bread and seldom eat meat. They do eat carrots or yams on occasion, and bananas are a staple. I do not believe they eat locusts, as does the Christian Filipino. Waste materials from the cooking braziers are thrown beneath the house between cracks in the floorboards. There it putrifies with the filth of the animals penned below. The brass bowls from which Moros eat are discolored with verdigris and I cannot help thinking that the use of these dirty vessels is the cause of the dreadful sores and eruptions which so many Moros have. They eat with their fingers and they seldom wash their hands. Moros are quite fond of the durian, a member of the breadfruit family. The taste of durian is pleasing if one can get by the smell. The odor of the fruit is simply appalling.

Moro men use pincers to pluck out hairs, and only the Datus [tribal chieftains], panditas and Imams have moustache or goatee. They also file their teeth, generally hollowing out the front surface so that teeth are concave in direct opposition to nature. Both men and women are constantly cracking their finger joints to make for supple hands. The men in walking throw their shoulders and swing their arms violently.

It would be hopeless to try to describe the intricacies of Moro thought, manner of dedication or way of arriving at conclusions. Like all semi-savage people the Moro is subject to superstition and fancy. You must not ask a man what his name is; this must be obtained through a third party. The deadliest insult, of course, is to call a Moro "babuy," or pig. They abhor pigs to the point of mania. The Koran teaches that the pig is unclean; in their zeal to follow this holy book they go to spectacular lengths. When our Moro packers found that our supply trains contained tins of bacon they mutinied and left in a body. We kept our bacon, but we had troopers handle the bundles.

The Moros made great sport of killing wild pigs. These drives called "saguiris," were the cause of great celebration and merriment by the entire tribe. A huge V-shaped bamboo enclosure was built, into which the pigs could be funneled by beaters. The wings of the "V" were frequently a thousand or more yards long, with a 500-yard opening on high, flat ground. Experience had shown the Moro that hogs usually made for high grass cover, hence the apex of the fence was so placed as to butt up against a rocky cul-de-sac.

At this open arena bamboo platforms were erected for

the accommodation of women, children and other spectators. The women played on agons and kulingtangs, dressed in their finest and most colorful sarongs. The men and boys would advance in a long skirmish line, carring spears, krisses and kampilans and shouting wildly. Boars and sows run before the line, squealing and dodging, but are caught and cut down in the end. It was not uncommon to round up and slaughter a hundred or more of these poor beasts. In sticking and hacking away at the animals, Moros made ghastly wounds, frequently lopping off a leg or severing an animal cleanly in two. These were not domestic pigs run wild, but the true Malay wild hog with great curving tusks. I attended one saguiri and saw thirty-seven hogs killed in less than half an hour.

Moros are not given much to athletics but are inveterate gamblers. He is fond of "tiangui" or cock-fighting and will bet everything he has on a champion cock. Contrary to Filipino custom, Moros do not fight their birds with steel spurs, preferring the natural claw. Hence his fights are longer than Filipino matches where a deft stroke with the steel spur can decapitate a bird in an instant. Where the Filipino employs a square pit some 25 feet on a side, the Moro uses a circular enclosure four feet in diameter. An excitable people, they create a cacophonous din as they gather in scores about these tiny arenas.

Not unreasonably, Moros do not care for intrusion upon their religious ceremonies. While I have never been molested at a Moro ceremony, I have always felt unwelcome. I would not have attended had official duty or chance not dictated otherwise. Fanaticism is always directly beneath the surface. Once, five officers from my regiment were invited to a Moro wedding. During the ceremony a zealous Moro drew his kris and lunged at the five seated nearby. One drew his pistol and shot the man down only a few feet away. Before he died, the Moro succeeded in wounding one of our men, slashing him viciously on the left forearm.

During Ramadan all mosques are centers for great activity in Mindanao. The chanting goes on throughout the night, and is weird and awe inspiring. It is accompanied with the beating of very large log-drums with carabao-hide heads. Deep and sonorous in tone, the drums can be heard miles away.

Following Mohammedan custom, a deceased person is buried in the vicinity of the house occupied during life. In Moroland you see tiny cemeteries all over the place, an interesting but sombre custom. Moro graves are wider and shallower than Christian graves, and contain a niche on one side where the body is placed lying on its side, facing Mecca.

Planks or poles are fitted over the grave and covered with three or four feet of earth. The earth is held in place by revetments at the sides and ends of the grave. The mound is then decorated with a large Chinese porcelain jar, with streamers and umbrellas mounted on poles. The umbrellas carry white streamers, the Moro color of mourning.

The grave is thus made hollow so that the angels Nakir and Munkir may visit the deceased, the former in the interest of Allah, the latter on behalf of Saitan, the evil one. After a thorough examination of the man's life, the two angels decide which of them shall carry the deceased away.

After the funeral there is a feast which lasts a week or more. Here many panditas and imams gather to pray, invoking the powers of Nakir to spirit the deceased on to Heaven. Participants chant and sway, trance-like, bending over from sitting positions until foreheads touch the floor. Great trays of food are consumed as the drumming and chanting go on and on. . . .

Moros believe that a Mohammedan who has lost a hand, foot or finger will not attain Seventh Heaven. Thus the criminal who is punished by mutilation automatically is barred from that joyous place. Once we wounded a Moro pandita in battle. That was at Taracca in April 1904. The surgeon had to amputate his lacerated foot. When he regained consciousness he berated all within hearing, dramatically thrusting his footless stump upon the ground in bitter frustration. He was subdued and tied down, but his ravings continued. Later, Datu Enoch lost his ear in a knife fight over a woman over in Cotabato Valley. In rude surgery, a Moro grafted the ear back onto the head, but some two inches below its proper place, on the neck just behind the jawbone. For the rest of his life he walked about an apparition, scaring people out of their wits. One hopes that his courageous attempt at preserving the whole body carried him to Seventh Heaven.

In addition, the Moro dress and weapons drew Corney's attention:

> Moros living in the forests wear very little. Residents in the coastal towns wear colorful garb. Both men and women are fond of bright, gay colors — red, yellow and green being the favorites. Both sexes wear the sarong, a piece of cloth about four by six feet. The two halves comprising it are sewed together along the long sides so that it may be slipped over the body and worn toga-fashion. Generally the sarong is made of silk, although some are a unique but pleasing combination of silk and hemp.
>
> Under the sarong men wear the "bengala," a tight-fitting shirt worn with breeches or trunks. Women wear a blouse and tight-fitting pantalets. Hair fashion for women calls for a tight knot set jauntily on the left side of the head. Lips are painted a vivid red. All carry betel nut boxes, made of silver or brass. Many are real works of art.
>
> The chewing of betel nut is a continuous affair. A mild narcotic, it stains the teeth black. Teeth are filed to points to make for easier chewing. Women let their nails grow to extraordinary lengths, protecting them with silver shields or fenders . . . .
>
> The chief weapons of the Moros are krisses, kampilans, bankau, glat and lantaka. They do not use the bolos, which is a Christian Filipino weapon. The kris is a long knife, with either straight or wavy blade. It is filed to razor sharpness, and can lop off a man's head at a single blow. The kampilan is a large two-handed sword, heavier than the kris and more devastating if handled skillfully. It is generally sheathed in an ornate wooden scabbard carried innocently over the shoulder. Only a few pieces of rattan bind the scabbard halves together. Swung downward in a swift arc, the blade severs the strings and bites cleanly into its target. The bankau is a spear used more for hunting than in warfare. The glat is a dagger, usually sheathed in a mahogany scabbard with hammered silver ornamentation. The lantaka is a brass cannon, fashioned after the small Spanish fieldpiece. A muzzle-loader, it shoots anything — ball, rocks, lengths of chain, nuts, bolts. . . .

The Subanos in Mindanao employ a weapon akin to the Roman spring-spear. The contrivance is placed on game trails, and has a tough piece of cane attached to the spear which is tied to a sapling under tension. As an animal touches the vine with hoof or snout the spear is tripped and the sapling hurls it into the unsuspecting beast with tremendous force. As the spearhead is barbed, extraction of the blade is impossible. In the early campaigns of 1903 Moros used this against us and we lost several men.

Moros also used puas, sharpened bamboo stakes driven into the ground and covered with leaves and twigs. Smeared with excrement they proved to be poisonous to any unlucky enough to step on one. Whenever Moros expected to make a fixed defense anywhere, they littered the ground with pua stakes. At Ambuludan in the Cotabato District in 1904 we found more than two thousand of these devilish devices before the Moro trenches.

When the Moros gathered, Corney posted sizeable guard detachments in town to disarm any one carrying weapons in defiance of the District Governor's edict. One exception permitted all tribal chieftains to carry arms.

Explaining his precautions Corney observed that:

The Moros are a savage and treacherous people, and we must ever be on the alert against them. I am not prepared, nor indeed inclined, to deduce why this is so. For the present, it is enough for me to know that we represent mortal enemies to them, and that they will kill us anywhere and anytime they can. Sophistry has no coinage at the moment. They hate. They kill, and until we put them down they will keep right on killing.

I have been told by a Spaniard that a Moro can cut a man in two with his kampilan. In addition to being a resolute and skillful warrior he is a religious fanatic, and he will kill as readily for one reason as for the other. In hand-to-hand combat our soldiers are simply no match for the Moro. If our first shot misses the target, we rarely have time to get off another.

They are as hard on their own people as they are on enemies. The Moro debtor who cannot pay his Moro lender becomes the latter's slave. Worse, his whole family goes into bondage until the account is squared. The debtor loses all rights and he and his children may be physically sold throughout the archipelago. Sometimes creditors will cancel the debt if the debtor will kill an agreed upon number of Christians. In this circumstance the debtor wins and loses. He loses his life but he gains Islamic Seventh Heaven. These are the people we are trying to "civilize." One wonders what will happen in the long run.

Iligan is a small but bustling place of some 2,500 people of divergent races and cultures: Visayans, Chinese, Hindus, and a few Spaniards. Moros do not live in town but surround the place in thousands up in the hills. The town is situated on a narrow strip of land jutting into Iligan Bay with a river of the same name on the south. This finger pointing into the sea is about a mile wide and two miles long. It is a Christian Filipino enclave surrounded by a vast sea of hostile Moros. It was founded as a Spanish penal colony in the early 1600s and has not improved to any noticeable degree.

The country around is truly beautiful, the luxurious vegetation something wonderful to behold. Animal life abounds, and the night brings on a wondrous din of screeching, howling, whirring, clicking and grunting. The Visayans who live in town are much like the Tagalogs of Luzon, but not so aggressive.

In November, the "sizing up" ended. General Wood led eight companies of the 28th Infantry, four of the 23rd, one battery of artillery, a detachment of engineers and Troops A and D of the 14th Cavalry from Marahui to attack the Sultan of Taracca on the east shore of Lake Lanao. The Sultan had sent insolent messages to Wood daring him to give battle. When Wood arrived with his army, the Sultan came out under a white flag and surrendered.

Wood then turned to the trouble in Jolo and engaged the enemy there with stunning results, killing over 300 Moros while suffering five casualties — one man killed and four wounded. Not until February 1904, however, were the Jolo Moros forcibly put down when Major Hugh Scott with Troops I, K, L, and M of the 14th Cavalry defeated Pangliman Hassan who died bravely in the savage fighting.

The first American killed in this vicious skirmish was Private Lewis A. Solomon of M Troop. A member of the advance party, he was surprised by Moros who sprang from high grass. Solomon suffered cuts on the head, arms and legs and had his left hand severed completely. One slash of a Moro kampilan cut through several ribs, his lungs, stomach and liver. Still, he drew his revolver and killed two of his assailants. He died twenty minutes later.

Christmas passed quietly in the Philippines but Corney recalled far different surroundings:

Last year, at Wingate, there was snow on the ground and we had a Christmas tree cut from the hills and a yule log and brandy. We had brandy this time too, but it was too damned hot to enjoy it. On the 28th we had an earthquake which lasted for about thirty seconds. The doors swung on their hinges and two pictures were shaken to the floor.

Corney also described the events of the New Year:

On January third, Lt. Holcomb, a Moro interpreter named Infante and I went fishing. We took along several troopers and two Spaniards from Iligan. We fished the Manduling River, a swift and treacherous stream emptying into Iligan Bay. Twice we tried to put our vinta [native canoe] past the breakers at the river's mouth and do some deep-sea fishing. On the second attempt our craft capsized and sunk. That finished our fishing expedition.

It rained from January third to January tenth, steadily, night and day. I thought I had seen rain in Cuba. This is rain.

Several nights ago a Moro prisoner escaped from the guardhouse. Not only that, he took with him a carbine belonging to a member of the guard. This was mortifying to me as sub-post Commander. The NCO and sentinel on post were a cheap looking pair trying to explain the incident away. The escapee, Magaglay, was a murderer. We have tried to track him down but the jungle has swallowed him up. Yesterday I went to a Moro wedding, having been invited by the Sultan of Pugahan to the nuptials. I took along an interpreter and three soldiers. The affair was indoors, in a house raised up on high stilts. Inside, men and women were seated around the walls on pillows, and several women were playing on small brass gongs and wooden xylophones. The Sultan offered anise and several sweetmeats. I had a thimbleful of the anise but declined the sweets.

The wedding was conducted according to Moslem ceremony by a sharif speaking in Arabic. The woman was little more than a child; the man, old enough to be her father. We shook hands all around afterwards and returned to camp.

In Iligan I found an old Spanish record book in the local church. It was interesting. One entry read:

"Today the Moro Donoo was killed by Guillermo Villanud of this town for stealing a carabao.

Iligan, July 24, 1876."

Another entry carried these words:

"Today Cerilo Lacond was murdered by Moros who came down from the hills. When our people kill Moros they are sent to prison. When Moros kill our people they go free. Where is the justice in that?

Fr. Clemente Ballesteros
Iligan, Dec. 10, 1884"

On December 1, 1890, an entry reported that Moros under one Amay Pap-Pag entered the barrio and killed twenty-five Christian men, women, and children and captured 130 others whom they led away as slaves.

The situation had not changed much by 1903. On January 30, Corney watched sixty Moros board a steamer which would take them on the first leg of a journey to the World's Fair in St. Louis. "I allowed these people to stay in the old barrack building here and found them to be colorful and interesting. They are under adequate supervision and should prove fascinating to people at home. Many who see their grinning faces will disbelieve the bloody stories printed about Moros, but it was ever thus."

Corney continued his observations and memories of life in the Philippines:

Yesterday I saw a small boy use his carabao as a boat. He crossed the river, some 100 yards wide, and very deep, by standing on the beast's back. Five natives hustled into a baroto [small boat] and the bowman latched onto the buffalo's tail. The patient beast carried the extra load across the river, slowly, but without hesitation.

Today (February 10) we received our first bulletin about the war between Russia and Japan. Russia has the manpower, but the Japs are tougher, I think. I think they will win and someday we may have to fight them.

Today (February 11) I heard of a trick pulled by Col. Wallace of the Cavalry detachment over in Jolo. It appears that three juramentados were shot by several soldiers in the market place in Jolo. Wallace had the bodies brought into a public place where hundreds of Moros were gathered. He ordered the digging of a communal grave, and placed the dead men in it. To the utter horror of the crowd he shot a hog, tied nearby, and tossed it upon the corpses. Through an interpreter he let it be known that every juramentado killed henceforth would be buried with a hog. To a Moslem, there can be no worse fate. The news has apparently spread far and wide. I'm not so sure it will halt Moro depredations: it might in fact cause more.

Today (February 16) we were in Cagayan on business and I was talking with a priest at the convent near the river. A man was gathering driftwood and swam out to retrieve a big length of bamboo. Suddenly the priest shouted: "Look out for the crocodile!" The man tried desperately to reach shore but was caught and carried under. Within moments men on the shore were firing volleys at the monster. The man's body was recovered downstream about twenty minutes later, horribly mangled. The crocodile was shot and dragged upon the bank. He looked to be about twenty-four feet from snout to tip of tail.

Today's bulletin (February 27) on the war indicates the Japs are getting the best of it. I'm not surprised.

Today (March 2) I finished my work in Zamboanga and took the transport *Liscum* for Malabang. From Malabang we went to Camp Vicars over a mountain trail through superb tropical forest. From Vicars some soldiers rowed us across Lake Lanao, a distance of about 18 miles. We landed at Marahui and from there proceeded to Iligan.

Crossing Lanao we were between two hostile strong-holds, Taracca on the east and Bacolod on the west. We were too far out on the lake though to worry — except for lake pirates. We saw none.

Corney's diary contained only a few items during April but in May he described a gruelling mounted exploration through the great forest. During the two-week trek the detachment ran low on rations and finally dined on monkey and locusts. The mosquitoes nearly ate the men alive, and leeches attacked troopers from every stream, river, and rain-drenched leaf. Field soldiering in the rain forest was a torturous experience.

Corney had been in the Philippines scarcely five weeks when a ghastly incident illustrated how dangerous service in the islands had become. Private Fernando Keithley was walking post in a supply dump about a mile from Camp Marahui. Three other soldiers of the guard were asleep in a tent nearby. With no moon, only a handful of stars broke the vast jungle darkness. Suddenly, nine Moros jumped from hiding places in the undergrowth, yelling and brandishing krisses and spears. In the confusion that followed, the three sleeping men were cruelly hacked to death. Keithley fought courageously, parrying sword slashes and spear thrusts with his rifle. Alternately firing and clubbing, he fended off his attackers. Fearing the arrival of some reinforcements from Marahui, the Moros drew off. Keithley was found a little while later in a widening pool of his own blood. He was rushed to the hospital at Marahui where he died the following day.

Near eight in the morning Major H. A. Barber of the 28th Infantry, temporarily in command of the post, called Corney at Iligan to inform him of the tragic episode and to discuss the apprehension of the criminals. They met at Marahui to plan for infantry from Marahui to join troopers from Iligan in tracking down the killers. The effort was unsuccessful for the murderers appeared to have vanished into thin air.

Seven years later while Corney was serving his third Philippine tour, a man named Usukut came into camp and told the commander that he knew where some of the Keithley murderers were hiding. The headman in the village of Bacarat, Amai Lobanku, had run Usukut out of town and disgraced him before his family and friends. Lobanku had hidden seven of the killers for seven years, permitting them to use Bacarat as a hideout. "All this time," bristled Corney, "he masqueraded as our friend, taking everything we had to offer."

Actually, the informer was little better than the protector. He was living near Lobanku on the morning of November 14, 1903, when the killers returned from their grisly work. Usukut recalled,

"They showed us the rifles and belts taken from the sentries. Lobanku praised them for killing the dirty Christian pigs. We all had something to eat and laughed about it." What ultimately rankled Usukut and made him an informer was Lobanku's taking one of his wives.

On the evening of November 11, 1910, Captain Smith led a detachment of troops reinforced by men from the Filipino Constabulary to Camp Tampanan. The column set out for Bacarat with Usukut as a guide. Arriving at dawn they surrounded the village and Corney marched a detachment up to Lobanku's house. Under questioning Lobanku pointed out the shacks of two of the murderers, who were apprehended at once. Four others were pursued and taken; one was never found.

The criminals were tried, found guilty and sentenced to life imprisonment. The poor 14th Cavalry trooper Fernando Keithley gained some measure of immortality. Camp Marahui was renamed Camp Keithley in his honor. If justice was a long time in coming, its vehicle was foolproof.

Even this incident, however, could not portray the savagery of the conflict. Corney described the Moros of Mindanao and one of their most dangerous customs:

> He is of low stature, generally slight in figure with small wrists and delicate hands. His face is Mongolian in cast, with a short nose, prominent cheek bones and flat features. He has jet-black hair and dark brown complexion.
>
> A peculiar custom of the Moro, directly traced to religious frenzy, is running amok. The Spanish named the custom "juramentado," from the verb "jurar," to take an oath. The oath in this instance was that taken to kill a Christian, by any means possible. In this grisly business, the killer is prepared by panditas (Islamic priests) for his mission, as it is assumed he will himself be killed in his attempt to slaughter.
>
> The juramentado seeks his victim or victims from Christians, generally in the crowded marketplaces of the larger towns. With stealth his guise, and with a razor sharp bolo or kris hidden beneath his garments, he awaits the opportune moment, then springs upon his victims like a tiger, slashing and cutting, stabbing and decapitating in a wild frenzy of blood and horror.

He believes that like the souls of the prophets and those killed in battle for the faith, his soul will be admitted at once to the full fruition of paradise. His soul will take flight directly to the Mohammedan Seventh Level of Heaven, a wondrous place filled with houris, streams of crystal purity and sweet-scented forests of ylang ylang. Here too he will find the Tree of Life, so large that a fleet horse would require a hundred years to cross its shade. Its boughs will be laden with the most delicious fruits, bending to the hand of him who seeks to gather.

Inhabitants of Heaven will be clothed in raiment of silk and sparkling jewels and dwell in fine houses. Every believer will be waited upon by hundreds of attendants, bearing dishes and goblets of gold to serve every variety of viand and beverage. He will eat without satiety and drink without inebriation, and the last drop and morsel will be comparable to the first. He will hear the sweet voice of Israfil, and the songs of the daughters of paradise. The rustling of leaves over his head will produce true harmony, and myriads of bells on the branches will play the sacred music of Allah.

Above all, the juramentado will be blessed with the most ravishing female society for eternity. Besides his earthly wives, who will join him in all their pristine charms, he will have 72 houris, resplendent women free from all human defects or frail-ties. These will be his adoring companions until the end of time.

That the juramentado may enjoy the blessings which await him, he will rise from the grave in the prime of manhood, at age thirty, of pleasing stature and possessing the faculties of complete manhood.

I knew one Moro who used his kris to kill two young Christian Filipino girls and two boys before he could be cut down. I saw two others "at work" on separate occasions in the market-place at Zamboanga. Both were killed on the spot, as they should have been. With all of the promise of heaven given these deluded souls, it is not difficult to see why they practise juramentado.

During almost six years in the islands Corney came to know both Moro and Christian Filipinos. He never liked Moros but respected them as courageous fighters and dangerous adversaries.

A bold, fanatical, wild lot, they were, by any standard, more colorful than the Christian Filipinos. Had the Moros been left alone, they would have been no trouble, but the Christianizing Spaniards bequeathed a bloody legacy, the worst of which was yet to come to Corney Smith.

CHAPTER SIX

Monkeys, Leeches and Snakes

EN ROUTE TO ZAMBOANGA to act as Trial Judge Advocate in the court-martial of an officer charged with dereliction of duty, Corney received the first inkling of the most arduous jungle expedition of his career. The trip from Iligan was made in March 1904 via a Coast Guard cutter in the company of Smith's commanding officer, Major F. H. Hardie, who was to serve as a senior member of the Board. Hardie proposed an overland march with Troops H and G of the 14th, moving from Camp Overton to Cagayan, inland to Lake Lanao, to Camp Keithley, and finally back into Overton.

When asked his opinion, Corney replied, "Well, the part from Overton to Cagayan ought to be easy, also the last leg, from Keithley back to Overton. So far as I know, no white man has ever been in the mountains between Cagayan and Lanao. It's right in the heart of Moro country, and I don't think horses can make it. One thing, Major — it would be one hell of a trip."

On the day after the court-martial Hardie outlined his plan to General Wood, who responded, "Hardie, I doubt if you can get through from Cagayan, but you may try if you wish. If you go, I'll want a full report at the end of your march."

A week later, the column left Camp Overton. Corney's G Troop included one lieutenant and forty-five enlisted men. Captain Adams commanded H Troop, a lieutenant and forty-eight men. As wagons were impractical, pack mules carried the provisions and ammunition.

As expected, the march to Cagayan was easy, much of it on hard-packed sand. A young American named Kauffman lived in Cagayan. After leaving the Army in 1900, he engaged in the manufacture and shipping of Manila hemp. He had seen no Americans for several years and was delighted to play host to Major Hardie and his officers.

Early the next morning the men saddled up and followed the Cagayan River in a westerly direction through a series of coconut groves. They were amused by a Filipino standing on the rump of his carabao in mid-river, guiding the beast by a rope through an iron ring in its nose. The two reached the opposite shore and the man turned to wave.

About six miles inland, the column began a gradual ascent along the narrow, swift river and through thick jungle. About a mile farther on, at a "treacherous, boulder-strewn crossing of the river," the soldiers came upon a party of Montescos going to market in Cagayan. A colorful lot, the natives were dressed in bright shirts and blouses and armed with wicked-looking krisses and kampilans. Each of the women wore a large wooden comb in her long thick hair, and chewed betel-nut with teeth filed down to sharp points. Corney described the meeting:

> These people paused to watch us cross over. The rocks were slippery as grease with moss and several horses went down, mine among them. No one was hurt, but it was damned embarrassing. Once assembled we proceeded up a narrow pitch of trail so steep we had to dismount and cling to our horses' manes to maneuver.

For the next several hours the column climbed: up one hill, down; up the next, down; and on into the gray, wet afternoon. The trail was narrow and the ground muddy from incessant rain. At a small settlement of three Montesco bamboo shacks the Major halted and made camp about four in the morning. As the shelter halves and the mess tents went up, the rain came down in sheets.

Everyone was soaked in minutes. Sleep was impossible as torrents of mud and water ran around the flapping shelters. Hardie called the officers together requesting their opinions on going ahead or turning back. Every officer voted to return to Cagayan.

The downpour had eased by dark, but a steady rain continued throughout the night. Near midnight as Corney was inspecting sentries, he saw Major Hardie studying a map on an upturned mess chest. Hardie asked, "Corney, you all voted to turn back, but I hate to throw in the towel. What do you think our chances are if we go on?"

Corney replied, "Well, I'll vote the same way again, but, if you do continue, I suggest you send a detachment on ahead. If the trail is passable, word can be sent back."

His superior answered, "Alright, that settles it. Wake up your first sergeant and tell him to roust out your Troop. Take half of the pack mules and get started at daylight. Have your QM Sergeant box up four days' rations and four days' half-forage. Go forward for two days. If you think we should follow, send me a runner. I'll stay here an extra day. If you don't come by then, we'll head on back for the beach, and you're on your own."

At daybreak Corney, with Lieutenant Davis, five mules, five civilian packers and forty-seven men, started up the mountain. Before long the narrow, twisted trail ended, forcing the men to use machetes to cut their way through tangled vines. After several hours of this exhausting work they found a trail on a narrow mountain shelf.

On one side, the mountain rose sheer for about 2,000 feet, and on the outside of the trail was a precipitous drop of more than a thousand feet. Suddenly one of our mounts pitched over this vertical cliff with a terrified scream. We could hear his body crashing through trees below; the poor animal must have been dead before he reached the bottom. Soon there was silence, except for the rushing of the river far below us. Fortunately the trooper was leading his mount and had the good sense to let go when the animal fell away.

With darkness approaching, there was nothing to do but go forward. To remain would force each trooper to spend the night standing on the narrow shelf holding his horse's reins. About a mile ahead, the trail widened and emptied into a small grassy flat just large enough to accommodate the small party. Corney recalled the campsite as "a veritable godsend." Soon the men tethered the horses and mules to a ground-line and put up their small shelter halves. Again the rain lashed the small camp with howling fury. With impassable terrain on either side, a rain-slick mountain trail fore and aft, and a thundering, drenching rain emptying the heavens, Corney recognized the true nature of the predicament: "We were in a fix, no damned doubt of it."

The rain finally subsided hours later, and the sounds of the jungle echoed from below: night birds calling, gecko-like lizards with their high-pitched squeaks and the drone of millions of insects, humming like a great, well-oiled machine. Near midnight, Lieutenant Davis nudged Captain Smith: "Sir, they have spotted us!" As the column was in Moroland, the news was alarming. From a little canyon leading away from the campsite came intermittent flashes of light, as though men with palm and resin torches were coming through the heavy forest.

Corney ordered the first sergeant to awaken the men. He and Lieutenant Davis then moved slowly toward the canyon to take a look. In a small clearing they found the answer to their fears. On a large tree, perched thousands, perhaps millions, of fireflies. As if on signal, the entire colony would glow with a ghostly white incandescence, lighting up the entire surrounding area. Lasting only a few magical moments, the light would disappear as though cut off by an electrical switch, only to reappear moments later.

Corney had seen fireflies in Baltimore, Washington and Tampa, but nothing like this. "They send forth their brilliance at once, at simultaneous and exact intervals, so that the night in one instant becomes a glorious vision."

Breaking camp in the morning, Corney sent two Montesco runners to Hardie with a message. The note said that the Troop would not recross the country it had come through and would go on. Corney's message described the loss of the horse, and suggested that H Troop make its way back to Cagayan.

By noon G Troop had progressed barely a mile. The river crossing took considerable time and every foot along the opposite shore had to be cleared with machetes. The van struggled to cut its way through jungle as thick as woven rattan and as dark and gloomy as night. Four days' rations stretched into eight; the horses and mules were out of fodder on the sixth day. The forest seemed full of deer and wild hogs. The men could see the graceful deer darting through dappled green light in the clearing and hear the pigs snorting in the undergrowth. But no man could get a clear shot at any animal. Great colonies of chattering monkeys hovered high overhead and the men shot a few. Corney described the meal and subsequent operations:

> With a little rice and seasoning, our cook made monkey stew which wasn't bad at all. You knew you were eating monkey, though, and that tended to make it less palatable.
>
> On the seventh day, I determined to make a reconnaissance on foot with Private Rapar, a husky, nervy and good-humoured trooper. The object was to find the highest tree in the forest, climb it and spot Lake Lanao, if possible. We were about 8,000 feet high now and Lanao should be below us — somewhere.
>
> Rapar and I left camp at daybreak. By noon we were on the mountain's top, a crag from whose fissures grew several large and sturdy trees. To reach the trees we had to hand-over-hand up some Bejuco vines which tumbled down over the crag in profusion. I climbed the tallest tree, and there, far below us, lay Lanao shining like a jewel in a vast ocean of jungle green.

Overjoyed, Private Rapar exclaimed, "Looks like we've made it, Captain."

Corney realistically cautioned, "Yes, but from what I can see from here, it looks like about four more days on the trail."

Corney had decided to send out a relief party from this mountain camp. Several men had dysentery or fever; and the food was gone, except for monkey and some locusts which were roasted on sticks. The forage consisted of tough fibrous underbrush which the horses and mules nibbled at only in desperation. Corney asked for volunteers. From these, he selected Lieutenant Davis and ten men to push through the jungle on foot to bring help from Camp Keithley. The remainder of the Troop, with the volunteers' horses, would follow Davis' trail as fast as possible. The Lieutenant and his small party soon disappeared into the dark forest.

The Troop followed Davis' trail to a small Moro rancheria the next morning. Davis had arrived hours before, apparently without trouble. The people were uncommunicative but showed no inclination to attack. They had no food, but the headman, who knew some Spanish, told of another rancheria miles ahead where the troopers might buy chickens, rice, eggs and bananas. For a fee, the Moro headman provided two torchbearers to guide the men to the next settlement.

Only 500 yards from the second rancheria, Private Price, riding at the tag end of the column, fell with his horse into the river. Though shaken, he was not seriously hurt; but the raging waters swept his horse away. Price accompanied the troops into the village where Corney and his men bought the first decent food they had eaten in over a week. The Moros seemed amazed that the men and riders had crossed the mountain from Cagayan. One of Corney's packers, a civilian named Dan Ming who had worked for Corney's father in New Mexico and Arizona, marvelled, "I've packed in the U.S., Mexico and Canada, but I've never seen anything like this." Before breaking camp the next morning, the troopers had a pleasant surprise. In a marshy backwater of the river, Private Price's horse, saddled with accoutrements in place, stood up to its belly in water and calmly munched tule grass.

The column travelled all day through dark, teeming jungle, but, by dusk, the trees began to thin out perceptibly. Just after dark the men could hear rifle fire and knew that the relief column was not far away. Within an hour, the party arrived with cargadores (porters) bearing food and forage. Corney recalled: "I wish I could describe adequately how the bacon, eggs, coffee, bread, and jam from Keithley tasted to us." A doctor with the relief party attended the sick. The following morning, after another hearty meal, the column started for Camp Keithley.

Soon the men emerged from hills into low swampy country, crisscrossed with waterways and covered with shoulder-high grass. In one low-lying place the column passed an old Moro cota (fortress) with crumbling stone walls surrounded by a moat with a single drawbridge. Several trumpet-mouthed lantaca cannon stood on battlements atop the walls. Vines, threaded among the falling stones, held the wall together. The place was as silent as the grave, an eerie forgotten enclave and monument to the centuries-old struggle between Spaniard and Moro.

The column reached Keithley the following morning. Corney found Lieutenant Davis and three of his men sick in the hospital. The remaining seven rejoined the Troop for the march to Overton. Corney telephoned the adjutant to indicate the column would arrive about noon.

As the men marched in, they were welcomed by the entire camp: soldiers, officers, ladies, children, even the inevitable dogs barking in grand excitement. In Corney's words:

> They must never have seen such a ragged, weary and footsore command. We looked like tramps. Our clothing was in tatters; our boot-soles were tied on with string and gunny-sacking; we were unshaved, and all horses, mules and men were gaunt as scarecrows. . . .

He later summarized the hardships:

> We had taken horses through country infantry would have found hazardous. In large measure we subsisted on the land, and while provender was unpalatable, it served. We could have eaten horses, but I'd have to be at death's door before I would order the shooting of these noble fellows. Most of them looked like Rosinante after the march, and all but one went all the way. The horses got so thin-bellied we had to make frequent stops, towards the end, to adjust saddles and cinch up the girth ropes.

Corney also described the insects and reptiles encountered:

> Mosquitoes, gnats and flies were ferocious. Up in the mountains big blue flies would blow our sweaty saddle blankets as they hung to dry. We therefore had to brush away the nit before maggots were hatched. I was always fearful lest one of these loathsome creatures might enter the nose, eyes or mouth of a sleeping trooper – since we had to use saddle blankets as mattresses.
>
> Mud-leeches were a problem. Black and ugly, about the size of a match, they would enter shoestring holes and work down to our toes. We could not feel them sucking blood, but ultimately felt the cold and clammy beasts as they grew larger. Removing our shoes and socks we would pull off these rubbery apparitions, now as thick as lead pencils. Worst of all was the fear of infection, because our feet were generally wet and

muddy, and because leeches live in thick, decaying vegetation. This was certainly not the most pleasant aspect of our jungle experience.

We saw numerous snakes in the forest, mostly brilliant green and sharp-snouted tree snakes, and giant pythons. Some of these big fellows looked to be 25 to 30 feet in length. Oddly, we saw few birds, although we could hear their raucous cries day and night. We did see some hornbills, very odd creatures. The hen goes into a hole in the tree which the cock blocks up with mud, leaving only a small aperture through which he can feed his mate and her chicks.

I would ride through the great forests of Mindanao and Luzon later on, in hot chase after Moro killers. In many ways those rides would parallel this one — in grim terrain, hunger, fatigue and physical stress. Still, this one would always remain special in one particular: it was the first. After a man does something for the first time, it is never quite the same again.

Corney Smith's effort with his Troop was long remembered in Army circles. The 14th Cavalry Roster for 1945 stated:

The Cotabato Valley expedition under Captain Cornelius C. Smith was a striking example of courage, determination, and endurance. Through the broiling sun and the pouring rain, through the cogon grass which commonly grew to a height of fifteen feet, through mud waist deep, in the face of tropical fevers and venomous snakes, in the midst of millions of mosquitoes, and through treacherous swamps, the column of picked men and officers under Captain Smith pushed on and operated in the Cotabato Valley from August 1903 until February 1905. These soldiers of the 14th operated, lived, fought and conquered under difficulties and hardships encountered only in the tropical jungle.

CHAPTER SEVEN

Into Moroland Again

IN JUNE 1904, GENERAL LEONARD WOOD gave Captain Smith
a special assignment which took him through country much like
that he had just negotiated from Overton the preceding month.

"Captain," detailed Wood, "you are to make a thorough reconnaissance of the interior of Mindanao. Proceed from here [Overton]
to Misamis then cross the island to Margosatubig. Choose your
own route and select your own assistant, one lieutenant. Take a
medical officer, ten enlisted men and as many cargadores as you
need. This is a peaceful mission, hence the small party."

Corney "thought these to be the most liberal instructions from
one of the finest men I have ever served under. The General
asked for an estimate of the expedition's time-frame, and I said
fifteen days."

Wood concurred: "Very well, in fifteen days I will have a boat
waiting for you at Margosatubig."

Corney chose First Lieutenant F.P. Holcomb and ten men
from G Troop, 14th Cavalry. He also selected First Lieutenant
J.M. Coffin with one enlisted man of the Medical Corps, one interpreter, one guide and thirty-five cargadores, making a total of

fifty-one men. The column would move through forests, swamps and mountains, and cross scores of rivers and streams in country never traveled by white men before, not even during the 400 years of Spanish possession. Mindanao, second largest island in the Philippine Archipelago, encompassed some 36,000 square miles, roughly the size of the state of Indiana. Until the American occupation, the island, like most of the others in the chain, was largely unknown except for the coastal regions. Satisfied with their coastal presidios, the Spaniards saw no need to explore the hinterlands.

Just prior to departure, Corney received a message from Captain Frank McCoy, aide-de-camp to General Wood, which read in part:

> Only wild tribe known in front of you is Subano, Chief Timay Umbing, living at Pang Pang near Dumanquilas Bay. Investigate his relations with Moros. Datu Dacula lives at Cumalarang. Head for his rancheria where vinta transportation permits. . . . Boat will pick you up at Margosatubig in 20 days. If in vicinity of Mt. Malindang or Mt. Tres Reyes, get information on them — height, forests, lakes, etc. . . .

The party left Overton in a Quartermaster launch on June 12, and steamed some forty miles across Iligan Bay to Misamis where they spent the night. The next morning, Corney picked up the interpreter and the guide. On June 13, the column headed for the interior. The first objective was Mt. Malindang, a peak of about 8,000 feet lying nearly forty miles inland. As far as Corney could ascertain, the mountain had never been climbed. The Moros believed that demons and evil spirits lived on the precipitous crag; the Spaniards simply considered any such venture foolhardy.

As the column approached the foothills of the mountain, a cloud of mist enveloped its upper ridge, probably the result of vapor rising from rain-drenched vegetation below. Gallardo and Pacasmo warned Corney of devils lurking in the ghostly upper air. Unconvinced, the column rode on but soon saw that Malindang was too steep for any sort of frontal approach. Scaling the mountain from the east would obviously require at least three days because of the dense jungle growth.

At midafternoon, Corney halted for the night in a jungle hamlet of some half-dozen houses "on the edge of Christendom" on the east slope. Beyond lay the country of the pagans and savages. In the evening, a woman and two of her daughters entertained the fascinated troopers with "weird songs, accompanied by a man playing a sort of banjo made of a coconut shell half covered with goatskin," with strings made of hemp. In a masterpiece of understatement, one soldier observed: "It sounded kind of flat."

The next day, the column entered Subano country, the domain of a pagan tribe worshipping birds, trees, mountains and rushing rivers. This sedentary people raised rice, corn and bananas on terraced hillsides, and hunted deer, monkey and wild pigs. About three in the afternoon, the column came to a creek and a Subano settlement governed by a datu named Danunto. The people were curious but friendly, bringing chickens, eggs, bananas and yams as gifts.

Corney noted that Subanos were much lighter in color than Moros or Christian Filipinos, somewhat shorter in stature, quite muscular and of almost benevolent expression. They professed great fear of Moros, who from time to time would raid their villages for women and slaves. In Danunto's rancheria Corney saw a "large bewhiskered baboon in a tree, fully as large as a four- or five-year-old child. It was the only one I ever saw in the Philippines, in almost six years of service there." A burden bearer brought Corney a comb of "inferior honey, dark and made by bees smaller than ordinary houseflies. The bananas, though scarcely larger than a man's little finger, were sweet and palatable. The whole stalk was about the size of a football."

The party set out again for Malindang the following morning and spent much of the day chopping out a trail with machetes. About noon the men came upon the skeleton of a python. Although the bones were scattered, it was apparent that the snake had been at least thirty feet long. Camped for the night at Malubug Creek, the men laundered and swam in the deep and clear pools.

Corney was impressed with his cargadores: "These men are experts in the use of bamboo, cogon grass and nipa palms. Within an hour after starting to make camp we have fine little shacks, impervious to sun and rain. These grinning little fellows really know their business."

Because the ascent of Malindang would begin the next day, the troopers hoped for a good rest. This was not to be. Throughout the night giant kalongs (fruit bats) crashed into trees "with a grace comparable to a brick landing in water." About half as large as a house cat with a wingspread of almost five feet, the bats flew slowly about the camp. Their loud squeals kept the men awake much of the night.

Proceeding as Corney put it, "up, up, up!" the column began climbing the worst portion of the east wall the morning of June 16. At about 2:00 P.M. they arrived at what they thought was the mountain's crest. To their dismay, they saw that Malindang was still miles away with an intervening chasm of vast, tangled jungle. Mixed emotions greeted the decision to forego Malindang as an objective.

Since the peak the column had climbed had no name, Corney christened it Mt. Lebo in honor of Colonel Thomas C. Lebo, regimental commander of the 14th Cavalry. Needing water, the troopers cut sections of bejuco vines from trees and "milked" them for cups of water. In the cold moments after dawn, Lieutenant Holcomb climbed a tree and saw Camp Overton, Misamis and Jimenez to the east, and the little town of Buliuso to the west. Buliuso became the party's new objective.

The ascent of Mt. Lebo helped dispel a myth for the ten frightened Subano guides provided by Datu Danunto. They had balked at climbing the mountain but were persuaded to do so. Asked about this reluctance, the leader told of a legend concerning a huge seven-headed, man-eating python living on the mountaintop. Although they did see a python about halfway up the mountain, it luckily had but one head.

In Buliuso, Datu Giligan staged a dance for the exploring party. In the large room of a nipa palm hut a woman played the kulintangan, an instrument resembling a xylophone with various-sized brass gongs instead of graduated wooden keys. Adding to the orchestration were several hollow-log drums and two brass gongs of considerable size. Torches of dry palm leaves dipped in copal varnish furnished the light. The scene was weird and barbaric. In the center of the room almost nude male dancers were writhing and leaping in cadence to discordant outbursts of drums and gongs, whirling spears around in great circling sweeps and thrusting wicked-looking krisses in vicious jabs. As the music increased in tempo, a slashing rain beat upon the roof sounding like millions of tiny hammers providing accompaniment. Several men admitted to being "queasy" about the spectacle. "A slip here, a thrust there — intentional or otherwise — and a bloody massacre could have ensued."

Several days later, Corney and his men came to the shores of a beautiful lake. Known only as Danao, the Malay word for lake, it was christened Lake Leonard Wood by Corney and so marked on his map. Steep, jungle-covered mountains surrounded the lake. Palms and other tropical vegetation grew to the water's edge.

No good camping place could be found nearby, and a boat was sent to notify the datu on the lake's opposite shore. A small flotilla of vintas soon appeared with wind filling their multicolored cotton sails of primitive Malay design. Soon the datu, Masau, stepped ashore and invited the entire party to cross the lake to his rancheria. The horses had to be taken in relays, and several hours passed before all had been transported from shore to shore. Men, women, and children clustered about Corney and his men, pointing at their outsize visitors and touching the peculiar white skin. Masau assigned houses to the party: officers and enlisted men taking quarters in separate buildings, and the cargadores sleeping on the ground under the raised floorboards.

June 26 was spent mapping Lake Leonard Wood. With Subano guides, Corney and Lieutenant Holcomb sailed around the entire shoreline mapping as they moved. They found that many streams emptied into the lake, but that the Kumalaran River rushed away from the lake in a swift torrent towards the waters of Dumanquilas Bay.

About noon, the mapmakers encountered one of the island's many dangers. Lieutenant Holcomb suddenly asked: "Captain, what is that thing going off the bank into the lake?" Corney recalled that:

> We could see only that part of the animal vertical to the three foot bank, as there was high grass on shore and the water was muddy near the bank. Holcomb thought it was a pig, but I saw at once that it was a huge python. Sergeant Lawrence and I took shots at it, he with his rifle, I with my pistol. As it was some eighty yards off, moving, and we were in canoes, we both missed. By the time we reached the spot he had entered the lake, he was gone; we did not see him again.

There were many of these monsters in the islands. The pack train employees at Iligan killed and skinned one, hanging the skin on a wall of their quarters. It measured just under thirty-four feet. I saw another one caged in Manila for shipment to a zoo in the states. It was over thirty feet long.

They possess terrible strength in their jaws. The opening capacity of the jaws can accommodate a muntjac or wild pig. They crush the food into lumpy, sausage-like shapes before swallowing. After working quantities of saliva over the carcass they begin to swallow, working the body into the maw with spasmodic ingestions aided by sharp inward pointing teeth.

Once, near camp Vicars we heard some pigs squealing. Not far away, in the brush, a python had one wrapped in its coils and was constricting to kill it. Around the snake danced five other pigs, bristles raised and tusks slashing at the snake. The snake would raise its head some five or six feet away from the coil and lunge at his tormentors. One of the men raised his rifle to shoot the python. I said, "No, that's nature's way: don't interfere with it."

Masau furnished the party with guides to a settlement some four miles north of Dumanquilas Bay. A little before noon the column came to Kumalaran and was met by its headman, Datu Bularong. He furnished a hot meal of rice and yams and offered a fermented drink as well. The liquor, an evil-smelling concoction, was served in a jar about thirty inches high. Eight or ten reed straws protruding from its surface enabled several drinkers to sip simultaneously. Several of the men tried the stuff but were repelled by its rancid odor. "I'd hate to probe to the bottom of that jug," said one. "No telling what you'd find there."

In Kumalaran, Corney saw three men from the neighboring island of Borneo. They had small holes bored through their upper front teeth, at the gum line. Brass-headed tacks inserted in these holes shone like jewels in the sun. Each man displayed intricate tattoos about his neck and shoulders.

Bularong would not permit his men to accompany the party to the shores of Dumanquilas Bay. "Moro Country, badman, kill Subanos, kill you." A few miles out of Kumalaran the men found a cluster of Moro houses. Moro men armed with spears, krisses, kampilans, bolos and firearms, quickly appeared wearing anting-antings [charms to fend off evil spirits]. Corney noted: "When some twenty-five of these dandies fell in beside us, I decided to halt and have them disperse as a body."

This maneuver required a little diplomacy for the Moros were in a half-exuberant, half-truculent mood and increasing in number. By the time the party reached Kumalaran, over a hundred well-armed Moros headed the column. Corney described the arrival:

> As we came into town a runner from Dacula met us. He was the most martial-looking Filipino I ever saw, well-built, straight as an arrow and with a keen, aggressive face. He wore dark-red tight-fitting trunks, a bright red satin jacket and a red fez. He carried a ten-foot black hardwood lance with a bright steel point about a foot long. Held close to his body was a handsome kris.

> He came up to me, saluted, and said in Spanish, "Datu Dacula says you cannot stop here. You have only a few men. You are of no importance. He will not receive you, but if you want a bicharra his younger brother will receive you." To this I replied, "Very well, you will please ask Datu Dacula to have three large sailing vintas prepared for my party so that we may leave Kumalaran this evening and proceed to Margosatubig." He saluted and was off on the run.

Within minutes Corney, Lieutenant Holcomb, and Doctor Coffin were ushered into a large house to meet with Dacula's brother and some neighboring datus. As soon as the conference began, Sergeant Redling informed Corney that the Moros outside were agitated and that the column's cargadores were very much alarmed. Stepping to the door, Corney saw at once the cause of the trouble. Several soldiers were cooking bacon over a small fire and the drippings were splattering and hissing in the pan. Strict Mohammedans all, the Moros could not countenance this defiling of holy Moslem ground. When Corney ordered the men to empty the pan into the river, tempers cooled.

The meeting resumed, dominated largely by Dacula's brother, an insolent and surly boy who spoke fractured Spanish. When Corney saw his vintas pull up to the river's bank, he thanked the datus for their courtesy and left the room with Holcomb and Coffin.

Corney assigned boat spaces so that he, Holcomb and Coffin were each in charge of a third of the party in a separate craft. As Corney prepared to embark he innocently offered his left hand as a gesture of goodwill to 'his insolent young host because his right hand, injured in an accident several days earlier, was bound in splints. Grasping the injured right hand instead, the savage squeezed with every ounce of strength, malevolent eyes gleaming with hate at the unintended insult. Corney, suddenly painfully aware of his error, nonetheless cooly withdrew his bleeding and swollen hand, nodded, and turning on his heel said, "All right, Holcomb, saddle up — let's get out of here."

It was a wise reaction. Only thirteen soldiers and native burden-bearers faced over 300 Moros on the riverbank, armed and itching for trouble. An overt though unintentional act on the part of any soldier would have spelled doom for the entire party. The party reached Margosatubig hours later, on June 28, twenty-four days after leaving Camp Overton. They returned to Overton over government routes in easy stages: sailing first to Malabang on Illana Bay, then traveling overland to Camp Vicars on the south shore of Lake Lanao, crossing the lake by vinta, and riding the twenty-five miles on into home base.

Unfortunately little rest awaited Captain Smith and his men. Within six weeks they would be on the trail again, not for a practice march, but on a search-and-destroy mission after the wiliest of Moro chieftains.

CHAPTER EIGHT

Datu Ali

DATU ALI OF TINUNCUP was possibly the most famous Moro that Mindanao ever produced. Wily, sagacious and tough, he had for years eluded all efforts to capture him, repeatedly slipping out of tight places where arrest seemed imminent. Because he claimed to be descended from Mohammed through Kabungsuwan, the priest from Johore who introduced Islam into the Philippines, the datu commanded tremendous respect among his people and wielded uncommon power. So awe-inspiring was his person that his subjects actually approached him on hands and knees when petitioning for an audience. All believed that if Datu Ali died at the hands of the hated foreigners, he would miraculously rise from the grave to ultimately triumph. Ali eventually was killed in October 1905, during a clash with an expedition led by Captain Frank McCoy. As Governor of the District of Cotabato, Corney Smith investigated rumors that Ali had returned to continue the struggle against the foreigners.

Corney's connection with the dangerous Moro began, however, after General Wood had issued orders that slavery and plural marriage be discontinued in Mindanao. Not unreasonably, given the time-tested customs of the land, Ali rebelled. He gathered 2,000 men in a fortified village called Saranaya, a day's march from Dulanan where his friend, Piang, was datu. Though American forces occupied a blockhouse at nearby Kudarangan, Ali believed Piang could handle the invaders in his sector and made no move to reinforce him.

As soon as Ali had gathered his men in Saranaya, General Wood marched out to meet him. The attack was made from the flat, open and swampy country on the river side of the stronghold. Although Wood killed or captured a few Moros in the engagement, the vast majority simply melted away into the jungle while the soldiers floundered in marshy water up to their armpits. The failure of the effort required a new expedition several months later.

At Camp Overton, Corney received orders from General Wood on August 9 to prepare to pursue Datu Ali. Corney's experienced jungle travellers were a logical choice for the assignment. Corney was directed to select eleven privates and one noncom from each of the four troops at Overton, plus a hospital sergeant and two Medical Corps privates. Ten cargadores, paid thirty-five cents "gold" per day, would accompany the force. The best possible men were selected for the expedition: physically strong, able to endure and willing to serve. Field equipment would be dangerously light. The only luxuries permitted were mosquito nettings. The column moved via Marahui, where it was joined by Lieutenants Hayne and Russell and men selected from the four troops in the garrison. Corney Smith commanded the entire cavalry detachment. By the time Corney reached Marahui, he decided that an additional fifteen cargadores were necessary and finally took the trail with 129 officers and men. Later, the number of cargadores increased to seventy-five to carry the plunder and provisions from enemy villages.

"My orders were liberal and satisfactory," said Corney, "in effect, they were to go out and get Datu Ali, dead or alive." Corney's base would be the blockhouse at Kudarangan. Each detachment commander could stay out ten, fifteen or twenty days, depending on his situation. After any such foray into the jungle, a detachment was, if possible, given three days' rest. The respite provided treatment for the sick, casualty evacuation and replacement.

As the detachments forming the expedition converged from widely separated places, Parang was designated as the rallying point.

It was a likely spot on the edge of Moro country. Here Corney issued additional orders to provide field rations for all hands (129) and designated one officer and an enlisted man to assume charge of all necessary operations in the field. Fifty bolos were distributed among the men for clearing pathways through the jungle.

While Corney's previous expedition with horses was "interesting," it had proved conclusively that the jungle was no place for cavalry. This expedition traveled on foot. Corney explained later, "It was hard enough for the men to look after themselves. Much of the time we were wading through nasty ill-smelling swamps, floundering through mud and soaked to the skin with driving rain, in dark jungle where the sun seldom filters through. Caring for horses on top of all this would have been impossible."

One week after receiving its orders, the command started from Parang into the Buldun mountains with Datu Ali's rancheria as its first objective. On August 21 an advance guard under Ali fired upon the column's point, then vanished into the bush. A small party scouted the area and returned in an hour to report many tracks on the muddy trail leading towards Ali's rancheria. Corney noted:

> On the next day we made a very early start and marched fast, hoping to find a lot of Moros in the open on the far flank of the range. By luck, Russell with the advance guard ran smack into a small party and, before they could get away, killed Datu Paniambang and captured his 15-year-old son. Paniambang was shot by Sergeant Heuser of my troop; he had twice won the "Buffalo Medal" as the best shot in the army.

The boy told Corney that his father's party of 200 men had only a few rifles. The mission of the force was to harass the expedition until Datu Ali could arrive with more men. Ali was supposedly in Saba with some 800 men. The boy was right; but when the command reached Saba, Ali had withdrawn, taking his little army with him. Although disappointed, Corney consoled:

> All was not lost, though; we burned his rancheria to the ground, destroying many great and intricately designed bamboo houses (in which were stored many thousands of pounds of rice), and commandeered all of the chickens and Muscovy ducks on the place.

The command reached Kudarangan on August 26 and rested there for five days. As Ali was not to be found in the immediate vicinity, Corney asked permission of General Wood to backtrack over some of the country already screened to destroy more enemy villages and crops. Normally, he would have burned these objectives en route, but could not as he was in "hot chase" after his adversary. Wood agreed and the command left Kudarangan at 6:00 A.M. on September 1. They proceeded down the Rio Grande eight miles by launch, then hiked some four miles inland to Saranaya, "the big fort where Ali had first defied our army." Here Corney's command was joined by Captain Kerth and his 23rd Infantry detachment.

That night, a Moro wielding a razor-sharp kris badly cut Kerth's interpreter. The Moro had been taken on the trail some days before; then, as he appeared docile and subdued, Kerth removed his guard. The Moro, waiting for an opportune moment, grabbed a kris from a cargador and slashed wildly at the nearby interpreter. Corney contended, "Kerth erred. I have not the slightest trust in the Moros. During our entire operation I kept my cargadores and guides under strict guard."

That evening Corney asked his guide where Balatalupa was, for he had been informed that it was only some two or three miles from Saranaya. At first the guide professed no knowledge of the place, then changed his story to say that it was a long day's march away. Although this was Corney's first experience with the man, he became suspicious. Through his interpreter he told the guide, "You have one more chance. Give me the proper information about Balatalupa right now, or you will be shot in the morning."

The bluff worked. Balatalupa was close at hand, and before daylight on the following morning, the command started for the new objective. At about 6:00 A.M. Lieutenant Lippincott fired at a Moro riding a pony along the trail. The man fell dead from his mount. It was Degababan, son of Datu Uata Mama, whose wife was one of Ali's sisters.

By the time the column reached Balatalupa, the entire population had fled except an eight-year-old boy "who had rickets and badly deformed legs." He was comforted, fed and taken back to Saranaya for proper disposition. The twenty houses in town were burned, tons of rice destroyed, and all of the village's chickens and ducks were taken.

In the last house of the village the men also found a woman cowering in the corner. She was suffering from paralysis and was "altogether a pitiable sight." She claimed that the village leader was one of Ali's henchmen named Cumatan. Corney had her placed on an improvised stretcher for the trip back to Saranaya.

On his return to camp, Corney learned of another settlement in the vicinity, a place named Sambulauan. He sent Lieutenants Hayne and Russell, each with thirty men, to capture any Moros present, sack the town and destroy its stores. They moved out at 4:55 A.M. on September 3, arriving at the objective within two hours. Not a soul was present. The detachment burned about 100 shacks and nearly a ton of "palay" (rice).

Corney sent Lieutenant Lippincott and a detachment of twenty-one men to escort four sick men back to Kudarangan the next day. Lippincott also took half a dozen cargadores to carry back supplies. He returned to camp that afternoon around 4:30 P.M. with the needed provisions in time to join the command on its next raid.

Corney had sent Lieutenant Hayne some eight miles ahead to a place called Buluan with orders to sack it and rejoin the column at the Pungadan River. Hayne burned twenty-five shacks and fired the stores of rice and camotes before rejoining the command. During this destruction, he killed two Moros and captured two small boys. The Moro "nursery" was growing. On September 7, the column arrived at a village called Boayaan. Also deserted, it was reduced like those occupied earlier. On the eighth the column reached Saban on the Nican River, and this tiny settlement suffered the same fate. Since other small hamlets were reported in the vicinity, Corney ordered Lieutenant Russell, ten men and twenty-five cargadores to forage and plunder. Russell's detachment returned to camp around two days later after burning twenty-five shacks and several tons of rice and pulling down all of the fencing used for livestock.

That evening, Dr. Coffin reported that Private Hodgden of B Troop had come down with typhoid and would have to be returned to Kudarangan as soon as possible. After a forced march of nine miles through the thickest jungle, over mountains and rivers, the command reached Boayaan early in the afternoon of September 11. Here Corney decided to send Hodgden on with a small detachment under Lippincott while the main body would continue on to complete its mission in the time prescribed by General Wood.

For the next several days the column averaged seven miles a day. On the fifteenth, the men arrived at the Matitiboc River where they discovered blaze-marks of the 22nd Provisional Infantry Company hacked into hardwood trees. The 22nd Company and Corney's combined command were to join forces a few miles ahead on the Maratagao River. It seemed obvious that the infantry company was a day or two ahead and would await the column in Pikit.

En route, the expedition found a hastily vacated Moro settlement with old baskets, pieces of cloth and other household goods thrown loosely about. A number of these baskets, generally used for carrying food, contained pieces of roots which indicated that the scorched earth policy, while cruel, was effective. Anyone reduced to eating roots instead of rice, manioc, camotes and other jungle staples must be having a hard time.

The place stank. Nearby, at the edge of a small clearing, lay the decaying body of a dead Moro. As the command resumed its course for Pikit, three Moros opened fire from the trees. It was a brave but foolhardy act for one was killed, one wounded, and the third escaped. The wounded man and the escapee were captured later in the day near Pikit.

Five other Moros were killed before the column reached Pikit, where it rested until the morning of the nineteenth. Corney took stock of the expedition to date:

From September 1, when we left Kudarangan to the 16th, when we arrived here in Pikit the results of our raids account for eleven Moros killed, three wounded, five women, one fifteen-year-old boy and four small children captured, one pony killed, seven captured, and some 300 ducks and chickens taken. Also we destroyed from 18 to 20 tons of stored rice, and totally destroyed Balatalupa, Sambulauan, Sulanan, Tinutunan, Boayaan, Saban and Nican.

I really dislike this kind of business and would rather

fight the Moros in pitched battle. I am under orders, however, and there is no doubt that this action will break the enemy's will to resist. If it doesn't, he's either very brave or very crazy.

On the nineteenth the troop followed the banks of the Rio Grande toward Kudarangan. About two miles out of Pikit the men suddenly encountered some twenty-five Moros working in a rice paddy. The Moros ran in every direction. Late in the afternoon the soldiers camped on the river at Ynoch's Market. Vintas loaded with rice en route to Piang's place near Kudarangan began to pass the camp. Corney decided to commandeer them to transport his men downriver; sitting in these graceful lateen-sailed craft was easier than hacking through the jungle any day. By nightfall a number of the vintas had been appropriated by "shots across the bow," but not enough to transport the entire command. Early in the morning, however, a big fleet of the slim craft was hauled ashore. All troopers embarked and by midmorning were stepping ashore at Kudarangan where the Troop rested for two days.

Corney described the next movement: "On September 23, we started out for Buluan, going up the Dansalan River in vintas towed by a small motor launch. We made our first camp at Sacapan." Corney's command was a day behind Lieutenant Feeters and the 22nd Provisional Company. Feeters had been grounded on a sandbar in the river but had refloated the boats and gone ahead to engage Datu Ampatuan in a firefight some three miles downriver from Sacapan. Although the natives had fled, they had no casualties and lost no prisoners. Feeters asked Captain Smith to join the pursuit of Ampatuan and his men. Corney replied that that was what he was there for and asked Feeters where the Moro chief was. Feeters admitted he did not know, but guessed that Corney's objective, Buluan, was as good a place as any to start. The two agreed to meet four days later in Catitisan.

The next morning, Lieutenant Lippincott wounded two Moros in the high grass near Pisalangan where the command crossed the river on a rude raft built by the cargadores. On the opposite shore was a Moro settlement, Dansalan. All of its inhabitants scattered as the first raft approached the bank. The column destroyed the nine well-constructed houses in the village, plus sixteen tons of palay.

Three days later, in camp on Sinabun Creek, Corney faced a

command decision. His guide informed him that they were still two days out of Buluan and that he knew how to get to Catitisan only from Sacapan, not from Sinabun Creek. Corney "decided to press on, anyway" but some ten minutes later met a runner with a message from Captain Halstead Dorey, Aide-de-Camp to General Wood. The note indicated that hostile Moros were gathered at Danualusan on the far side of Kiyu Kiyu, and would probably fight. Wood directed, "If possible, find Feeters and cooperate with him. Chenowyth says Feeters will be near Ampulan. The foregoing is not applicable so long as you are in contact with the enemy, or know where he is so you can strike him."

Dorey's note changed the situation. Corney returned to Sacapan but could find no trace of Feeters. Two days later, another runner arrived with news that Feeters was upriver, heading for Kudarangan, burning as he went. Satisfied that Feeters could make it on his own and would not intercept the Moros at Danualusan, Corney decided to return to home base himself. Both parties arrived at Kudarangan on the morning of October 1. Corney shortly received good news as Lieutenant Smyser and twenty men of the 14th Cavalry joined his command. They had come as replacements all the way from Jolo.

Near midnight Feeters received a call from Major Chenowyth, 17th Infantry, in Cotabato, advising that Datu Ali would be at Piang's village across the river and that Feeters ought to attempt to catch him by blocking off all escape trails. The task was complicated because Piang, supposedly friendly, could not be antagonized.

Feeters immediately asked Captain Smith to assist the infantry. Smith replied that he was anxious and willing, but could not move unless ordered. Chenowyth and Feeters were Infantry; Corney, Cavalry. While the two branches often worked together, no great love was lost between them. "Not that I mind working with them, even for them," commented Corney, "only that I want the situation spelled out in advance, so that there will be no recriminations later, on who should have done what, where, when and how." Feeters placed a call to Chenowyth, who "directed" that Captain Smith cooperate in the mission. There were no explicit orders. As senior officer, Smith assumed command and the column made ready to move out.

Corney felt that the orders to block the trails without antagonizing Piang were insufficient and contradictory. He knew that the Moros could escape by vinta or launch as well as by trail and that Piang was known to be an Ali collaborator. Why placate him? Just before departing, Corney received a telephone message from Captain Dorey telling him to "use your judgment in what should be done at Piang's."

In a sense, Captains Smith and Dorey were working in opposite directions. Smith had no liking or admiration for Datu Ali, regarding him as a despot and rebel, and wanting to get him "dead or alive." Dorey felt that he might bring peace to Mindanao by inducing the powerful chieftain to surrender. He had met with Ali earlier and been presented with a beautiful brass lantaca (cannon). In this meeting, Ali had asked that his wife (Piang's daughter) and children be allowed to join him. The request was refused but with courtesy which Ali interpreted as weakness. During a second meeting with Dorey, the Moro conducted himself with such aplomb that his followers were emboldened to hold out against any American attempts to capture them. In any case, Dorey gained no advantage from either encounter.

Perhaps Dorey had been convinced of Datu Ali's sincerity by a letter the old man had sent him. Written in Arabic, translated into Spanish by an interpreter and then into English by another man, it read:

> This letter is from me, Datu Ali, to Captain Dorey and to the Civil Governor. Respecting what they tell me, that they have no ill will, I will say that I might live on any site within my jurisdiction, but would prefer to be near the Americans. I am now old, so would select Sacapan, Buluan, Lipasan or Saranaya as my home.
>
> Respecting my family, you may send them to me, or I will send after them. I propose this as I know that Piang hates me. I wish to do nothing without your knowledge, and this is the truth.

The letter may have lost some accuracy in two translations but it seemed correct. Captain Dorey, one of the two addressees, accepted it. Ultimately, however, Datu Ali's wife, Minca, made her escape from Piang's settlement taking her children and several articles of value. Dorey, meaning well, had been hoodwinked.

Minca's escape was followed by the flight of over 500 men, women and children, all of whom joined Datu Ali. Captain Smith, in total disagreement with Dorey's actions, could do nothing but follow orders:

>I was to keep my troop in readiness to embark on the launch *Guardoqui* and wait for a whistle from the gunboat *Pampanga*. The *Guardoqui* would steam across river, land at Piang's place and we would disembark and go after Ali. Should Ali fail to surrender, Dorey and party would kill him right there in the wardroom of the *Pampanga*. I waited until dark for the *Pampanga*'s signal. It never came.

The reason the signal was never given was because Dorey, after accepting twenty-three rifles surrendered by Ali, permitted the wily chief to "go and get" hundreds more. Ali never returned; he had again outsmarted his host. He had his wife, family and 500 or more followers; all for only twenty-three rifles. Smith was appalled. "I have always held that in dealing with Moros you must never, repeat never, cater to one. Consistent with honor, you must beat him at every turn. He understands no other language." Later, assessing Dorey's part in this affair he said, "I consider this affair so poorly conducted as to merit a full account of it being kept for subsequent reference   should my views ever be sought in the matter by proper authority." He added, "Captain Dorey is an officer and a gentleman; he simply chose the wrong way to deal with Datu Ali."

Still, the possibility that Ali might be ashore in Piang's village dictated that Corney's Troop had to search the village. "We took advantage of every tent, shack and tree in Kudarangan," said Corney, "to keep from being seen from Piang's across the river." The column sneaked into the bush and proceeded to a point two miles downriver where it would be picked up by the *Guardoqui*. The launch, riding high in the water without troops, would appear to be making a routine trip to Cotabato.

The launch picked up the troopers as planned and ferried them to a spot directly across the river. There it waited for an hour to give the men time to surround the village. Then it steamed back up the river and into the mouth of the Dansalan to block any attempts to escape by vinta.

By dawn the Troop had surrounded and cut off the land side of the village, blocking all jungle escape routes. The *Guardoqui* was in place "in the stream," as was the gunboat *Pampanga*; any Moros attempting to escape by river would be blown out of the water. Seeing his predicament, Piang sent two emissaries to Captain Smith. One was the sharif (high priest), the other a Hindu named appropriately enough, "Bombay."

Corney minced no words: "I am going to make a search of your place, and I want you to turn out every man, woman and child in the village. I want them to congregate right here in the village square. You have half an hour. I want no treachery. If there is treachery, I will wipe out the village. Go."

Within twenty minutes nearly 1,300 people were milling around the square: about 475 men and boys, the remainder women and small children. Corney sent Lieutenants Hayne, Lippincott, Norwood and Smyser, each with small details, into the houses to search and ferret out laggards. With the exception of a few invalids, none were found. Datu Ali was not in the village. Months would pass before he would be caught; the sly jungle fox had slipped the noose again.

A brief lull set in. For the next six weeks no excursion ventured into Moro country and Corney rested his men, replacing those who had contracted fever on the trail. There was also a general turnover in officer personnel. Hayne, Lippincott and Russell were relieved and Lieutenants Poillon, Castleman and Smyser were assigned. Dr. Love replaced Dr. Coffin. By December, Smith was the only remaining original member of the Provisional Troop organized in September.

On November 14, the troop embarked on the steamboat *Santa Cruz* and sailed up the Dansalan River to Sacapan, again searching for Datu Ali. As the *Santa Cruz* made ready to pull away, Corney turned to Colonel G. K. McGunnegle standing at dockside with Dorey and asked, "What are your orders, sir?"

"Any Moro more than two miles away from Kudarangan who will not surrender on order will be shot. Is that clear?"

"Yes sir," was Corney's only response.

At Sacapan, Corney found the usual lot of sullen and apprehensive people but no Moro men, and no Datu Ali. Corney decided to use Sacapan as a base of operations for a few days and had his cargadores create clear fields of fire in all directions by cutting away all of the undergrowth around the town's edge.

A patrol was sent out, but recent heavy rains and general swampy conditions eliminated any chance of following Moro tracks. The patrol burned ten shacks and two tons of rice. On the sixteenth, Corney went out with Lieutenant Smyser and eighty men, leaving three officers and thirty-five men in camp. About two miles into the jungle they came upon a sizeable Moro supply depot. Warned of the patrol's approach by the usual noise made by white men moving in the jungle, the Moros fled. All houses and many tons of rice were burned.

Hayne, Russell and eighty men made a similar foray on the following day, destroying thirty houses and five tons of rice. On the twentieth the Troop was ordered back to Kudarangan where it rested until December 9 when it took the trail again to police the country between the mountains and the southwest shore of Lake Buluan. The soldiers enjoyed a more leisurely patrol, travelling in a long string of native vintas, pulled by the launch *Polloc*. After a seemingly fruitless mission, the Troop was returning to Sacapan; from there it would go up the Catitisan River and then inland to Lake Buluan. As the launch neared Sacapan, Corney spotted four Moros on shore some 800 yards upstream. The crew manning the Colt automatic gun mounted on the *Polloc*'s bow fired several futile rounds at them; none were hit. After the Moros escaped, troopers picked up several bolos and a pouch with eleven rounds of Remington ammunition.

Starting up the Catitisan, the waterborne expedition soon found that the narrow, swift and crooked stream made canoe travel impossible. Corney ordered the vintas burned and the detachment went on by foot. The next day, two troopers were wounded by bamboo spikes planted in the trail. Although the stakes had not been poisoned, the wounds caused by the sharp spikes were deep and painful. Later the same day, Smyser jumped a party of Moros in fixed positions and wounded several before the others vanished into the jungle.

Soon the Troop came upon an extensive series of Moro trenches, measuring 250 yards in length and placed to cover the trail with excellent fields of fire. Luckily for the invaders, the Moros were not in force. Some men, guarded by several riflemen, were working on the parapets. First Sergeant Randall rushed the trenches with a detail of twenty men, wounding two Moros; but the party again disappeared. A shack near the long trench contained hundreds of newly cut bamboo stakes which Corney ordered burned.

On the twelfth, six Moros were killed at Ambuludan and the town burned. A thorough search was made for Ampatuan, one of Ali's chief henchmen, but he was not found. Two more Moros were killed between Ambuludan and Budoc. Corney noted that "for fighting Moros our light carbine is really not effective. Many of the wounded get away, and sometimes they turn and get our men before another round can be fired."

The next day the Troop destroyed three small villages including Budoc. At Catitisan the men found several newly dug trenches about one hundred yards long, paralleling the Catitisan River and commanding the trail leading into town from Buluan. Wire entanglements surrounded the trenches. Fortunately, no one was in them. Here the men discovered and destroyed twenty-six crates of charcoal used in making powder.

During the next forty-eight hours the command destroyed over 100 houses and burned about sixty tons of rice. The homes in this area were not mere palm shacks but were intricately designed places constructed of native hardwoods. Corney, dedicated to putting down Moro insurrection, was reluctant to employ the scorched earth policy. "Why don't these bastards stand and fight — I hate this business of burning houses and food."

The Troop ran into resistance near the Allah River, a tributary of the Catitisan, whose banks were swampy and partially hidden by tall grass. Seeing several Moros on shore, the advance guard began firing but drew no response until the main body arrived. Then a heavy volume of rifle fire came from Moro trenches placed on a slight rise just behind the swampy terrain. "I made the men sit down low behind two small wood piles near the bank and on the trail, and directed the First Sergeant to cover a small detachment sent out to flank the trench." The Moros had no intention of playing Corney's game. While the flanking party was working its way into position, the Moros left their trenches and disappeared into the jungle. They had left their mark; Sergeant Price was seriously wounded in the chest.

Inspecting the rifle pits, Corney found three dead and two

wounded, an unusual circumstance since Moros normally carried away their casualties. Also in the rifle pit was a piece of paper with Arabic writing on it. Corney put it in his pocket and later had it deciphered. It read:

> We begin our task and I know that no bullet can harm me. God and Mohammed will allow nothing to harm me. I see the great Abu Bekar and am defended by Osman and Ali. Allah delivered me from evil. I praise Mohammed because of his wondrous works and ask his protection.

The prayer had failed. It lay crumpled in the palm of one of the dead men in the trench.

Corney asked Dr. Love if it would help if the Troop remained in camp for a day or so to rest the wounded man. Love answered that Price must be taken to a hospital at once. Price then said to Smith: "I am afraid, Captain, that I will be a lot of trouble to you now. If I die, please don't bury me out here where these people will dig me up and insult my remains." "You won't die, Sergeant. We're taking you to the nearest hospital right now. You'll be up and around in a week or two." Corney was wrong; Price died the following day. Corney sent a message to the commanding officer at Kudarangan requesting a coffin and authority for the entire Troop to attend the funeral. The raiding party arrived at Kudarangan two days later as the launch *Woodruff* was tying up dockside with Price's coffin. Like so many before him, Price died in the service of his country in a faraway place, but he was not forgotten by those who had marched beside him.

In his report to the Provisional Field Commander at Kudarangan, Corney summed up the ten-day expedition:

> I consider the work done by the Provisional Troop of much value to the government. We got right into the heart of Moro country, and would have accomplished more if we had had guides capable of taking us into other regions where Moros are holding out. I firmly believe that Ali is in the mountains west of Catitisan, from which place he has been drawing his supplies. If another expedition is contemplated, I suggest the procurement of able and willing guides and the inclusion of one or two Hotchkiss guns as arms.

On this expedition we killed 15 Moros and wounded five. We captured 22 rifles, two carabao and five ponies. We burned about fifty houses and destroyed some 70 tons of rice. We had one man killed, Sergeant H. F. Price, and two men wounded by stepping on bamboo spikes.

We found that the woolen puttee is better than the canvas legging, for general wear and keeping out leeches. We augmented daily rations with native rice, corn, camotes, sugar cane, coconuts, bananas and papayas. Green papayas are better than ripe ones. They should be peeled and sliced up like fried potatoes, then fried in bacon grease. The leaves of wild red pepper bushes, boiled and seasoned, taste not unlike spinach. The red bulbous banana blossom, chopped up and boiled, makes a good substitute for cabbage. The Bejuco vine, plentiful in the forest, furnishes potable water in surprisingly large quantities.

We found that experienced cargadores can carry 50 to 60 pounds for distances up to twelve miles per day. In rapid marches, the weight should be reduced to a maximum of 40 pounds.

Banana stalks make excellent rafts. The rafts should not be too large or attempt to carry too much. Five stalks, pointed at the prow, secured with two binders, and covered with a flooring of split bamboo will actually carry seven men with equipment and rations. In using vintas, it is generally best to lash them together. Also, it is best to use those which can accommodate from six to seven men. The larger ones are too narrow and unwieldy. It is best to place cargadores in the bow and stern of each canoe since most are experienced rivermen. Bejuco vines or bamboo poles serve well to lash these craft together. When towed by a launch, vintas ought to be in single column about six feet apart; this allows ample space for making sharp turns as dictated by the river's course.

Khaki shirts are better than blue flannel shirts for obvious reasons. Blue shirts scratch and irritate the skin and the skin festers. Khaki trousers are better than breeches, which bind. Khaki shorts are the most comfortable but leeches are a problem when the bare leg is exposed.

Field rations are good but monotonous. We augmented

our field ration diet with wild hog, deer, young carabao, chickens and ducks. Fruit was plentiful and tasty.

Cargadores are invaluable in the field, knowing a great deal about jungle-lore, rafting, vintas, vine bridges and such. Viscayans are the best, Tirurays next and Moros last. Once I saw a book on the Moros written by a Jesuit priest who had been in Moro country for forty years. It was leather bound and titled *What I Know About the Moros.* Inside were some 300 blank pages. All should be placed under the direct supervision of a competent officer or noncom and kept busy.

My officers and men behaved splendidly. I would be glad to go out with any or all of them again, any time.

Smith was not yet through with the Moros. On January 27, 1905, the Provisional Battalion left Piang's village for Sacapan, and the next day went on to Kaya Kaya and Ambuludan. The 14th Cavalry and 23rd Infantry companies under Captain Smith raided the villages of Taragat, Natubuc and Kapaia. All were reduced to ashes and the inhabitants scattered. Next came Dimasisig where a Juramentado Moro crept stealthily through the brush trying to kill a member of the advance party. He was dropped in his tracks by the wary trooper who wheeled and fired point-blank.

The command proceeded up the Guinibun River and marched to the Kabulanan River, destroying villages as it went. Near Sacapan forty-two banana tree rafts were built to ferry men and equipment over the swift waters. The men returned to Kudarangan on February 1, having travelled over 100 miles in four days.

Corney took the Provisional Troop out on its last expedition from February 4 to 10. Most of the time was spent retracing trails covered in September to determine if the Moros were filtering back and rebuilding; they were not. Sambulauan, Balatalupa and Saranaya were "ghost towns, forlorn, silent, with weeds and jungle creepers closing in all around."

On February 10 the Provisional Troop ceased to exist and all units were returned to their home stations. In his assessment of Captain Smith's part in the Provisional Troop expeditions, Colonel G. K. McGunnegle wrote:

Captain Smith is one of the very best of officers, accomplished, painstaking, industrious and progressive. He will fill any position to which he is assigned with credit and honor to the military profession. During the past five months he has been in command in the field operating against hostile Moros. This service has been difficult and onerous, probably as much so as any which our soldiers have ever had to contend with. Captain Smith has performed his duty faithfully, honestly and well under circumstances calculated to try the mettle of the best of soldiers.

Datu Ali remained at large until October 1905 when he was finally run down and killed by Captain Frank McCoy, the Aide-de-Camp to General Wood, in a fight at Malala. A year later, Corney, now District Governor at Cotabato, heard rumors that Datu Ali had risen from the grave to lead his people against the hated American invaders. Smith decided to prove, once and for all, that Ali was dead.

His interpreter was a friendly Moro who had been with McCoy at Malala and seen Ali killed. He also knew the two Moros who had dug the grave in which they had buried Ali and three of his sons also killed at Malala. In addition to the gravediggers the interpreter located three other Moros who had been present at the interment. All five were brought before a general gathering of Moros at Cotabato to verify Ali's death. According to Corney, "The faces in the crowd were impassive; I had not the slightest inkling whether they believed their countrymen or not."

The Moro raids and cases of Juramentado declined dramatically after Malala. It had been a bitter campaign. If Cuba had been the "splendid little war," the Moro campaign might aptly be called the "savage little war."

A Maguindanao Moro, Iligan, Mindanao, 1903. (Photo from personal files)

A Moro Grave, Iligan, Mindanao, 1903. (Photo from personal files)

CHAPTER NINE

The Philippine Constabulary

FOR THE NEXT SEVERAL MONTHS things were quiet in Iligan and Corney's Troop settled down to routine garrison duty. Several patrols were sent into the field but none lasted more than a few days. In October, Corney received orders to return stateside for recruiting duty at Jefferson Barracks, Missouri. While the bright lights and diversions of St. Louis were better than the steaming jungle and incessant rain of the Philippines, recruiting duty was boring. Corney lamented, "It's necessary, and someone has to do it, but I don't have to like it — I'd rather be where the action is." The tedium consisted in saying the same things over and over to prospective recruits in an attempt to "sell" the Army. Corney disliked this public relations aspect of the service. Only the frequent trips kept life from becoming too jaded. On December 18, 1905, he took a group of new recruits to Vancouver Barracks, Washington, and saw some friends he had made there twenty-one years earlier. In March 1906, he escorted recruits to Fort Rosecrans, California; in June to the Presidio of Monterey, California; and in August to Fortress Monroe, Virginia.

These were not trips in poor rolling stock nor "here today — gone tomorrow" deliveries. The trains were comfortable and the travel pleasant. After delivering his charges, Corney spent several days enjoying the town. Regulations were less stringent in 1906 than in the 1970s, giving officers latitude unknown in today's army. Corney took the next available train and he did not spend two or three days worrying about how to "justify" his leisure in the city.

Within weeks after his return stateside, Corney resumed work on a Maguindanao grammar for use by troops in the field. He had found in Iligan a translation begun many years earlier by a Jesuit priest named Juanmart, converting Spanish into Maguindanao. Corney had started the English version in March 1905, acquiring a basic knowledge of Maguindanao as he went along. He submitted the translated text to the War Department early the following year and was informed by the Military Intelligence Division of the Chief of Staff's office that:

> The Chief of Staff has approved the printing of the grammar, and requisition has been made, therefore, to print 1000 copies of this work for issue to the army.

The book was published as Document 270, Government Printing Office, in February 1906. General Leonard Wood wrote from Manila: "Please accept my congratulations on your success in this work. I turn over the government of the Moro Province on April 15. It will give me great pleasure to commend you to General Bliss, who follows me. . . . I believe your return to duty here would be for the best interests of the people in any district to which you might be assigned."

Another congratulatory note came from Colonel Langhorne in Zamboanga: "I am glad to see that you have been recognized as a prominent author. If you come out here again there are some twenty-eight dialects you can work on."

Spurred on by this hint of a possible return to the Philippines, Corney wrote to General Wood, Colonel Langhorne, and others requesting a transfer to the Islands. "My dear Smith," wrote Langhorne, "I am very glad to hear from you and will bear in mind your wish to return to Mindanao. Should anything occur here to make possible an appointment for you I shall take pleasure in presenting the matter in your behalf."

On July 31, Corney received a wire from the War Department stating: "Do you desire detail as governor of Davao, Philippines. Wire answer." He sent a seven-word reply minutes later: "I desire detail as Governor of Davao."

By the time Corney reached the Philippines in October his orders had been changed; he would serve as District Governor of Cotabato, not Davao. He provided his own opinion of the assignment:

> The government of the Moro Province in my time was practically independent of the Governor General in Manila. It had its own legislative council, consisting of a law member, doctor, engineer and several others. The Provincial Governor (in my case the officer in Zamboanga) had a comparable staff including secretary and treasurer. The Provincial Governor was always a general officer of the Army. In my almost six years in Mindanao I served under Generals Leonard Wood, Tasker H. Bliss and John J. Pershing.

> The legislative council of the Moro Province made its own laws which were sent to Manila, to the Civilian Governor General for approval. As it developed, this became largely a matter of form. Really, the government of the Philippines and that of the Moro Province constituted a dual authority – the former legislating and controlling the Christian and Pagan tribes in the north, the latter the Mohammedan peoples in the southern islands.

> The Moro Province consisted of five districts: Zamboanga, Jolo, Davao, Lanao and Cotabato, each under an army officer serving as governor. I had the honor of serving as Governor of Cotabato during 1906 and 1907, and as Governor of Lanao in 1910, 11 and 12. Of the two districts, Cotabato was the more civilized. Lanao was turbulent, and our troops were in the field most of the time.

Aside from the honor and degree of autonomy involved in the District Governorship, an additional reward developed. Although a captain in the Regular Army, Corney now became a major of

Filipino Constabulary with full pay and allowances. Later, in 1909, he would command the First Battalion of Filipino Scouts at Camp Vicars, and in 1910 command both the First and Second Battalions in Lanao.

The Constabulary had been established by an Act of Congress on January 30, 1903. An armed police force, its purpose was to maintain order and enforce the laws of the Philippine Islands. Enlistments were available to any male citizen of the Philippines who — providing he was of average intelligence, able-bodied and of good character — would take an oath of allegiance to the United States. Appointees could not be under twenty nor over thirty-five. Testifying to the small stature of most of the natives was the height and weight chart for enlistees which began at 5'0" and 100 pounds and ended at 5'8" and 120 pounds.

These rugged men proved as good as, and frequently better than, the larger Americans who served beside them. Khaki breeches and shirts were neatly worn and well pressed with puttees wrapped smartly around the legs. Headdress was either turban or fez for the Moro scouts. Disliking footwear, men wore shoes only at parades, inspections or whenever they felt like wearing them in the field.

Moros in U.S. employ were occasionally cruel and treacherous against their own people. As Governor in Cotabato, Corney had to deal with a Constabulary agent named Pasalandan and an alleged criminal, Pacasmo. Pasalandan had tired of his wife, Apunta, and cast her off. Several months later she met and married Pacasmo. Although the former husband did not want her back, he was crazed with jealousy. Pacasmo was employed by the government as a laborer for the quartermaster at Cotabato and was known as hard working and inoffensive.

One day Pasalandan brought him in, charged with murder, theft and possession of firearms. In the preliminary hearing before Corney, Pacasmo, wild-eyed and terrified, readily confessed to the charges. It seemed all too pat. Between the hearing and the trial, Corney had a lieutenant question Pacasmo further and a grim story unfolded:

When Pasalandan arrived at my home, said Pacasmo, he had eight men with him. I was seized and bound with a rope and hanged by my arms behind my back, and pulled up so my feet were well off the ground. Then I was twirled round and round and struck with rifle butts. Pasalandan asked where my revolver was. I have never owned one in my life. I want the judge to know I never had one. But they spun me more and hit me more and so I said I would admit owning a gun. I was hanged like this three times, once at Titay, once on the Agus River, and once at Pasalandan's house. At Titay they hit me on the head and cut my head open, making it bleed all over my shirt and pants.

At the Agus River they hung me and built a fire under my feet. Then they said I would confess to killing a Chinaman or they would kill me. I said I would confess to anything. That was a lie. I killed no Chinaman. Here I am. I beg your mercy.

A trial followed in which both Pasalandan and Pacasmo were thoroughly questioned. Pasalandan's witnesses were glib and confident; Pacasmo's frightened but resolute. Apparently many had been victims of Pasalandan's cruelty. Pacasmo was acquitted and Pasalandan convicted. He was removed from his position, fined and jailed.

While serving as Governor at Cotabato, Corney made several interesting observations about various tribes:

The Bagobos, like the Sioux and Cheyenne Indians, are great bead workers, the attire of both men and women being very elaborate and strikingly colorful. Bagobos are strong, robust and relatively tall. Many are noticeably lighter in color than the average Filipino. Men wear trousers with bead work and don kerchiefs or turbans and stick long knives into their pants. The men also wear ear-discs of ivory measuring about two inches in diameter. This is connected to a second smaller disc which fits into a hole in the earlobe, like a collar button. Beautifully carved, these discs are prized possessions and may be worth one or even two carabao.

The Mandaya man wears an odd-shaped wooden hat topped off with a wild cock's plume, which gives the wearer a jaunty appearance – like an Austrian jaeger or an Italian Biscegliari.

The Manobas, Bukidnons and Montescos worship

forest spirits. They live in a region of profound silence, broken only occasionally by the sound of a hog or deer running through the forest or the discordant cawing of a hornbill.

The Bagobos, Subanos and Mandayas are poor in material wealth, living from hand to mouth. Not much is known of them, and accounts made by the Spaniards are fragmentary and contradictory. I have found Subanos to be friendly and gentle people, inclined to hospitality and good fellowship. If a man's face is an index to his feelings, then these are happy people. They are continually smiling. They are like children when compared to the Moro, who are treacherous, crafty and sullen. Again, like children, they display an almost touching affection for flowers, birds and music.

Tirurayes, Bilanes, Bagobos, Mandayas and Atus are superstitious. The supernatural directs their daily lives to a marked degree. When they dance they are often "moved by spirits" which propel them on to wild energetic gyrations which cause them to topple over in exhaustion.

Among the Tirurayes the insane are treated with deference and respect. This is because they are believed to house spirits which may not be offended. I have seen mild cases so treated, but cannot help but wonder what happens when the deranged person is wild and violent. Tirurayes and Subanos are poor warriors, abjectly fearing the Moro. Thus they remain in the deep gloom of mountain forests, away from coastal settlements where Moros abound.

The poverty of Subanos and Tirurayes borders on misery, but it is a matter of choice. They are indolent, eating whatever nature has to offer and pass a great deal of their time in sleeping, lounging about or paying one another visits. I must say, though, that they treat outsiders with consideration. They are pure children of nature, asking nothing and willing to share what little they have.

Bilanes are a physically beautiful people, clean of limb and well muscled. They seem to be a pure and unmixed tribe, living quietly on rice, yams and forest game. They live in such isolation that no proper census has ever been taken. Historically, the Moros have raided Bilane villages for slaves. They still do, but infrequently, now that we are here to prevent such things.

The Bagobos make human sacrifices when times are bad. Several such sacrifices have been brought to light recently. Interestingly, the perpetrators cannot understand why we object so strenuously to a custom which to them is natural and proper. The Bukidnons ("Mountain people") are tall for Filipinos. Women are handsome, most having slender hands and feet. Bukidnon men are supposedly monogamous, but many have copied the Moros and have several wives and several concubines. The warriors equip themselves with a sort of rude armor made of kapok and large intricately carved wooden shields.

These people love music and dancing, and there is one dance in which the women and girls manipulate shawls between extended arms and fingers to a peculiar rhythmic and gliding step seen nowhere else.

Visitors approaching a Bukidnon town are met by a fully armed warrior who brandishes a formidable lance carrying a bell on the shaft. He dances about in astonishing fashion, makes faces, thrusts out his tongue and shakes his lance as though to impale the visitor. The intruder is expected to smile appreciatively at this wild display. I have always done that, but I have never forgotten that these men are wild savages. My pistol was always within easy grasp; fortunately I never had to use it in visiting Bukidnon settlements.

A Bukidnon Datu, especially one who has killed enemies in battle, wears a beautiful gold headdress, strung with red, white and blue tassels.

The Mandayas are fine looking people with almond-shaped eyes and long straight lashes. Both men and women go fully clothed, and the women often have their arms loaded down with ornaments of brass and shell. The hair is banged squarely across the forehead and worn in a knot at the back of the head. Into this is thrust a silver mounted wooden comb. At the waist there generally hangs a huge mass of ornaments and charms.

The Mandayas use bows and arrows with consummate skill. Their shields, long and slender, are not unlike those carried by Ilongots. They are great silversmiths, working beautiful mountings into spears, knives and other weapons. They are good fighters. Recently I met a man carrying a scarlet Bagani coat, the garb of a man who has killed six persons. I asked him why he was carrying the Bagani garment, instead of wearing it. "Because," he answered, "I have only killed five people."

The Subano houses contain almost nothing in the way of furniture but are often abundantly supplied with china plates, brass betel nut boxes and trays, brass gongs, and large brass jars. The latter are especially prized. I have heard that Subanos practise polygamy but have no evidence to substantiate the assertion.

Corney spent most of his time in Cotabato arbitrating civil cases involving Filipinos but was often in the field. Cotabato was a large district, extending from Illana Bay on the west to Davao District in the east and bordering upon Lanao District in the north. With his staff members and a detachment of the Filipino Constabulary, he made many trips into the uncharted wilderness of central Mindanao. He later observed that his most interesting and rewarding experiences in the Philippines were those periods spent as District Governor.

In June 1907, he received orders for stateside duty with the 14th Cavalry at the Presidio in San Francisco.

CHAPTER TEN

The City by the Bay

ARRIVING AT THE PRESIDIO in July 1907, Corney settled down to "humdrum garrison duty." Still, the assignment had its advantages. The social life was gay and there always seemed to be something to do. The city had not yet recovered from the earthquake of 1906. Great piles of rubble lay in many places, particularly along streets like Post, Geary, Sutter and O'Farrell. Many of the buildings on Russian Hill and Nob Hill were blackened hulks, and some stores along Lombard Street were shuttered and vacant. The constant banging of hammers and the sawing of wood indicated that a new San Francisco was rising from the ashes.

Since there was no post school, the Smith boys, Gil and Graham, attended a school on Nob Hill about two miles from the Presidio. One of Graham's classmates was a daughter of Ghirardelli, the "Chocolate King." Invited to her sumptuous home for a children's party, the size and splendor of the mansion overwhelmed him. Graham later bubbled, "Gee, Dad, they've even got trees growing in the house!"

Shortly after arriving at the Presidio, Graham stood side-by-side with his father at the northernmost tip of the adjoining post (Fort

Winfield Scott), and watched the "great White Fleet" steam into the harbor. In later years, Graham would often remark "how pretty the ships were steaming along in line — the *Iowa, Oregon, Brooklyn* and the others."

A few days after witnessing the fleet sail through the Golden Gate, Graham watched a giant parade swing down Van Ness Avenue to honor the fleet: "Troopers, sailors, marines and cadets — men by the thousands marched down Van Ness that day. As far as I was concerned, Dad's G Troop was the smartest looking unit of all. San Francisco had never seen such a parade."

Corney settled in the Presidio, then busied himself with the usual round of training, honing and polishing his outfit, trying to make it the best one in the Army. If "emulation is the sincerest form of flattery," then a comment of Captain J. G. Langdon could be counted as such:

> Dear Captain Smith: I would like to take my noncoms through your stable and let them look at your saddle rooms, just to show them what I believe to be the only model outfit in the army. Could you give me this permission for 10 o'clock this morning?

In the summer of 1908, Corney was given an unexpected and pleasant assignment. From June through August, he would be Superintendent of Sequoia National Park and the General Grant National Park in California's Sierra Nevada Range. His command included several civilian park rangers plus two troops of cavalry to assist as rangers, firefighters, road builders and tourist guides. It promised to be an enjoyable summer; Gilbert and Graham were especially enthusiastic and impatiently waited for the school term to end.

Fanny and the boys made the trip by Doherty Wagon, a paymaster's wagon built like a stagecoach, equipped with comfortable leather seats and drawn by four big mules. Gil and Graham rode horses about as much as they rode in the wagon. Corney was a stickler for making camp early and getting up at the crack of dawn. Generally, therefore, the train stopped at about 3:00 P.M. and was up, breakfasted and on the move by 6:30 A.M. The leisurely trip averaged perhaps fifteen miles daily.

Corney noted that:

> At that time, regular army troops were a rarity in California's interior towns and rural districts, and our arrival in small towns along the way was the cause of considerable excitement. We were treated royally. Dances were given and a man's uniform was his ticket of admission. So kind and generous were our hosts that our money was practically worthless. The enlisted men were on an equal footing with officers where attention from townspeople was concerned. This was interesting since in the larger coastal communities only the officers were sought out. I had pondered the inequity of this before, thinking of Kipling's famous poem *Tommy Atkins.*
>
> In several of these towns merchants loaded the men with tobacco, candy, ice cream and beer. Restaurants gave the men free meals, and at Dinuba farmers came into camp with great wagonloads of oranges, grapes, and watermelons. Frequently we returned these favors, asking our benefactors to share our mess. They had many questions about Cuba and the Philippines.

Gil, now eleven years old, had become a fairly proficient bugler, and persuaded the military bugler to permit him to blow first call and reveille. One morning, according to Graham, "Gil hit a clinker, and Dad said, 'Bring that man to me!' " When the "man" appeared shamefaced, everyone laughed, adding to Gil's mortification. "Chambers," the Captain informed the bugler, "I don't mind you and Smith swapping places, but you take him out and practise him some; I don't want any more sour notes — understand?" Practice improved Gil's ability. "By mid-July he was blowing as many calls as Chambers," said Graham, "and was especially good on tattoo and taps, letting the long sweet notes hang out there in the cold night air."

The family had a wonderful summer, enjoying the cool, clear midsummer days of the High Sierra. Beautiful mountain scenery, forest animals for company, fresh trout frying in the breakfast pan, and songs and stories around the nightly campfire provided a serene existence. Unfortunately, sorrow soon visited Corney's household.

In February at the Presidio, Fanny suddenly suffered a ruptured appendix and immediately was rushed to the hospital. Despite the best efforts to save her, she died several days later. Although Corney and the boys spent another summer at Sequoia, it was not the same carefree place for them.

During the latter stay, Corney met Walter Fry, forming one of the closest friendships of his life. Fry was the Chief Ranger at Sequoia and served Corney as a sort of Chief of Staff. Writing about his companion years later, Corney said:

> Fry is a remarkable man, big, openhearted and honest. He seems to have taken his stature from the mountain crags and the giant sequoias around him. He is rugged and brave, yet like so many men of that stamp is gentle, kind and considerate. As my assistant he has been exemplary. Once, on a ten-day inspection of the park he astounded me with his knowledge of botany, geology and natural history. I don't know when I have spent a more delightful ten days — listening to dissertations on bear, white-tailed deer, rattlesnakes, trout, sequoia trees, Douglas fir and all of the small animals of the forest. Also, he told me all about the early days of the California Highwaymen, Evans and Sontag, and of the Mexican bandit Vasquez whose severed head is displayed in a pickle jar in a San Francisco Medical Museum.
>
> Born in Illinois, he became Sequoia's chief ranger in 1892. He knew Muir and Burroughs intimately, and he knows people. I have not known a finer man.

Three other civilian rangers, C. W. Blossom, H. T. Britten and L. L. Davis, who served with Corney during the summers of 1908 and 1909 left favorable impressions. They cooperated with the troopers working on the roads leading into the General Grant Tree area. The men also served as fire watchers from vantage points positioned throughout the park. The troopers built observation towers some miles away from the main camp. Telephone lines and heliograph provided communication links. A German private named "Shorty" Hengst was the Troop farrier. Hengst was also an amateur carpenter and built a supply shack near the road leading into camp. Years later, during a visit to Sequoia, Graham recalled Hengst and his Teutonic thoroughness: "That shack, for instance, he even put lathe-turned decorations on the eaves and ridge crest." The shack presumably had long been blown over or had been torn down after twenty-three years. As the Model A swung around a bend in the road, Graham shouted: "By God! There it is — there's Shorty Hengst's shack!" Shorty's handiwork, weather-beaten and gray, stood proudly beneath the great redwoods soaring above it.

All was not fun and games at Sequoia. In 1909 the troopers had been in camp only a month when a huge forest fire swept the area. Both G and H Troops manned the fire line for the better part of a month before the devastating blaze could be extinguished.

Even when conditions were "normal," the troopers kept busy. Averaging fifteen miles per day, Troop rangers accumulated an astonishing number of miles patrolling the park. During the tourist season, men rode over 1,128 miles patrolling General Grant Park, 1,132 miles in and around Buck Canyon, 1,200 miles for Rocky Gulch, 1,236 for Cold Springs, 1,250 for Atwell's Mill and 1,224 for Clough's Cave. This riding was "routine only," and did not cover messenger service and unforeseen or emergency details. Corney moved his men from station to station once a month to change the scenery and forestall monotony.

Captain Smith enforced a rigid set of rules and regulations for all visitors to Sequoia or Grant Park. Item 13 specified that:

> Persons who render themselves obnoxious by disorderly conduct or bad behavior, or who may violate any of the foregoing rules will be summarily removed from the park, and will not be allowed to return without permission in writing, from the Secretary of the Interior, or the superintendent of the park.

The regulation also provided humorous sidelights. When a trooper ordered one camper to dig a pit for his kitchen garbage, the offender replied, "I came here for a rest, not to dig holes." The soldier replied, "Well, the Captain ain't gonna like it, so dig one anyway!"

During another incident, a woman could not understand Captain Smith's disapproval of her dumping dish water and bath water on flowers bordering her family's tent. An interesting conversation developed when Corney reasoned, "Well, if nothing else, madam, it will kill the flowers."

"Well, it ain't killed me."

"No, but you don't drink dish water."

"Well, sir, you got me there."

Both visitors stayed on, but Corney ejected two others for breaking the seals on their firearms and one family for keeping a slovenly campsite with an open garbage pit and generally unsanitary conditions which attracted not only flies but also hungry grizzly bears.

Corney normally applied logical rules for camp sanitation. He could not, however, enforce the rules on private land adjoining the park and commented that:

> There are no hotels in either park. In Sequoia the firm of Broder and Hopping maintains, under contract with the department, a transportation and permanent camp service. This establishment is, in my opinion, remote from first class. I believe the members of the firm are thoroughly honest and good people, but they do not seem to understand the proper running of a mountain resort.

> They have a few cheap tents, a cookhouse, a dining cabin and a small store, the group being called Camp Sierra. A good many people from the small towns of the San Joaquin Valley use this place improperly, and sanitary conditions are very bad. As the firm of Broder and Hopping is on patented land, and as neither member is in sympathy with the rules and regulations of the Interior Department, enforcement of rules in this camp is difficult and embarrassing.

Predators and wild game were almost superabundant. Corney reported: "Mountain lions, wildcats, wolves and coyotes are troublesome. I have ordered rangers and soldiers to shoot them wherever found. Rattlesnakes are to be exterminated on sight, and I will add wolverines, skunks and hawks to the list."

Corney also described fishing in the park's icy streams:

> There are myriads of tiny trout in the streams hereabout, due to the planting last year by my predecessor, Captain Kirby Walker. Hence, fishing is excellent. It is particularly good around Hockett's Meadow, Quinn's Horse Camp and Cabin Meadow Country. Five men and one lady personally known to

me took 242 trout from Aug. 22 to the 24th. Some were fourteen inches long, and most were over ten inches.

By the following summer, he confirmed that predators were still a problem but fishing was better than ever:

> One reason for the numerous mountain lions seen throughout the area is the unusual number of deer. I recommend that the government purchase a pack of hounds and conduct a campaign to cut down on the number of lions, lynx and wildcats. I feel that dogs constitute the only means of solving this problem, since the cats are too wary to take poisoned bait and eat only what they kill.

Arguments among Park visitors whether Yosemite's "Grizzly Giant" tree was larger than Sequoia's "General Sherman" tree prompted Corney's evaluation: "I've seen both and say without hesitation that the General Sherman is the larger tree. We have measured it to be 36 feet in diameter six feet from the ground, and 20 feet across 100 feet up."

In August 1909 one of the enlisted men at Sequoia died of stomach trouble. The young corporal, John Paul O'Brien, was the son of Charles A. O'Brien, a prominent Pittsburgh attorney. In informing Mr. O'Brien of his son's passing, Corney ended his letter:

> Having lost my dear wife and good mother within the last six months, I can but offer you the consolation of a man who knows what grief is but who has never questioned the will of God, who knows when to take our loved ones from us. If I may be of service to you, please command me.

Answering, the boy's father wrote:

> Please accept a loving father's gratitude for your tender ministration to my lovely boy and your sweet message of sympathy and consolation for myself. . . . He had nothing to repent of, for he never caused me pain or sorrow, except now that he died in the springtime of what I know would have been a splendid manhood.

The editor of the Pittsburgh *Gazette Times* was impressed by Corney's letter to the bereaved father, and he informed his readers that:

DON'T SETTLE FOR SECOND

Some there are who hug the delusion that when a man becomes an officer in the army he is transformed into a martinet or a cad. Certainly Captain C. C. Smith of the Four-teenth Cavalry is not such a man. In his letter to City Solicitor Charles A. O'Brien, telling of the death of the latter's son, there speaks the gentleman as well as the soldier.

Few finer samplings of the English language come to one's notice in a lifetime, and between the lines there is revealed unmistakably the impulse of a gentle and chivalrous heart.

During his long service, Corney Smith addressed many letters of comparable sorrow to bereaved loved ones. He received many answers, some polished, some semiliterate, but all carrying the same heartfelt message from sorrowing but grateful wives or parents. Perhaps the O'Brien letter was special because it came at a time when his own loss was so recent. In one sense, the time at Sequoia and General Grant Parks had been idyllic, a sort of pristine paradise of fresh pure air, sparkling streams and giant trees which dwarfed the body but elevated the soul; in another, it had been a lonely and heartbreaking experience. As any man might, Corney wished to get away from the scene of his poignant memories. A return to the Philippines provided the opportunity.

CHAPTER ELEVEN

Our House at Marahui

IN OCTOBER 1909, after twenty-seven months stateside, Corney Smith once again sailed for the Philippines. He welcomed the diversion. The summers at Sequoia had been enjoyable, but the loss of Fanny at Letterman was a devastating blow. He longed to get far away from the bitter memory and begin anew. With no mother to care for them, Gil and Graham stayed behind with their grandparents in Leavenworth.

As Captain Smith stepped aboard the transport *Thomas*, he did not know that a beautiful passenger from New York would shortly provide the love and companionship that he missed so keenly. On the third night out of San Francisco, Corney met Kathleen Crowley, daughter of Republican Congressman Richard Crowley, at a ship's dance. From that time on the two were inseparable. They were married at the Cathedral in the old Walled City of Manila. For his honeymoon, Corney arranged for a leave of absence before settling down in Marahui as District Governor of Lanao.

A leisurely cruise to the Orient took the newlyweds first to Japan, where they relished the comforts of Tokyo and other major cities. They went next to China, stopping in Shanghai where the full-bearded, meticulously dressed Sikh policemen directing pedestrian traffic amazed Kathleen. Later they traveled to the Great Wall of China and marveled at its brutish magnificence and at the thousands of grave mounds stretching away from its base. From Canton, where Kathleen had her fortune told by a soothsayer who promised long life and many babies, they went to Hong Kong, Kowloon and Macao. Riding in rickshaws, feasting on exotic foods and watching the endless procession of life on shore and on the bobbing sampans in the bay, they enjoyed their honeymoon.

After six weeks, the Smiths arrived in Marahui and set up housekeeping in a comfortable white bungalow sitting on a sweeping lawn shaded by frangipani and ylang-ylang and covered with bougainvillea. In a circular flower plot out front, Corney mounted a lantaca cannon, the gift of a Subano chieftain. "It was not the grandest place we ever had, but our house at Marahui was the first. I'll always think about it with a twinge of nostalgia." In the weeks that followed, old friendships were renewed and new ones formed. Picnics were held near the post and the women and children were taken along in carriages or in great two-wheeled carts drawn by carabao.

On one such outing, while Corney and Kathleen were sitting under a tree, rustling leaves overhead startled them. Suddenly a python dropped at their feet. Kathleen shrieked and remained terrified despite Corney's assurances that it was "only a little one." She considered any snake ten feet long to be a monster.

Soon Corney assumed duties as Governor of the District: listening to complaints, trying cases, putting down rebellions, and making inspections into the hinterlands. General Pershing, an acquaintance from the Dakotas, was now Corney's boss. A good friend, Pershing was stern yet tactful. He liked and admired Corney Smith but warned him against being so forceful and direct: "My God, Smith, ease up — your honesty is appalling."

Their friendship proved invaluable many years later. When Corney died, Kathleen had a difficult time proving that she was Corney's legal widow. The marriage certificate had been lost; the priest who married them was dead; and the Cathedral in the old walled section of the city had burned and with it all the records. Finally, in desperation, Kathleen wrote to Pershing in Walter Reed

Hospital asking his assistance. A phone call from him to the War Department unsnarled Army red tape. Within days, a special delivery letter brought all back pension and current entitlements.

Meanwhile, however, Corney grappled with the problems of the Lanao District, a product of the Organic Act of June 1, 1903, which created the Moro Province. It became a full-fledged political district on December 17, 1903, with the passage of Act 25. This legislation of the Moro Province Council established the forces necessary for running the Lanao District. In 1909, when Corney assumed command, some 50,000 Moros, a few pagan tribesmen, and about 3,500 Christian Filipinos inhabited the area.

Confusion reigned during the first few years of the district, as little or no understanding existed between the governed and the governors. The passage of time stabilized conditions somewhat, but even in 1912, Constabulary police scoured the territory for brigands and pirates.

One of Corney's major problems was Amai Detsan. This ruler of a turbulent district of Moros on the northwestern shore of Lake Lanao had never acknowledged the Spanish as overlords and saw no reason to acquiesce to American demands. He pursued, as the poet described, "the even tenor of his way." Ultimately, Detsan acquiesced to American rule, but it took a decade to accomplish the feat. Finally, diplomacy succeeded where force had failed.

Captain Bayard Schindel, 6th U.S. Infantry, was stationed at Tampanan, an American enclave not far from Detsan's headquarters at Ramain. Schindel gained the Moro's confidence by entering his rancheria accompanied by only an interpreter and a private. Impressed with the Captain's pluck, Detsan befriended him and returned the visit. He came to Tampanan not once but numerous times thereafter. In their subsequent talks, Schindel impressed upon the datu the advantages of recognizing American authority.

One day in the latter part of 1910, Schindel brought Detsan with a retinue of his followers to the office of the District Governor at Marahui, Captain Cornelius C. Smith. The datu and his men put on their finest garb to meet Smith and discuss American rule. Captain Smith told Detsan that in recognizing American authority he would open the door for aid to his people, including hospitalization, schooling, roads and economic assistance. Also, he would be named as undisputed chief of all of the datus in the area.

The only condition was that he would be expected to preserve the peace in his fiefdom and to eliminate the piracy and robbery then flourishing in Mindanao.

Detsan agreed to the proposal but questioned the American system of trial by jury. Smith warned the datu that he would not be permitted to shoot or spear criminals, but must apprehend and bring them in.

"What if they resist?" asked the Moro. Corney responded, "Then you must use your judgement, but you must make every effort to capture rather than execute. If you are forced to kill, then we must have proof that you have taken the right man."

Detsan's reaction to these conditions was soon tested as a bandit named Manganitza was terrorizing the countryside. He seemingly robbed and murdered at will in the little barrios scattered throughout the forest. Manganitza habitually waited in high cogon grass along some lonely stretch of road or trail, then killed his unsuspecting victims and escaped with his booty.

Shortly after Detsan's meeting with Smith a detachment of soldiers en route from Keithley to Overton found the body of a badly butchered Chinaman. The Governor then dispatched Lieutenant Hoffman to pick up the killer's trail and capture him. If the trail continued into Detsan's territory, the young officer was to report the fact immediately so that the Moro could continue the pursuit. Now was the time to find out whether or not Detsan would fulfill his pledge.

Hoffman found the killer's trail and saw that it led directly into Detsan's domain. Subsequently, Smith called the datu into his office and relayed the news. Detsan quickly led a small party after the bandit. Around noon on the following day, he and his sacopes returned by vinta on the lake and beached the vessel about one hundred yards from the Governor's office. He requested that Governor Smith be called to the boat to see something. Within minutes, Smith and two junior officers stood nearby.

"I have evidence," asserted Detsan reaching into the canoe for a gunnysack. With a flip, he opened the sack and rolled a human head at the Governor's feet.

"This is Manganitza, man who killed Chinaman."

Before reporting this bizarre event to General Pershing, the Provincial Governor at Zamboanga, Smith had to confirm that this head was indeed that of Manganitza. The interpreter in the District Office, Thomas Torres, had seen Manganitza several years earlier but was not sure that he could identify him. He did recall, however, that Manganitza had served Nusca Alim, a Mohammedan priest who lived for some years near Marahui. Surely, Nusca Alim would remember him.

They summoned Alim who arrived about an hour later. He was told that identification of a human head was necessary, but that he should be absolutely certain before speaking. With that the sack was opened and the head rolled out. Alim grabbed the long black hair, thick and full as a horse's mane, and held the remains aloft. After looking at the ghostly face, Alim spoke a single word, "Manganitza!"

By March 1912, Corney had tired of Philippine service. He longed to rejoin his old unit and addressed the Adjutant General in Washington asking for a transfer:

> I request that I be relieved from duty as a Major of the Philippine Scouts and returned to duty with the 14th Cavalry. Reason for this request is probable service on the Mexican Border. As I was born in Arizona, have served in New Mexico, and speak Spanish, I feel that I may be of some service on the border.
>
> On April 3, I will have been two years and five months in this district. I was detailed as Major of Scouts on September 8, 1909.

The Army agreed. Colonel Lea Febeger endorsed Corney's request citing his subordinate as "an active, energetic, and most intelligent officer, intensely interested in his profession. I shall regret losing Major Smith as a member of this command."

A few weeks later, Corney and Kathleen were bound for Fort Huachuca, Arizona.

Captain and Mrs. Smith and Corney, Jr., Naco, Arizona, winter 1914. "Home" was Southwestern Box Car 1113. (Photo from personal files)

Colorado National Guardsmen riding to a strike-torn area in the Southern Colorado coalfields, April 1914. (Photo courtesy *United Mine Workers Journal)*

CHAPTER TWELVE

Border Towns to Mining Camps

CAPTAIN SMITH DID NOT REJOIN the 14th Cavalry as he had hoped but, at Fort Huachuca, was assigned to the 5th Cavalry. Corney had already ridden in three proud mounted regiments, the 6th, 2nd and 14th; now he would serve with another.

When Corney arrived in Arizona, however, the 5th was still in Honolulu which prompted him to take a leave of absence until the command returned stateside. While he rested, long-simmering trouble below the border boiled over. In 1910, President Porfirio Díaz, "the Grand Old Man" of Mexico, was deposed after nearly thirty-five years of absolute rule over his people. For the next ten years the country crumbled — literally torn apart by those jockeying for political power.

Trouble between Mexican Federals and insurgents endangered the area from Matamoros to Tijuana. To protect American lives and property in the Arizona communities, troops of the 5th Cavalry moved to several border towns. In the autumn of 1912, Captain Cornelius Smith accompanied Troops A and G to Nogales.

Corney quickly encountered a remarkable individual, Colonel Emilio Kosterlitzky, Commander of La Gendarmería Fiscal of the

DON'T SETTLE FOR SECOND

state of Sonora. Kosterlitzky was a Russian who had deserted from the Imperial Russian Navy. On December 3, 1872, he had jumped ship at Puerto Cabello, Venezuela, then worked his way north to Mexico where he joined the Army. Catching the eye of President Díaz, he rose from the ranks to gain a commission. From then on his promotions were slow and steady until in March 1913, he became the Commander of Gendarmería's Third Zone.

In October 1912, Corney met Kosterlitzky in Nogales and they took an immediate liking to one another. As each of their units maintained its own officers' mess close to the border, frequent visits ensued. During these social affairs the two men talked long and earnestly of Mexico's problems. Kosterlitzky expected a decisive action with the rebels soon and told Smith that if forced to surrender he would cross over and give up his arms to the Americans. Ultimately, his 285 Federal soldiers were no match for the 900 men of Alvaro Obregón. After a bloody all-day fight on March 13, 1913, Kosterlitzky, his rurales and about eighty-five regulars crossed the international line and surrendered to Captain Smith. Corney posted A and G Troops along the two streets to take the Mexicans into custody, stack arms, and lead them away.

Corney summarized the Kosterlitzky story in a 1932 letter to a writer:

Dear Mr. Chisholm: I have read your Kosterlitzky article in *Touring Topics* with great interest. When I tell you that for many years he was my friend and that he surrendered to me in Nogales, Arizona, on March 13, 1913, you will, I feel, not take it amiss if I point out a discrepancy or two in your story.

I feel that I knew Kosterlitzky about as well as any American in Nogales at the time, as I was in intimate contact with him for several months, while he commanded in Nogales, Sonora, and I in Nogales, Arizona. On the morning of March 12, 1913, he sent an orderly to my camp with a note inviting me to lunch with him in his quarters. He added that he had some information for me. As it turned out, I had already received the information from our secret service. This was the news concerning Obregón's advance upon Nogales.

I had lunch with Don Emilio. As closely as I can recall his words, they were about as follows: "Obregón is on his way here with about 2,500 men. I will fight him, of course, but am at a disadvantage with less than 300 rurales and a few regulars under Reyes. If I have to surrender, I'll cross the line and surrender to you."

Just before dark on the following evening, both Kosterlitzky and Reyes came across the line with their forces after an all-day fight with Obregón. A place was designated to deposit their arms and equipment, and a place appointed to take their horses. I then asked Kosterlitzky which of his officers he wanted paroled. He gave me a list of fourteen, including three lieutenants whose names I recall were: José de la Rosa, Rafael Contreras and José Galas. . . . That night, in my camp, Kosterlitzky presented me with his sabre and sombrero, not as trophies of war, but simply as gifts. I still have them.

During the next few weeks, and before I left Nogales to return to Huachuca, Kosterlitzky spent a lot of time with me. I learned to know him as a gentleman and a soldier. He once told me of challenging Pancho Villa to personal combat and I believe it. He said nothing of any "running fight" with Villa, where he "threw his pistol at him." He said Villa was "cold-footed," and I believe that, too. The part of your story about Kosterlitzky talking with Harry Carr about a plan for the conquest of Mexico — I doubt very much. I always thought, and still do, that when Kosterlitzky left Mexico it was for keeps.

Kosterlitzky and his men were taken from Nogales in August 1913, and incarcerated at Fort Rosecrans, San Diego, California. In October of the following year, a general Mexican amnesty permitted their release. All of the prisoners except Kosterlitzky returned. He moved to Los Angeles and served as a special employee of the U.S. Justice Department for twelve years. He died on March 2, 1928, and was buried in Calvary Cemetery in East Los Angeles.

Corney returned to Huachuca in April 1913, and settled down to the post routine. Kathleen's days, however, were not so dull. She was expecting their first child which caused the usual flurry concerning layettes, bootees and sundry paraphernalia. On July 18 Kathleen gave birth to Cornelius Cole Smith, Jr. Corney's namesake quickly experienced the rigors of Army life.

The Smith family left Huachuca with the Second Squadron of the 5th Regiment in December 1913, for Fort Leavenworth, Kansas. Corney barely had time to unpack his bags before he was again on the move. In April 1914, he took the squadron to Walsenburg, Colorado. That beleaguered community, like others in the southern Colorado Rocky Mountain area, was an armed camp amid conflict between mine owners and their employees.

By the turn of the twentieth century, the labor movement had become such a factor in American economic life that the great anthracite coal strike of 1902 led owners to try to protect their economic hegemony. They formed trade associations, compiled blacklists of troublemakers, and organized strikebreakers. Increasingly, violence became the hallmark of economic disputes. The threat of radicalism provided some industrialists with the excuse for the ruthless suppression of the labor movement. In September 1913, some 9,000 miners in Southern Colorado went on strike to protest deplorable working conditions and to win company acceptance of their union, the United Mine Workers. Knowing that the employers would remove them from company-owned houses, the strikers put up tent cities nearby and walked off the job.

Strikebreakers constantly harassed the tent camps at Walsenburg, Ludlow, Forbes, Trinidad and other communities. On April 20, 1914, about 200 company guards attacked the main portion of the Colorado Fuel and Iron Company Camp. Pouring a withering fire into the canvas city, the guards watched while helpless women and children ran screaming from the makeshift camp. The guards then sprayed the entire area with kerosene and set it ablaze. In all, some twenty-five people were killed and more than 100 wounded. Eight days later, President Woodrow Wilson declared an emergency in Colorado and called on federal troops. Captain Cornelius C. Smith led G Troop of the 5th United States Cavalry into the troubled area to help restore order.

Federal troops began arriving in the strike zone during the last week in April — elements of the 12th Cavalry from Fort D.A. Russell and troops of the 5th Cavalry from Fort Leavenworth, Corney Smith's among them. The April 29 *Post* published a page-one cartoon showing U.S. troops marching in to the cheers of jubilant Colorado citizens shouting: "Hurrah! They're here!" Even the yapping little dog muses: "Now, they'll be good!"

The Federal Task Force was commanded by Major Willard A. ("Hunk") Holbrook, whose soldierly appearance and bearing caused one enthusiastic reporter to compare him to Lord Kitchener of the British Army. Holbrook established the ground rules at once:

> We are here to preserve order, not to take sides. It is not the purpose of the United States to inject itself into the controversy existing between miners and their former employees. The President looks for a quick return to normal conditions, brought on without further bloodshed. To accomplish this, every citizen is expected to read and comply with the provisions of a proclamation which has been sent to your postmaster for posting in your cities and in all surrounding camps.

The federal troops had been in Denver less than two hours when Holbrook assigned areas to his commanders. Corney was sent to Walsenburg and arrived as the last of the state militia departed. Captain Smith moved his men to the park in front of the courthouse and ordered an immediate conference of strikers, mine representatives and peace officers. When the men had gathered, he outlined his position, explaining as Holbrook had done, that he was not in Walsenburg to take sides but to eliminate armed conflict.

The conferees listened attentively, asked a few questions and departed. That night, however, Corney's troopers arrested six drunken National Guardsmen who had broken into a saloon, looted it and were giving away bottles of whiskey. The culprits, all privates, were escorted to jail and ultimately had to reimburse the saloonkeeper for fifty quarts of whiskey and twenty-five boxes of Havana cigars.

Corney worked diligently to reestablish order. He observed that railroad and express companies ignored Holbrook's order to stop the transportation and delivery of arms and ammunition. Corney rounded up and jailed the careless officials.

Holbrook also ordered the closing of all saloons to prevent idle miners from using these places to while away time and console themselves. Drunken miners had often stormed out of the bars spoiling for trouble. The saloonkeepers ignored the initial order but learned an abrupt lesson. After jailing several of Walsenburg's more volatile citizens, Corney Smith gained the reputation of a "hard-nose." Told about it, he replied, "Good, maybe that will keep others sober."

The *Denver Post* declared that "war and carnage in the Walsenburg District have been succeeded by the effective regulation imposed by United States Troops. Uncle Sam's cavalrymen are patrolling the streets, and since the arrival of Capt. C. C. Smith and his Troop, this former war center has become as quiet as a duck pond."

Amid a driving rain on the morning of May 9, Corney Smith, accompanied by strike leader Dan McGregor and a detachment of cavalry, left Walsenburg to tour the strikers' camps. They hoped to arrange the surrender of all arms held by the strikers. Understandably, the miners were reluctant to make any such gesture in the absence of similar action on the other side. The UMW leaders rejected any possibility of peace while mine guards and National Guardsmen remained armed in the strike zone. Major Holbrook reportedly stated that strikers should disarm, but mine guards ought to retain their weapons for the protection of property. Corney had difficulty "explaining" this erroneous rumor to outraged strikers. The miners asked: "Why not disarm both sides – or neither? It is said that guards need arms to protect mines. We had thought that federal troops would oust these professional gunmen. If they will not, we miners need guns to protect ourselves."

Corney saw the merit of the strikers' position. "If I were in their shoes, I'd do the same damned thing." Still, to enforce the peace, he took guns and ammunition away from the strikers and mine guards as well.

The arrival of elements of the 11th U.S. Cavalry from Fort Oglethorpe to join the troops of the 5th placed some fifty coal camps in Huerfano and Las Animas counties under federal surveillance. Within days, armed conflicts between operators and strikers dwindled and soon the sound of gunfire disappeared. With the restoration of peace, Corney's Troop became little more than a garrison force, with decreasing patrolling to do and fewer arrests to make. He turned to training his men in the rugged Colorado terrain.

Of particular interest to him was getting horses to swim in deep water. "Anybody can wade a horse through shallow water, or raft one in deep water; swimming is another matter." In the mountains near Walsenburg, Corney found a clear, deep lake ideal for his experiment.

> We made a raft of four empty wine barrels and some 2 x 6 planks, placed it in the middle of the lake and anchored it. A pulley was attached to one corner of the raft and another pulley made fast to a heavy post on the shore. A heavy rope was run through the pulleys and the ends spliced, thus providing an endless rope from raft to shore.
>
> Horses were tied to this conveyor-rope and pulled out into the water by a squad of men on the raft. At first, horses were timid and skittish but feeling the help given by the men on the raft, were soon swimming, albeit thrashing and wild-eyed. Another squad was present on shore to pull the horses back in, but only in one or two instances was its service required. As a horse heads for the barn at feeding time, so does it head for shore in deep water.
>
> Rafting is not plausible unless the water is very wide or very swift, and the raft is stable. Also motive power for the raft is a problem. It will take "forever" to row horses over a wide expanse of water, and the attachment of marine engines to rafts is virtually impossible in field conditions. This leaves the pulley method, and we found it practicable. Because of weight and tensile strength, wire-cable is better than rope, although normally it is not carried as field equipment — too heavy. It can be used for swimming horses; we did it in the Philippines in 1910.

In September 1914, the Walsenburg episode ended and Corney returned with G Troop to Fort Huachuca, Arizona. By November, the Smith family was living in a boxcar on a railroad siding in Naco, on the Mexican border. Once again the Mexican upheaval spilled over the boundary and U.S. troops were dispatched to protect American lives and property.

One day the besieging rebel force was firing wildly, with some bullets entering Naco. Under President Wilson's policy of "watchful waiting" the shots could not be returned unless they came as a result of a direct attack upon American troops. Angered by the situation, Corney's commander, Colonel Wilder, called him aside saying, "Smith, you speak Spanish. Go on over there and warn those people. Tell the first officer you see that if this keeps up we're going to fire back."

Getting to the firing line was not easy. Corney had to cross a zone swept by both factions, a no-man's-land of some seventy-five yards. Using the few bits of cover, he sprinted across.

Corney quickly reached a gun pit occupied by a German-American. "He was from Milwaukee, and he listened courteously to what I had to say. He said that he would change his direction of fire, and he held up the fire in his sector until I scampered back to safety." The foreigner's presence in Mexico did not surprise Corney because:

> We had learned from our Military Intelligence Department that there was considerable German interest and participation in the Mexican Revolution. Later we found that Villa was egged on by German propaganda before his raid on Columbus. Villa was not at the siege of Naco in 1914, but between then and his raid on Columbus, on March 8, 1916, had plenty of time to become saturated with German sentiment.

This meeting with the Wisconsin German was Corney's first contact with Teutons but not his last. Serving as Military Attaché in Venezuela and Colombia, and travelling extensively throughout the Caribbean during the period May 1915-July 1917, he witnessed much of the German agitation against the United States. The only trouble with this fascinating bit of "gumshoeing" in the Caribbean was that it caused him to miss the punitive expedition into Mexico in 1916. Corney rationalized: "I suppose I couldn't have done much there anyway — they kept Pershing under wraps. Given his head, he could have dealt with Carranza and beaten Villa easily."

Captain John Brown Kerr, Commanding K Troop, 6th U.S. Cavalry, during engagement with Sioux, White River, South Dakota, January 1, 1891. (Photo courtesy National Archives)

Fort Wingate, New Mexico, 1895. (Photo courtesy Marjorie Smith, Leavenworth, Kansas)

Major General Arthur MacArthur and officers of the
14th U.S. Cavalry, Fort Wingate, New Mexico, 1902.
General MacArthur is third from left, front row; Captain Cornelius C. Smith is third from left, rear row.
(Photo courtesy Marjorie Smith, Leavenworth, Kansas)

Second Lieutenant Cornelius
C. Smith on "Blue" at Fort
Wingate, New Mexico, before
beginning his 1,000-mile ride
to Fort Sam Houston, Texas,
in April 1895. (Photo from
personal files)

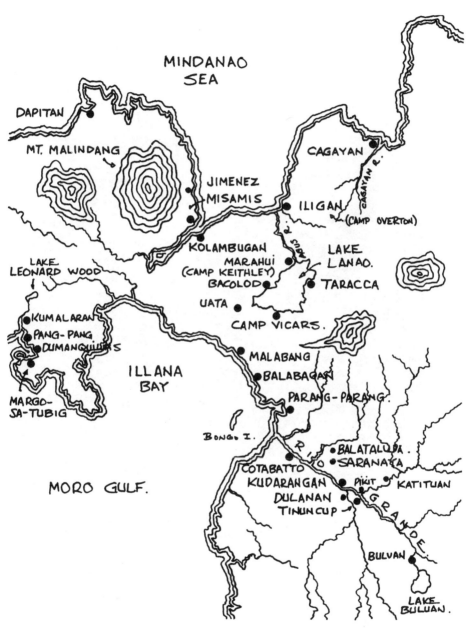

North-Central Mindanao where Captain Cornelius Smith's expeditions took place, March-June 1904.

Captain Cornelius C. Smith (center) leading Provisional Troop of the 14th U.S. Cavalry in the Datu Ali Campaign, Mindanao, 1904-05. (Photo courtesy National Archives)

Vintas tied up along shoreline at Moro marketplace, Cotabato, Mindanao, Philippine Islands. (Photo from personal files)

Moro constabulary with prisoners, Mindanao, 1905. (Photo from personal files)

Smith family, Sequoia National Park, summer 1908.
Captain Smith seated next to wife Frances, right.
Gilbert seated next to his father; Graham 8, mounted,
behind. Other figures not identified. (Photo courtesy
Marjorie Smith, Leavenworth, Kansas)

Kathleen Crowley Smith,
Manila, 1910. (Photo from
personal files)

Brigadier General John J. Pershing and Captain
Cornelius C. Smith with Moro Datus, Mindanao, 1910.
(Photo from personal files)

Departmental Election Board, Granada, Nicaragua. Seated, left to right: General H. Rocha (Conservative), Dr. Horacio Zavala (Conservative), Colonel Cornelius C. Smith, Carlos Locayo Vivas (Liberal), E. Arguello (Liberal). Standing: Ensign R.C. Brixner, Ensign M.R. Stone. (Photo from personal files)

CHAPTER THIRTEEN

The Unwelcome Guest

IN APRIL 1915, CORNEY RECEIVED orders for South America: "Pursuant to a request of April 7, from the Secretary of War, you are hereby designated to be the Military Attaché to the American Legation at Bogotá, Colombia." The new assignment meant a desk job in a diplomatic post, neither of which he sought. Still, it would broaden his career and provide a means for determining the extent of German activity in the Caribbean.

Corney recognized the tenuous background of Colombian-American relations and the difficult posture forced upon the attendant U.S. diplomatic mission. President Theodore Roosevelt's support of Panama against Colombia had assured Panamanian independence and the building of the Panama Canal but created ill will. He further enraged the Colombians when he bragged in 1911, "I took the Canal Zone." One of Corney's legation associates remarked: "Roosevelt was right. If we had negotiated on Colombia's terms the canal would have been held up for years, with mountains of Colombian red tape and never-ending demands for more money — maybe it would not have been built at all!"

Nevertheless, Corney was not prepared for the climate of over-powering hatred. He remembered:

> You could cut it with a knife. I came here wanting to like the country and the people; after a week here I must confess I like neither. I am insulted daily in my contact with the Colombians, as is the Minister, Mr. [Thaddeus] Thompson. Kathleen would be, if she were allowed the normal movements of a housewife in a free society; she is essentially a prisoner in our home. The press, arrogant and opinionated, reeks with anti-American propaganda. Colombian officials barely remain within the limits of protocol; some do not even bother to try.

Thaddeus Thompson explained: "They are of course bitterly resentful over Panama still, and our seizure of Vera Cruz last year has put some coals on the fire."

Corney later wrote:

> I can't blame them for exhibiting national pride — after all, all nations are egocentric. But this mass choleric behavior borders on the psychopathic. They act as though our army was on their border, ready to march in and take over. Why should we want to establish a protectorate in this primitive place? We have plenty to do at home in developing our own resources and raising the living standards of our own people.

For the next year Corney tried everything possible to surmount his personal feelings and serve the diplomatic mission as best he could. Though never losing his temper in a sudden outburst, he approached it almost daily. Ending his tour in April 1916, he wrote: "It is the first negative portion of my life. I have done the best I could, but I cannot leave with any feeling of success."

Conveying much of the exasperation experienced in dealing with people who hated America and Americans, Corney wrote to Gil and Graham in Leavenworth:

> My dear boys: Here it is Christmas and how I wish we were with you. Tomorrow the mail goes out and I want you to have a newsy letter, so here goes. Historically, Colombia is an interesting country, chiefly with reference to its struggle for independence from Spain in the early part of the nineteenth

century. The main figure then was "El Libertador," Simon Bolívar. Near our legation stands his old mansion, now used by the government as its Foreign Relations Office. Other Colombian heroes were Sucre, Santander, Nariño and Ricuarte; I am grieved to say that such men do not walk the streets of Bogotá today. This letter must not fall into Colombian hands, for I tell you that the leaders here are corrupt, venal, malicious and weak.

Certainly the land has had its share of civil wars, intrigue and bloodshed, and that added to its isolation makes it a truly godforsaken place. Ironically, it is full of rich natural resources. Sadly, the present government, and perhaps more importantly, the present level of civilization and development here are such as to assure its hopeless condition for many years to come.

You have asked about Bogotá, so I will tell you. It is a city of about 125,000 people, and it is unprepossessing, dirty, ill-smelling and with but few redeeming features. There are no places of amusement except movie houses, and there are only two or three of these. The climate is generally cold and the houses, including ours, most uncomfortable. Since few houses have either fireplaces or stoves people go about in overcoats most of the time.

Only a few homes have bathrooms, most using privies in the interior courtyards, and some places do not even have these. Policemen never interfere with men, women and children who make public toilets of the streets, a filthy and degrading "costumbre del país." The only truly picturesque drive in the city, Paseo Bolívar, is disgusting on this account. There are no sewers and sewage is carried away in carts drawn by undersize, underfed, spavined little horses which seem always on the verge of collapsing in their traces. The water supply is limited and dangerous. We use it only after it has been boiled thoroughly.

With these conditions it is no wonder that the death rate here is appalling. In 1914, 400 more died in Bogotá than were born, and I have seen many more funerals here in the five months since our arrival than I have seen during the rest of my entire life.

The stores are small, the goods shoddy, and the prices high. This is on account of the exorbitant revenues charged by the government and the killing freight rates for goods carried on the Magdalena River. The government is indeed poor and needs all of the revenue it can get. As always, it is the people who bear the brunt.

There is no such thing as a delivery wagon, nor is credit given. One buys and pays for his food daily, a most inconvenient system. The markets are a sight to behold, and the smells in these fetid places are overpowering. Meat is exposed to the dust and flies of the open street and it is always eaten on the day the animal is killed. There are no markets with refrigeration of any kind. Colombian butchers know nothing of meat cutting; they simply hack carcasses into unappetizing chunks.

With but one or two exceptions the streets are poorly paved, or not at all. They are fearfully dirty in dry weather and become bogholes when it rains.

The Colombian peasant is cruel and merciless to his beasts. Time and again, I have seen some poor overloaded burro prodded with sharp sticks or beaten until I had to turn away. The irony is that most of these poor creatures falter not because of stubbornness but because they are on the edge of starvation. The drivers simply are too ignorant to perceive the difference. At home if I saw a man mistreat an animal like that I'd take a cane to him. Here a foreigner on a diplomatic mission, I can do nothing.

Few kitchens have ovens, hence there is no such thing as hot bread or biscuits. Bread is furnished by the bakeries, cold. Moreover, the flour is improperly ground and so the bread is coarse and tasteless.

Servants are cheap, but so many are required to run a household that you wind up paying a considerable amount for domestic help. The girl who makes the beds, for instance, cannot wait on table, and vice versa. The laundress cannot iron; the gardener cannot do handy-work, and so on. What it amounts to is a bureaucracy of small skills, and with just a few exceptions these single-minded people cannot seem to perform their own chosen tasks with any type of efficiency.

Not only that, they are insolent. I've discharged several for that reason, but the replacements are just as bad. There is one bright spot. Corney's nurse is a good and kindly woman, quiet and able. She is teaching him Spanish.

Customs here are interesting. It is improper, for example, to take a lady to a restaurant after the theatre. The cafes are filled with men only, and the women are sent home to feminine isolation behind locked doors and barred windows — a heritage of Spain whose people picked it up from the Moors in the 7th Century.

The country is controlled, absolutely, by the Church. It is obvious to me that if more money was spent to alleviate the impoverished condition of the people and less on new churches and gaudy ecclesiastical trappings, everyone would be better off.

Well, my dear boys, I must close now. I know that this letter is oppressive, but our spirits are not. I've had good duty and bad, and will probably have more of both. I dislike the animosity here and the disorder, but the place is fascinating from the historical viewpoint. Besides, I like and admire Mr. Thompson and will give him all the help I can. Give our love to "Dat." Affectionately, Dad.

Expanding on this general disenchantment, Corney wrote to his great-uncle, Cornelius Cole, in "Colegrove," California, in July 1916. The long and acrimonious letter was perhaps as true an indicator of his feelings as anything could be in the circumstances:

I came here thoroughly prepared to like the country and its people. My reception here has endeared me to neither. It is not a personal issue; all Americans, from the Minister on down, are objects of scorn. In such a climate it is not possible to be enthusiastic.

Bogotá is one of the most remote capitals on earth and one of the most difficult of access. This tends to make it a backward place, with the people introverted and sullen. Interestingly, I have talked with people of other legations here, French, British, German — and all say unhesitatingly that of all the South American countries they know, this is the most primitive. . . .

Their dislike and suspicion of us makes them impractical. Although they need foreign capital badly they are reluctant to let it in, throwing up all sorts of picayune barriers. Part of this seems to stem from a desire by the Church to keep the country in a kind of medieval stranglehold. The country is truly "priest-ridden," and the people, poor, superstitious and fearful, seem uninclined to make any changes. . . .

The prevalence of disease and deformity is alarming. Syphilis is rampant and leaves its horrendous mark in spectacular ways. In the streets, particularly the little alleys of the poor, it is not uncommon to see people crawling along on all fours, unable to stand or walk. Club-footed people are common, as are the blind. Last week I was horrified to see a man with no eyes nor were there sockets where eyes should be. His face, in the region of his eyes was entirely smooth, merely a transition of skin from cheeks to forehead. Most must beg for a living, but few seem to receive much from their countrymen.

Many small "tiendas" (stores) seem to serve a double purpose. One may purchase goods in front or repair to a brothel in the rear. This is particularly true around the big market places where the country louts become fair game for the sharp city girls.

A few days hence I visited the city's main abattoir [slaughterhouse]. For cruel and crude methods of killing, I have never seen anything to equal it. The slaughterhouse was a long shedlike building with seven separate killing areas. It looks as though it has been used for perhaps a hundred years.

Each compartment was about 36 feet square and floored with large stone flags. In the center, slightly depressed, was a four-inch sewer drain for the running off of blood. Steers were dragged (literally) into these compartments from adjoining corrals — always in the presence of several other beasts just killed or being skinned. Naturally, the creature is in mortal terror and slips around grotesquely in the blood of his fallen comrades.

He is thrown and tied. The attendant then takes out a small patch of skin near the clavicle and pushes his long blade into the heart. The blood gushes out under pressure and is caught by an urchin holding a tin can. The poor, dirty people hanging around for these handouts, the dogs, the buzzards hopping about clumsily on the roofs, and the blood-smeared butchers give the place a fearful character. It is like a scene out of Dante's Inferno. In the manner described, some sixty steers are killed daily except Saturday. Then 120 are killed. On Sunday, those who can afford it go to the bullring and see more animals despatched, this time for sport.

Chicha is an intoxicant made from corn and the heavy black molasses of sugarcane. It is the national drink of Colombia. I have seen ten- and twelve-year old boys lying stupified in the streets from Chicha. A medical doctor of Bogotá gave it as his opinion that much of the physical abnormality seen in the lower classes was due to Chicha. Cohabitation by parties drunk with the liquor makes for defects in mind, body or both, according to the physician.

The national coat of arms bears the motto "Libertad y Orden." Unfortunately, the poor country has little of either. . . .

Interestingly, policemen are perfectly innocuous when it comes to crowd control. The police, many of them mere boys, will rarely arrest a boisterous man; he is at his constabulary best, however, with women, bootblacks and newsboys.

Here a man's business is everyone's business. If I ask a man for a direction, everyone within earshot crowds around giving directions. If a man pulls the bell-rope on the electric car, everybody yanks it — just to make sure the conductor gets the word. The motorman spends a great lot of time turning around and talking to passengers. Consequently, street accidents are plentiful.

The papers here are filled with terrible poetry and anti-yanqui diatribe. Censures, lampoons and libelous attacks upon their own political leaders fill up the remaining columns. . . .

You might not think it, but for convenience, comfort, and more importantly, people, the Philippines are far superior to Colombia. I have knocked around the world a bit; for sheer backwardness this place has no peer. For example, I have seen Filipinos blacken their teeth with betel-nut, but I have never seen one spit while seated at a table. Men and women do that here, frequently. In the Philippines we had American Commissaries for the purchase of good food, and one could take a shower bath. Here good meals are all but non-existent; all foods are either fried or boiled, and it is very difficult to bathe. Water pressure is low and frequently shuts off completely.

The government seems incapable or is unwilling to halt

mob action on political and civil disputes. It is simply a "way of life." Whenever the masses here have a grievance they organize "mitins" (meetings) wherein they simply gather, mob-like, harangue a spell and then go stone the edifice or home of the opposing party. Like as not the police join right in with them. Recently a man named Martín was employed by our government to help build an electric rail line here. One day while riding on one of the cars, checking it, he witnessed a Colombian Army Officer pestering a woman. He threw the man off. Since then, not only has he been deported, the company has been hounded and badgered by government officials to the point of disrupting its service. Martín had to take refuge at our legation until we could get him out. In the melee, Mr. Thompson was hit by a stone and confined to his bed for several days.

Corney had kept a voluminous collection of notes on his observations and travels in Colombia and complied with a War Department request to make a full report on his findings before he left Bogotá. He wrote a long and scholarly paper of some 250 pages, titled simply "Monograph on Colombia." The comprehensive narrative dealt primarily with a rundown on the Colombian government but also had exhaustive accounts of the country's topographical features, forests, coastlines, river systems, cities and towns, mines, industries, agriculture, and ranching. He devoted many pages to the flora and fauna of the country. These were not "Encyclopaedia re-writes" from a desk in the legation, but original writings from notes taken in the field.

Most interesting of all were his opinions and observations of the people and their customs. He had been asked to "tell it as it is" and consequently furnished frank observations:

I have read the Colombian Constitution from beginning to end. On paper it is a noble instrument. The trouble is, it is followed only when it meets the immediate requirements of those who employ it. Also, there seems to be no adhesion between the several departments of government. For example, the Cauca District talks incessantly about seceding and setting up a separate republic. This causes sides to be taken between the executive agencies, and I fear that in case of secession by Cauca the apparatus of government would fall apart.

Moreover, the black departments of the coastal regions hate the white departments of the interior, and vice versa; Antioquicans hate Bogotanos, and vice versa.

The constitution guarantees the life of the individual citizen, or at least reasonable freedom from anarchy and crime — yet there is no death penalty and murderers cannot be sentenced to more than ten years' imprisonment. In practise, they average two to three years, if indeed they are convicted and sentenced at all.

The constitution guarantees the "unrestricted profession, in public or private, of any religion whatsoever — so long as such worship is not incompatible with the sovereignty of the nation, or does not disturb the public peace." Contrary to what you may hear, this simply is not so; the Archbishop here does succeed, absolutely, in making Catholicism the state religion. So far as I can see, laws here are for the amusement of the politicians and the rich; the poor have all individuality crushed from them by a venal and paralyzing bureaucracy. . . .

Governmental appointments here constitute an unending game of musical chairs. No appointee seems to stay for very long, especially if he displeases the Press. Señor Rueda Acosta was fired as a cabinet member one day and appointed as Consul-General in New York the next; Dr. Miguel Abadia Mendez, the President's right-hand man, forced the resignations of four cabinet members, Isaius Lujan, the War Minister among them. Lujan was succeeded by José Cadavid who soon resigned. Salvador Franco became the new Treasury Secretary but soon became the War Secretary, vice [succeeding] Mendez who had spelled Cadavid. This is not unusual. Something like it goes on just about all the time.

Bogotanos take pride in calling their city "The Athens of America." No comment . . . .

The people here pride themselves as being members of a democratic republic. Yet seldom have I seen more distinct caste lines. The distance between the rich (a few) and the poor (most) may be measured in light years. No Colombian gentleman would ever carry a package in the streets. He employs a servant or urchin to carry it. No Colombian lady will ever go to market, no matter how much her criadas steal from her. Even house servants are caught up in this game. None of them will carry a bundle if someone of lower station is about to do the job.

This tends to make the upper class not only indolent but helpless — women especially, who do little else but sit around all day gossiping. They seldom read a book. Carrying on a conversation with one at dinner is a one-way street.

Whether intentionally rude or merely curious, Colombians are nosy. My wife has been asked, on first acquaintance, if we had any means other than salary, whether or not either of us had been previously married, had there ever been a miscarriage, etc.

With such laxity in law enforcement as exists here it is not surprising that the crime rate is high. Petty theft is a way of life, and larceny, mayhem and murder frequently go unpunished. In cases of theft, the formalities, red tape and presentation of witnesses is so complicated as to make charges not worth the bother. On the river steamer between Barranquilla and Bogotá I caught a man in my stateroom. I turned him over to the Captain. On returning to the stateroom I found that I had been robbed for forty dollars. The Captain dismissed the matter. When we got to Bogotá I preferred charges against both the thief and the Captain. Two other steamer passengers, Colombians no less, had been robbed by the same man. The three of us appeared as witnesses against him in court. He was dismissed with no fine. None of the stolen goods were returned. The Captain was not even called to testify.

In Mexico and in the Philippines people love music and dancing. Probably the abject poverty of the people here, or perhaps something in their physical or psychic makeup seems to preclude that in Colombia. During all my months in Colombia I saw not a single dance and heard music only on rare occasions. That in itself is sad; it is doubly so when one considers that most Colombians are old at forty-five. Add to this the fact that there is not one decent hospital in Bogotá, the capital, no trained nurses, and only a handful of doctors.

Probably diet has much to do with the poor state of Colombians' health. They eat potatoes, corn, plantain and yucca, and almost never see anything like lettuce, spinach, cabbage, turnips, beets or onions. They make no jellies, jams, pickles, bacon, ham or corned beef. They do make a mushy and inferior sausage. . . .

Garbage is removed from the streets in small carts. These are drawn by poor undersized creatures which so far as I can see are not fed oats, grain or hay. Cart drivers use filthy little gunnysack nose bags for the horses stuffed with the junk they pick up in the streets — potato parings, corn husks, banana peelings, etc. I cannot tolerate abuse of animals and wonder how anyone else can.

The people, generally speaking, are irascible and excitable, exercising no self-control at all when emotions are aroused. Children resent correction, as all children do, but here they are allowed tantrums hence become miniature tyrants.

There are no "seasons" here except two: wet and dry. In the valleys and on the plateaux between the cordilleras these periods are well marked. The dry season lasts about 90 days coming with the solstices; the wet issues in the equinox and lasts for a similar period. Hence, there are two rainy and two dry seasons in these places. There are places on the Pacific Coast where it rains practically all of the time.

Rolling stock is of the English type, now old and rickety. There is not a standard gauge. When the British companies put roadbeds down they used several different gauges. Hence in traveling between points changing trains becomes a fairly common event.

The principal steamboat. lines plying the Magdalena River are the Prieda López Line and Compañía Antioquia de Trasportes, a German concern. When boats of these companies are moving, things are pretty comfortable. When they stop to take on wood, the mosquitoes eat you alive. Also, many river Captains will not travel at night. Again the mosquitoes hold high carnival.

Concerning transportation, the principal means seems to be the back of the peon woman. It is she who lugs everything to market and thence home again to the shack high on the mountainside or in the jungle. Loads carried by these women are astounding. The men do a lot of directing but very little toting. Next after the woman comes the burro, the mule, the horse and the pack bull.

There are practically no wheeled vehicles in the country other than oxcarts. One exception is Barranquilla which is fairly progressive and does have some motor traffic. Barranquilla really is the best place I've seen here. Bogotá has a grave, "Inquisitor-like," medieval air; Barranquilla is fairly modern, with many automobiles and good streetcars. Bogotá has gone to sleep; Barranquilla is up and doing.

Dugout canoes are used on the rivers; some of them are quite large. In Bogotá men carry a contraption named "parihuela." It is something like a sedan chair, except that in place of a chair there is a platform for carrying loads. Braces attached to the parallel poles go around the shoulders of the wearers. Men using the parihuela can carry astonishingly heavy loads.

Owing to graft and maladministration in all departments, coupled with the honor accorded the military throughout Latin America, it is safe to say that the army is the best of the public institutions. Still, there are shortcomings in this branch which are astounding. For instance, they use the heavy, cumbersome German uniform and accoutrements simply because they are pro-German in sentiment. Light headgear is called for, but they use the abominable German helmet, spike and all, since everything here is not "military enough." Actually, the Colombian army is patterned after the Chilean army — which in turn patterns itself after the German Army. . . .

Notwithstanding its popular place in the scheme of things, there is not much of a budget for the army. A visit to any military installation proves this: ramshackle barracks, shabby uniforms, crowded conditions and so on. All things considered, it is a pretty fair institution.

Corney had been in Bogotá one year when he received orders to proceed to Caracas, Venezuela, for a similar attaché mission. His job in Bogotá had been one of utter frustration as neither he nor Minister Thompson could reach the inhabitants — they simply did not care to listen. Nevertheless, Thompson's send-off was rewarding. In a letter to the Adjutant General in Washington the Minister wrote:

I wish to express to you my appreciation of the happy selection made in detailing Captain Cornelius C. Smith as my

Military Attaché at Bogotá, Colombia. Captain Smith will have been with me a year in April. I have found him to be most industrious, painstaking, and efficient in performing all duties assigned to him. I regard him as a man in every sense of the word; honorable, trustworthy and a very capable officer.

One of his last official duties was to write a monograph in Spanish on the American Army. Titled "El Ejército de Los E.U.A.," it was a straightforward paper describing the army, its component parts, tables of organization, arms, and methods of enlistment. It had no bombast, braggadocio, recitation of battle honors, or anything of the sort, but was criticized by the press as "overbearing" and "insolent." "Well," said Corney on departure, "I would have been roundly surprised at anything less." Neither Corney nor Kathleen shed any tears over leaving Colombia. Corney Junior, however, experienced a tearful parting from his nurse María, who kept murmuring "pobrecito, pobrecito."

The one blessing to come from the frustrating South American experience was the birth of Corney's only daughter, Alice, on July 16, 1916, in Barranquilla. By law she would have been a Colombian citizen had she not been registered with an American Consul within one hour after her birth. "I damned near broke a leg getting to the Consulate," said Corney, "but my little girl had papers with about ten minutes to spare."

Major Cornelius C. Smith, Military Attaché, Caracas, Venezuela, 1917. (Photo from personal files)

CHAPTER FOURTEEN

What Are the Germans Doing?

COMING FROM THE CRISES and frustrations in his first diplomatic assignment, Corney was delighted to find that his second offered no such prospect. The reservoir of "anti-yanquiism" found in any Latin American country was generalized, not personal.

While Kathleen had remained in virtual isolation in Bogotá, in Caracas she attended parties, made friends and rode the handsome streets in a horse-drawn carriage. In addition, Corney found in his new boss, Minister Preston McGoodwin, a man of principle and character. Much alike, the two became fast friends. McGoodwin gave his subordinate the usual list of duties but permitted him a free hand in the execution of these tasks.

Following the sinking of the Cunard Liner *Lusitania* in May 1915, the American press continued its charges of unrestricted German submarine warfare. The subsequent sinking of the passenger ship *Arabic* and, early in 1916, the French liner *Sussex* inflamed the issue. Rumors spread that German submarines were sailing the Caribbean coastlines in search of harbors and hiding places in case of war with the United States. One of Corney Smith's first assignments was to find out if the reports were true. He stated:

Early in 1916 rumors came to us in Caracas that German U-boats were working the Caribbean in the lanes of steamship travel and that one or more bases were hidden away in coves along the Colombian or Venezuelan coasts. It was not hard to believe; both countries were pro-German. Each morning when I went to my office in the legation it was the Minister's custom to call me in for a brief chat on the day's problems.

One morning I suggested to Mr. McGoodwin that in view of the persistent rumors concerning U-boat activity along the coast it might be well if I should make a personal search. I proposed to him that I would examine the stretch of Venezuelan coastline extending from Paraguaná Peninsula to La Guaira. "What do you suppose the Germans are doing?" I asked. "Well, why don't you go and find out?" I made plans then, and would travel under my own passport as a naturalist working for a scientific expedition.

The next step was to get away without exciting suspicion. To this end it was announced that I was going on an official visit to our Consul in La Guaira, Homer Brett. Once with Brett I would arrange for passage by ship to Curaçao. This would be easy since American vessels laden with cargo and traveling between La Guaira and Willemstad would have to obtain clearance papers from Brett.

Both Brett and his vice-consul, Robert Daley, were apprised of my plan. On the day after my talk with them a tramp steamer came into port for clearance papers. She was bound for New Orleans with coffee and sugar and would stop at Willemstad and Kingston en route. Daley made all arrangements with the tramp's skipper, telling him of my mission. He was English and so was the crew, sailing under American registry. He refused to take payment for my passage.

At around eleven P.M. I boarded his vessel, disguised as a crew member, and went immediately to the Captain's quarters where I remained until he sailed the following morning. Before leaving Brett's office I arranged for him to send a coded message to George Messersmith, our Consul in Curaçao. As I knew Messersmith, I presented no disguise in Curaçao but went directly to his office, ostensibly as his guest.

Closeted with Messersmith, I was told that two men

were registered in a hotel nearby; that they were registered as Americans but spoke English in harsh guttural accents, unmistakably German. He suggested that I find out what I could.

I found that the men were employed by a New York firm, but were using this cover of legitimacy to hide efforts to purchase a ship from the Colombian government to be put under German registry, probably for use in supplying U-boats in the Caribbean. We did nothing in Willemstad but kept close watch on these two men during their stay there. Learning that they were to return to the states on a vessel bound for New York, Messersmith cabled the Justice Department people there; the two men were arrested as they came down the gangway in the Battery.

I remained in Curaçao for a week or so before going on to Aruba and the Venezuelan Coast. . . .

I learned from Messersmith that a man named Crabtree lived in Aruba and would help me with my plans. Thus, Messersmith obtained for me a boat to make the 60-mile sea trip to Orangestad and gave me a letter to Crabtree. The small sailing vessel had a Negro Captain and four black sailors. Around midnight, we shoved off.

Once out of the Waigat our one sail was hoisted and a fair wind carried us along. The sailors were respectful and solicitous of my every comfort. Some fell asleep and did not waken until the sun was up.

The cook brought me a mug of steaming hot coffee and a bowlful of dry crackers. I found the sailors to be friendly and cheerful. They asked many questions about America. When they spoke in Papaimento I was hard-put to understand. All spoke some Spanish, though, and we made out.

About ten o'clock we came alongside a huge monster lazing in the sun. Its huge head and broad, flat back could easily have been touched with a cane from my position in the bow. The skipper said "malo!" It looked to be about thirty-five feet long. I think it was a basking shark. It gave us no trouble and we continued on.

Around noon we came to Aruba and pulled up alongside a vessel loading goat guano. Messersmith had said that Crabtree was in the guano business; I reasoned that this might be one of his vessels. I boarded the ship and asked if Mr. Crabtree might be aboard. Answering my hail, a fine-looking bronzed man of about 60 announced he was Crabtree and what did I want? I replied that I had business with him and he said: "Come aboard and have lunch with me."

I went with Crabtree to his quarters and had a delicious meal. My crew was taken to the ship's galley and fed. During lunch I told Crabtree of my intention to scout the Venezuelan Coast. He seemed very enthusiastic about it, saying that he had gangs collecting goat guano all along the Venezuelan coastline and that I might use these camps as way stations if I chose.

I was invited then to spend a day or two with him in his home in Orangestad. "This is just my little place," he said, "my real home is over in La Vela de Coro on the coast." The "little place" wasn't bad, having a wide, comfortable porch and several Carib Indian houseboys. Crabtree worked between Aruba and La Vela running his guano business. From the rocky crags of the Venezuelan coastline he collected goat guano from the thousands of goats wandering in these lonely places, took it in lighters to ships waiting offshore, then transferred it to Orangestad from whence it was sold. In Orangestad, I simply announced to port officials that I was visiting Crabtree.

On the next day, Crabtree and I were invited to tea at the home of the Lieutenant Governor. He and his wife were most cordial. He presented me with a beautiful gold nugget found in one of the dry washes of the island's interior. It is odd that these islands lying so close to the equator are semi-arid. The reason is that prevailing air currents which drench the west coasts of Panama and Colombia with almost perpetual rain, keep it from falling here.

Crabtree was expecting his launch from La Vela but it did not come. Later, it was learned that it was laid up there dockside, undergoing emergency repairs. Thus we put to sea in another of his boats, a small one, which would take us from Orangestad along the eastern shoreline of Peninsula de Paraguaná to La Vela.

We very nearly didn't make it. We had boarded the tiny vessel at around six P.M., and even then white caps were running on the waves. The sky behind us was black. "It's only fifty miles," said Crabtree. "We'll be in La Vela before anything breaks." He was wrong. The wind was in our favor though, and for a while we skimmed along briskly.

Presently it began to thunder and now it was pitch black and the only illumination, except for a feeble lantern swinging in the wheelhouse, came from great jagged bolts of lightning ripping the sky. There were only four of us in the boat, Crabtree, two Negro boatmen and I. We could no longer control the craft. Tossed about like a walnut shell we would climb to the top of a mountainous wave, pause for what seemed an eternity, then swoop down into the trough like an express train.

Our sail tore into ribbons before we could get it down. The spar broke like a matchstick. We were pitched and tossed thus, in utter darkness throughout the night and until about noon on the following day. There is a famous painting by Winslow Homer entitled "The Gulf Stream." It pictures a Negro boatman in a storm-battered craft surrounded by sharks. Water-spouts are all about and the waves are angry. By comparison, his boat sails on placid waters. I despaired of our lives. Only a merciful providence carried us through.

At around three P.M. we limped into La Vela, wet, hungry and exhausted, having taken over twenty hours on a trip usually requiring seven or eight. We went directly to Crabtree's house, a beautiful spacious place with huge patio, and flowers and bird cages everywhere. My room had its own shower-bath. After a bath and some rest I went to the dining room, attended by an absolute corps of servants. We had a sumptuous meal.

It became known immediately that Crabtree was home and that an American was with him. On the next day, therefore, the Governor of the state of Falcon drove over from Coro in his Model T. He and Crabtree owned the only two cars (both Model T Fords) in the state. The Governor, a huge Negro dressed impeccably in white, was cordial and not overly inquisitive. He invited us to dine with him on the following day and we did.

Arriving in Coro we went directly to the Governor's place, a fine old Spanish edifice of Moorish influence with a huge ornate brass knocker on polished mahogany doors. The door opened directly onto a patio which was a veritable fairyland of exotic plants, trees, orchids and cages filled with exquisitely plumed parrots and rare jungle birds. In the center was a Moorish fountain, filled with carp, goldfish and small turtles.

Soon the Governor's wife appeared, a charming white woman of the Venezuelan aristocracy. Her English was flawless. The lunch was leisurely and of many courses. Conversation ranged from South American customs to the war in Europe. I must say my hosts were genial and charming. Still, I did not think it pertinent to tell them why I was there. I simply said that I was visiting Mr. Crabtree and in a day or two would take a boat for Panama and later return to Caracas. That ended it. . . .

It was now time to take up my solo trip, incognito, along the coast looking for German submarines. I would travel on the shore, from La Vela del Coro to La Guaira, a distance of some 240 miles, and pass by Cumarebo, Tocopero, Chichiri- viche and Boca de Aroa. Most of the trip would be in desolate uninhabited stretches though, with only an occasional flock of goats for company or perhaps birds wheeling overhead.

My plan was to hire horses or mules as I went along, and where I could not do so, walk. As it turned out, I walked most of the way. I carried a plant manual with me, several notebooks and several jars for bottling insects in case I had to employ the "naturalist" masquerade.

Farms or ranches renting me horses or burros would permit the beasts to go but a few miles, having a natural aver- sion to straying too far from home fires. At Crabtree's sug- gestion, I acted as his agent in seeking and giving orders for goat guano from goatherds along the way. Also, I stopped at his camps, wild, dirty little places perched up in the cliffs overlook- ing the sea.

On the first day out I came to a small town, Puerto Cumarebo, a run-down-at-heels little place, desolate and gloomy. Here I hired a mozo and two decrepit little burros, the only ones in town. Both were laden with faggots which I had to buy before I could rent the animals. It was not a total loss, however; I traded the wood for "almuerzo" at an inn on the edge of town.

After this lunch of fried eggs, rice, coffee and "dulce," we continued eastward along the beach, Juan, his two burros and I. We travelled at the rate of perhaps 2½ miles per hour, and by six P.M. had gone about 12 miles. We stopped on the beach where a little stream emptied into the sea. Juan was reluctant to camp there lest a jaguar steal upon us in the night. We went on for several hundred yards and made camp.

All day I scanned the horizon for signs of submarines, and poked in and out of coves where these trim craft might hide. I saw nothing.

Two days later we were at Punta Zamarro and here Juan left me to go it alone, on foot. Still no signs of subs. At Aguide I rented another burro but had it for less than a day. I walked then, into San Juan de las Cayas, another forlorn village, quiescent as though time had pulled a sheet over it. All along the route were rocky coves where submarines might hide. It is possible that some had, or even would; during my trip, though, there were none to be seen.

Fourteen days after leaving Crabtree in La Vela I came into Puerto Cabello. It had been a weary, exhausting, yet interesting journey. Here I rested for several days before starting out for La Guaira, still almost one hundred miles away. Puerto Cabello was a pretty little place, dating back to the days of the Spanish Main. I wondered what it might have looked like in 1872 when my friend Kosterlitzky had jumped ship from the Russian Navy. I would guess that with the exception of a few improvements it hadn't changed much.

The next eight days were much like the first couple of weeks, probing the coastline for submarines and sweeping the water with my binoculars. Nothing. Occasionally I would see fishing smacks and even a few dugout canoes at river estuaries, but never a submarine. Well, it had been a good idea. It simply hadn't paid off.

Corney had been back in Caracas for several months when he heard a fascinating story about two old spinsters living on a mountaintop near La Guaira. They were Josephine and Amalia Weisman, the foster daughters of Dr. Gottfried Knoche who had brought his family to La Guaira in 1847. Practising medicine and engaging in the export-import trade, Knoche had made a fortune by 1880 and decided to devote the remainder of his life to the one subject which consumed him — preservation of the human body after death.

Knoche built a home on the precipitous side of a mountain overlooking La Guaira, and with it a medical laboratory and a mausoleum. He settled in this aerie to study his voluminous collection of books on the mummies of Egypt, Mexico, and Peru. He became known, in a semi-fearful way, as "El Sabio de Buena Vista de Cariaco" [The Wise Man of Buena Vista de Cariaco].

He also instructed his wife and daughters in the lost art of Egyptian embalming. With the permission of government authorities, he embalmed two Indian corpses, dressed them in Spanish armor and placed them on either side of the door leading into the mausoleum. His wife died in 1885 and Knoche placed her preserved body on display. When Knoche died in 1901, Josephine and Amalia embalmed him and placed him next to his mate.

With Dr. J. N. Rose, a botanist of the Smithsonian Institution, Corney visited the Weisman sisters in August 1916. The old ladies, who had not been off the mountain for years, received them cordially, escorted their guests into the mausoleum, and showed them the well-preserved bodies of Knoche and his wife. Next to the raised marble sarcophagi holding the mummies of Herr and Frau Knoche were two empty ones waiting in icy silence for the sisters who would one day lie in them. "I had not the heart to ask," said Corney, "but I could not help but think — who prepares the last one to die?"

In October 1916, Corney accompanied Dr. Rose on a more mundane field expedition near Puerto Cabello. Rose found a hitherto unknown species of cactus which he named Cephalocereus Smithianus. In his long report on his expedition findings the botanist wrote: "This particular species was found by Smith on October 28, 1916."

Generally, Corney's stay in Venezuela had been pleasant. Considerably less tension existed between the U.S. Diplomatic Mission and the Venezuelan Government than had been the case in Colombia. Still, some stiffness developed in the months just prior to U.S. entry in the Great War. Ultimately, Corney felt his usefulness to McGoodwin and to the United States had come to an end and he requested a transfer. McGoodwin wrote:

I am in receipt of your despatch to the General Staff asking for relief from this post because of disinclination of

Venezuelan military authorities to deal with you officially.

You know how much I appreciate your presence here. Not only in your relations with this Legation but also with the Venezuelan Government, and especially with those in charge of the Military Branch. You have displayed rare tact and inordinate patience.

... When it is considered that the Inspector General, the dominating influence in the army here, holds his position by reason of being the older son of the ruler of the country, it seems quite natural that he will have no disposition to take any American Army officer into his confidence. You are sure to have observed that there is no personal animosity toward you. I have observed repeatedly that resentment is directed toward the U.S. Government. Three years ago an identical situation concerned the Military Attaché to our Legation in Lima. Life was made so miserable for him that he quit in disgust, making no effort to conceal his chagrin. A good soldier, you have kept your feelings to yourself.

Personally, I shall regret seeing you go, but your repeated efforts to secure any sort of cooperation with Venezuelan Army officials render your task here hopeless. I quite understand your desire to be relieved. You are at liberty to transmit this letter to your superior in Washington if you see fit.

In a final effort to bridge the gap, Corney stayed for awhile, but to no avail. When he finally left, McGoodwin wrote:

Having just been advised by Major Smith that he is under orders to proceed immediately to Washington, I deem it my duty, and therefore have the honor to state that he has rendered very valuable service to this Legation, especially since the severance of relations between United States and Germany, endeavoring to checkmate renewed efforts upon the part of German propagandists in this country. For months he has undergone all manner of discomforts in sailing vessels, and in long journeys on foot along the desolate desert coast of Venezuela. From the day of his arrival over one year ago, Major Smith has never failed to cooperate readily and loyally with this Legation. I am glad of this opportunity to express my sincere appreciation.

Corney was leaving a good friend. For several years the two men corresponded, then, with the passing of years, exchanged Christmas cards. Corney was saddened to learn from McGoodwin's wife, Jean, that her husband had passed away in Lynchburg, Virginia, on September 26, 1935.

CHAPTER FIFTEEN

The Best Damned Regiment in the Army

THE AMERICAN DECLARATION OF WAR on Germany on April 6, 1917, increased Corney's desire to quit his attaché post and rejoin the troops in the field. Grudgingly he labored in Caracas until July before receiving stateside orders. He avidly followed America's preparation for war and the conduct of Allied operations. In June General John J. Pershing landed in France with the first contingent of the American Expeditionary Force. Corney, spurred on by the news of his old friend, wrote again to the War Department. The conflict was warming up everywhere — and Corney was not in it.

The western front in France had been stabilized for more than two years in trench warfare. Movement of forces was measured in yards and feet, and casualties were astronomical. Cavalry had no place in this situation. On the eastern front the war was fluid with rapid and far-ranging movement of cavalry by Russians and Austro-German forces. In the desert, the British field marshal Allenby used English and Indian cavalry to rout the Turks.

The American horsemen, with the exception of the 2nd U. S. Cavalry, remained on the Mexican border. Under the circumstances, this decision seemed warranted. Mexico was full of

German agents. Should the U.S. be attacked on its southern flank, experienced troops were poised there to repel the invasion. Many of the veterans had been on the Punitive Expedition of 1916 and were smarting to get a "real crack" at the Mexicans. Most justifiably felt that Wilson's policies had hamstrung any real effort to punish Villa for his raid on American soil.

Despite the readiness and desire of these troopers to give battle, two new weapons were revolutionizing warfare. The airplane and the tank rendered cavalry as archaic as the crossbow. Whether Corney knew it or not, the day of his beloved cavalry was nearly at an end.

Still, the passage of the National Defense Act in June 1916 increased the cavalry arm from fifteen to twenty-five regiments, each to be composed of twelve troops plus a machine gun unit. Before the act could be implemented, the U.S. declared war on Germany and entered the conflict with only seventeen cavalry regiments. Meanwhile, Corney was en route to Camp Grant, Rockford, Illinois, to assume command of the post and to train infantry. He had been offered the job as Military Attaché to the American Embassy in Madrid but he turned it down in order to serve with troops. He wanted an overseas billet but was assigned a training mission.

Corney lost no time in putting his command on a war footing. He introduced rigid training schedules and maintained an almost constant state of readiness. Most of his men were big, husky farm boys from Wisconsin, coming to Camp Grant from that state's 32nd Division ("Red Arrow"). Corney formed the recruits into the brand new 341st Infantry Regiment, which became a part of the 86th Division. A feature article in the *Chicago Tribune* in February 1918 described the work of the new unit:

> From barracks to troop train in forty-five minutes is the remarkable mobility record achieved this morning by the 341st Infantry Regiment. Top notch military efficiency was for the "Wisconsin Eagles" in this competitive drill considered one of the most important phases of the Division's War schooling. Under the direction of Colonel C.C. Smith, Company Commanders and men evacuated their barracks, sweeping out all traces of occupancy and falling into column fully equipped for

action between "assembly" at 6:15 A.M. and 7 o'clock. By seven, first battalion men, bearing regulation packs and fully armed, were swinging past the regimental reviewing stand on the way to the station.

The maneuver included the packing of barracks bags by all hands, collection and loading of all regimental equipment, packing and lashing of wagon trains and supply trucks, and the clean sweepdown of all quarters. Every last vestige of personal equipment — photos, calendars, clippings and other personal gear — was packed in special bags and tagged for shipment to individual homes.

Said one reviewing general: "This is one of the most remarkable achievements of the entire training period. A regimental movement is always estimated in hours, and I have seen a seasoned regular army outfit spend two days in getting away from a given point. The regiment that can swing into action in less than one hour will hold a vital advantage in war."

Corney, however, saw nothing particularly noteworthy in this maneuver. He had always trained his commands to travel light and move fast. To take two days to move a regiment was unthinkable. He told a subordinate: "Yes, training is hard — I'm going to make this the finest damned regiment in the Army."

Reasonably concluding that men in the field might not always have war field kitchens, Corney schooled men of the 341st in individual field cooking techniques. He wrote the order and then supervised as his subordinates carried it out. The exercise was complete, beginning with men digging shallow trenches, building small individual fires, cooking bacon and potatoes, and making flapjacks. Asked by a brother officer if such things as cooking should not be left to the individual, Corney answered: "Hell, no, I'm not running a chef's school, but these men will at least learn the rudiments of food preparation. I think that's important."

Corney considered professional soldiering a way of life and this war gave it a new dimension. He had never really had personal feelings in his dealings with Sioux or Moros, whom he considered tough and able adversaries. The Germans were different. He saw them as a Christian people, nurtured by centuries of progress and culture, now degrading themselves in a war against helpless people.

In a letter to his uncle, Cornelius Cole, from Camp Grant he wrote:

> I am really anxious to get to Europe to aid in punishing that race of vandals. I am, I am sorry to say, bitter in this matter, and I think it will be unfair if the Germans are not made to suffer some of the devastations they have visited upon France and Belgium. They have been preparing for this war ever since the Franco-Prussian War of 1871; it's time someone brought them to heel.

In May Corney received a letter from his old friend, John J. Pershing:

> It gives me great pleasure to inform you that I have recommended you to Washington for the promotion to the grade of Brigadier General, National Army. I am satisfied that, if the recommendation is acted upon favorably, you will prove equal to the responsibilities and duties of the higher grade.

Corney was not promoted to general officer rank, then or ever. He certainly rated it because of his demonstrated ability to plan, organize and execute military programs of large and complex nature. His misfortune was that he, along with several others, ran headlong into an internal feud between Pershing, Commander of the A.E.F., and General Peyton C. March, Army Chief of Staff.

Pershing and March discussed their bitter feelings in subsequent publications. In his book *My Experiences in the World War,* Pershing related how his requests from France were "emphatically overruled" by both March and the Secretary of War, Newton D. Baker. President Wilson chose not to intervene; hence March and Baker had things pretty much their own way concerning the conduct of the war.

In *The Nation at War,* March spoke forcefully about favoritism in the matter of military appointments and promotions. Much of this text dealt with favoritism concerning relatives of congressmen, a most natural and commendable position as assumed by the Chief of Staff. Corney, an experienced and able senior commander, was not in that category; he was simply a "Pershing man." For all practical purposes that was enough to keep him from attaining higher rank. Pershing wrote:

After frequent attempts to obtain the promotion of several Colonels whose abilities had been thoroughly tested in active service, and having failed to get their names on a recent list of promotions, I sent a cable asking for a re-consideration of my recommendations, suggesting that it be shown to the Secretary in person.

I also wrote the Secretary immediately giving him my point of view, and explaining just what the promotions of tried officers with the armies would mean to efficiency in my command. In a letter from him, sometime later, it was clear that the cable had not been submitted to him, as he stated in his usual cordial manner that it was his full intention to give every consideration to the men of proved efficiency, which was, on principle, all that I could wish. In practice, however, his subordinates did not carry this out.

Asked later if he had any resentment to those men promoted to general officer by March, Corney said: "No, most of them I didn't even know. I would have done my best as a Brigadier as I did when I was a Corporal, Captain, or Colonel. My conscience is clear."

If General March wanted to pass Corney by, others were of different persuasion. In a letter to Corney on November 25, 1918, Lieutenant Colonel Charles Burnett wrote:

As Division Inspector of the 86th Division from September 1917 to February 1918, I saw a great deal of the administration and methods of instruction of the 341st Infantry under your command. From my observations the unit was excellent in every respect and could well form a model for other National Army organizations. Comparing it to the other infantry regiments of the division I considered it the best and so reported it, both to the Division Commander and to the Inspector General's Department, Washington.

Lieutenant Colonel Gordon N. Kimball, Judge Advocate of the 86th Division, gave a similar assessment:

In my opinion the 341st Infantry was the best in the Division in training, administration and instruction. The training was evidenced by the appearance of enlisted personnel, which was superior. The discipline, as evidenced by courts-martial was excellent, and the administration exceedingly good. The initiative of the Regiment and its officers and men were surpassed by none. During Colonel Smith's time of command the 341st Infantry was excellent in all respects.

As the months passed, battles raged at Verdun, Cambrai, Ypres and Amiens, but still Corney could not secure an overseas billet. It was the first time in his career that he was on the "home-front." Corney recognized that "somebody had to do it, but I'd have given anything to take a regiment against the krauts." In a brief time span, he had done a creditable job at Camp Grant. New regiments forming in Texas needed the strict, experienced hand of the professional soldier.

CHAPTER SIXTEEN

From the Ground Up

IN FEBRUARY 1918, A BOARD of five officers convened at Fort Sam Houston, Texas, to discuss the formation of new cavalry regiments. The exploratory nature of the idea and lack of men and equipment to support it limited the initial plan of instruction to officers. The six-week training period included such things as cavalry drill regulations, "hippology," and stable management, equitation and other items pertaining to the military employment of horses.

In March the War Department directed the organization of a Third Squadron of the 312th Cavalry, and the formation of three new regiments — the 313th, 314th and 315th. The squadrons of the 312th would join the parent organization at Fort D. A. Russell, Wyoming. The 313th would form at Del Rio, Texas, the 314th at Fort Bliss, El Paso, Texas, and the 315th at Fort D. A. Russell, Wyoming. All regiments would attain maximum strength under a colonel, lieutenant colonel and major from the Regular Army.

Commanding the 341st Infantry at Camp Grant in December 1917, Corney wrote to General Tasker H. Bliss, Chief of Staff, to obtain command of one of the new regiments. Bliss replied:

I have just returned from Europe and find your letter of Dec. 19 in regard to commanding one of the new cavalry regiments. I have placed your application on file with the Adjutant General with a statement from me that I think you well qualified for the position and desire that your application receive full and proper consideration.

Bliss' endorsement bore fruit. Corney was assigned to command the new 314th Cavalry at Fort Bliss. The Regiment would be made up of replacements from existing units plus recruits. Also, it would have a band — the infantry band of the 1st Ohio National Guard.

Corney immediately began making a plan of organization and training. This work resulted directly from experience gained with the 341st Infantry. He also obtained an early release from that unit to proceed to Bliss with a cadre of selected officers to provide them with about six weeks of intensive training before the arrival of troops. Corney held both morning and afternoon classes but "recitations were not allowed to overshadow practical exercises held outside."

In making his plan for the development of the Regiment, Corney kept two things in mind: the effective training of officers, men and animals, and the proper arrangement of buildings, tents, corrals and stables to provide smooth handling of all elements. Contrary to present-day procedure wherein civilian contractors build military bases at enormous cost to the government, the officers and men of the regiments formed in May 1918 built their own facilities. "Thus," wrote Corney, "in building the camp it was necessary that time laid out by the government for training should not be usurped by construction work. That is, all of our improvements had to be accomplished outside of instruction hours."

An old camp about two and one half miles from Bliss known as Owen Beirne proved to be the only available site. It contained a line of dilapidated old mess halls, nondescript shacks, huts and rows of weather-beaten tent frames. It had been used by a brigade of national guardsmen from Kentucky, then reduced to ruins by time and weather. Doors swung crookedly on hinges, where there were doors; windows were shattered; and tumbleweeds gathered in piles against fences and adobe walls.

Still, given some ingenuity and a little bit of help from the

Quartermaster, Corney saw in this skeleton the makings of a first-rate cavalry camp. He had talked with the Quartermaster stationed with the 7th Cavalry at Fort Bliss and ascertained that it would take about $20,000 to renovate the ramshackle barrack buildings and construct new officers' quarters, latrines, fencing and stables. As it turned out, the government supplied only a token amount for this work, the bulk being paid for by the sweat of officers and men of the 314th. Corney remembered:

> At Rockford we had an excellent cantonment, but no room for adequate training. At Beirne we had no cantonment, but all of the room in the world. I see the construction of this camp likened unto a ship, where the captain, holding forth on the bridge, may witness all that goes on around him and act accordingly. I will therefore build a tower, centrally located, from which platform I can see the entire flat countryside stretching away in every direction. In this way I and my staff may witness construction and training as they progress.

The tower was built by officers and men working from 6:30 P.M. until dusk each afternoon, and on Saturdays. The sixty-foot "Bridge" proved so useful that Corney successfully petitioned the Commanding General of the El Paso District to permit the Regiment to remain in Owen Beirne rather than move to Fort Bliss:

> I believe that the war training of a new regiment is aided by camp rather than garrison conditions. With draftees, who know little or nothing of military life, a camp symetrically and systematically laid out as this one [Beirne] is, is superior to the sprawling formless general government installation, which affords maximum comfort while providing minimum training.

When Corney put his men to work, Camp Owen Beirne was an assemblage of run-down buildings, hardly portending an effective military installation. Before long, all of the spadework and after-hours labor paid off as the commanding generals of both the Southern Department and the El Paso District wrote favorable reports about the camp. It even became the model for five more camps to be built in Texas.

The 314th Cavalry basically followed the system of instruction put forth in cavalry training publications of the General Staff,

United States Army. Yet as an old cavalryman with years of experience, Corney put his own interpretation on these schedules. Having a large body of men to train in a limited time, he used the tower to effect. Whenever he wanted to teach a maneuver, he gathered his officers to watch a picked squad or detachment go through the motions on the drill field below. Signals might be relayed easily to the model outfit, questions asked and discussions held by students on the tower. This obviated paperwork, the issuance of written orders and the usual administrative paraphernalia.

From his vantage point on the tower, Corney witnessed the entire program, from start of the drill to watering and feeding of horses. The horses were fed and watered again, after retreat at 6:10 P.M. "I always watched this — it was interesting to see the entire regiment moving to feed at the same time, and see the horses all diving into their nose bags at once."

Corney held at least one call "to arms," "to horse," or "fire call" per month. Calls were sounded either day or night. All hands fell out, men with belts and rifles, officers with sidearms. Sounded at night, the call permitted no time for dressing. Such drills were helter-skelter affairs at best, but the troops seldom failed to be in place within the time allotted. "This is a unique sight," said one reporter from the *El Paso Herald* in June 1918. "The Colonel has 950 men here now, mostly raw recruits from the Eastern states. To see them scramble out of tents and 'fall to' in company streets is something to see."

Corney considered attitude and deportment as important as training and conditioning. He issued orders specifying that no soldier could leave the post unless properly attired, and slovenly personal appearance would not be tolerated. "Uniformity of dress throughout this command is absolutely essential to discipline." Elaborating on the subject to one of his junior officers he said: "When men of the same command are seen in town, like some other outfits I see, with some men wearing campaign hats, others Red Cross helmets, others stocking caps, and others bareheaded — it looks like hell. Also, you can bet the Command is a sloppy one."

Corney conveyed his philosophy when he wrote:

Military men will agree that soldierly discipline of an extraordinarily high degree is necessary to steel a soldier for battle service. The Inspector General and our allied visitors repeatedly state that the greatest weakness in recruits throughout the land is discipline.

Explaining these sentiments, Corney added:

We're not running a popularity contest here. We are getting men ready for war. To be good soldiers they must look like soldiers, act like soldiers. That is impossible when every man does what he pleases. I may be liked or disliked here. That's unimportant. It is important that I be respected, and that my officers and non-coms be respected. That much achieved, we will turn out proper soldiers for the United States Army.

Of some moment in the area of discipline were the fleshpots offered in El Paso. Some were reputable; many were not. The latter were placed off limits and posted with Military Police. Members of the Regiment were not permitted to cross the line into Juárez nor could they bring liquor into camp. Though he agreed with both prohibitions, the edicts were not Corney's but were issued by the Commanding General, Southern District.

In the World War I era, troops moved either by rail or steamship. Depending upon the location of his command, Corney planned for either. Prearranged orders were always written, prepared for tailoring and immediate issuance. A typical example was the order for movement by rail. It formed a part of Corney's "Scheme of Instruction for a Cavalry Regiment," a long and interesting treatise on military logistics.

When a move by rail is anticipated it is necessary for the commander to apprise the railroad company of his needs. Thus when the movement order comes he will have (or at least have a better chance of getting) the proper number of passenger cars, freight cars, stock cars, and flatcars.

If no kitchen cars are provided it is the duty of the Regimental Mess Officer to wire to stops along the way, arranging for coffee and something to eat. The adjutant will determine the exact number of officers and men boarding the train and figure out sleeping arrangements and storage space. To calculate the number of baggage cars required he may assume that each man will have about two cubic feet of plunder. Having obtained the cars he will see that each one is marked properly on the outside with chalk: baggage, A Troop, 314th CAV.; 48 men, B Troop, 314th CAV., etc.

In the stock cars, twenty horses or mules may be loaded, head to tail. Three supply wagons, tongues removed, may be placed upon each flatcar (two if tongues left on). If possible, load the wagons, thus cutting down on baggage car requirements. On long trips, stock should be unloaded for exercise every 24 hours.

Corney elaborated on the lessons he had learned:

When troops are going into the field or the war zone, there is no valid reason to take a lot of gear. This pertains to men carrying individual equipment, and organizations carrying boxes of stuff. Within the limits of reason, the rule should be "the lighter, the better." At Grant, we were always ready to move out for an Atlantic port on several hours' notice. This included taking everything we really needed.

I may not know everything about transporting animals by rail, but what I know I learned the hard way. During the Spanish-American War I was in charge of moving animals from Mobile to Tampa, and then getting them stowed properly aboard ships for transfer to Cuba. I had over 1,000 mules to move in fifteen separate pack trains. I take no credit for the breakdown; a War Department order specified that each train would carry sixty-four mules and one "bell horse." In each train, therefore, I put fourteen saddle mules and fifty packs. Saddle mules were ridden by a packmaster, a cargador, blacksmith, cook and ten packers. Each packer looked after his mule and five others, but as the diamond-hitch requires that packs work in pairs, it worked out that each two men cared for twelve mules. There was always rivalry among packer teams to see which ones brought in the freshest animals on the march.

The maximum load for mules was laid down at 250 pounds. This did not include the "aparejo" or packsaddle which weighs about 30 pounds. We never weighed our old fellows down like that, although foreign armies did — and then some. Maximum loads for us in the Cuban occupation was around 200 pounds. One reason for this, aside from considerations of mercy, was that pack-gear was put into standard-sized packages, small increments easy to get at.

When our mule trains were loaded, in 1898, a train of 50 fully loaded animals weighed in at about six and one-quarter tons. I quote these figures to show what supply officers may count on if called upon to move animals by rail.

I recall a portion of George Steunenberg's famous poem "All Hail the Army Mule!" It is an apt description of the high regard old army hands had for these patient, tough old fellows:

> He's been an unsung hero for a thousand weary years,
> and now that he's been glorified we give three ringing
> cheers,
> No more he'll be the object of rude joke and ridicule,
> He stands the king of quadrupeds — All hail the army
> mule!

Another poem that comes to mind is "The Packer." I don't know who wrote it, and it's too long to recite in toto. It went something like this:

> I wouldn't be a soldier if they made me a brigadier!
> and I'd die before I wore a uniform — gimme the old
> blue overalls for twelve months in a year
> and a slicker when we ride into a storm.
> We ain't so much to look at, and our ways is rather slack,
> and along the trail you're apt to hear us swear,
> but when your out of rations, and your belly rubs your
> back,
> You can bet you'll find the pack train there.

And we could — the pack mule and the packers were indispensable. They are gone now, but they were one hell of a pair for a long, long time.

In a continuing effort to keep troop commanders on their toes, Corney distributed a series of questionnaires dealing with daily life in camp. All had to be answered and carried such questions as:

(1)   What is the general fitness of your command for the service, especially the cavalry?

(2)   Do the new men complain a lot?

(3)   If so, are their complaints justified?

(4)   What have you done to provide amusement and diversion for your men?

(5)   Has anyone in your command failed to pass the small arms firing test?

(6)   Why?

(7)   Do you have any money lenders or "bankers" operating within the troop?

In July, the War Department, impressed with the whole operation at Camp Owen Beirne, ordered Corney to make a personal report. He replied:

I arrived here on April 4 and met on the 6th with seven officers at Headquarters of the 5th Cavalry at Fort Bliss. At that meeting I announced that formation of the new Regiment might be considered as having begun. I named an acting adjutant and supply officer and assigned the remaining five officers to troops.

On the 5th I had been informed by the Commanding General, El Paso District (General George S. Read) that I could establish my officers in the old School of Mines at Fort Bliss or at an abandoned campsite called Owen Beirne, formerly used by the 15th Cavalry. I chose Owen Beirne.

The camp was a ramshackle affair, with gutted buildings, most of them demolished for lumber. My request for lumber and building materials was cut back severely by the District Quartermaster, but we went ahead anyway, improvising as we went. The attached blueprint shows all reconstruction and new building. The last adobe set of officers' quarters will be finished by the 25th inst., and the camp completed. Our camp is neat, symmetrical and military. Visiting officers from Washington and several foreign mission people have labelled it the best one seen in recent inspection tours. No instruction time was taken for building. All orders for training were, and are, carried out to the letter. I must give credit and thanks to Lt. Col. Wagner, and Captains Dascum, Schille and Foster of the area QM Department. Although unable to furnish me with sizeable amounts of material, they did what they could, making our task easier. Apparently they are willing to act on the theory that they will help those who help themselves.

By April 15 all officers had arrived here. They were put immediately into an intensive six weeks' course of cavalry training. During this time enlisted troops were coming into camp, the first being aliens as specified by the general order establishing the Regiment. In this first lot we received 106 aliens from Douglas, Arizona; Camp Greenleaf, Georgia; and El Paso.

On May 4th, the First Ohio Infantry Band arrived, an excellent aggregation. They came in from Camp Sheridan, Georgia. On May 13 the Medical Detachment arrived from Columbus, New Mexico, and on the 26th we got 202 draftees from Jefferson Barracks, Mo. These were followed by volunteers and draftees from Fort Logan, Colo.; Chickamauga Park, Ga.; Fort Oglethorpe, Ga.; and Fort Slocum, N.Y.

Weekly drill schedule began on June 3. These schedules have been sent to the Director, War Plans Division, General Staff, Army War College as directed. Training is progressing satisfactorily and so is the Regiment's state of readiness. It assembles, each troop to its own parade, on alarm call within two minutes. Average time to respond to "to horse" call is eight minutes.

The camp has some amusement accommodation for the men, a fine Y.M.C.A. building, billiard rooms in a recreation hall, and a small library. I am informed that citizens in El Paso are raising money to donate for the erection of an outdoor movie.

Great stress has been laid on training, readiness and fitness. Also on uniformity as it affects military matters. That is to say, all garbage stands and incinerators are similarly placed with respect to company areas; saddle-racks, picket-lines, forage corrals, and latrines are uniform. In effect, the Regiment operates as one immense troop.

The report was longer, going into detail concerning training and improvisation concerning building. When Corney left the Regiment to go to Huachuca, Major General Robert A. Howze wrote:

Upon relinquishing command of the El Paso District, I take occasion to commend the work of Colonel C.C. Smith, Cavalry. He has built up a new regiment of raw material. By his energy and ability for command he has inspired his officers and men with the highest ideals of a soldier — duty and obedience. He possesses to a marked degree the quality of leadership.

Attesting to General Howze's remarks, the newly organized 31st Cavalry won four cups in regimental competition with the 5th and 7th Cavalry Regiments and the 82nd Field Artillery. The Regiment accomplished this feat between arrival of troops in May and Corney's departure in October, a fitting going away present for a tough commander.

CHAPTER SEVENTEEN

The Buffalo Soldiers

LEGEND HAS IT that Plains Indians likened black cavalry troopers to buffalo because both had short, kinky hair. Another plausible story holds that the Indians called Negroes "Buffalo Soldiers" because when under attack these soldiers would fight fiercely until victorious or overcome. Always the term "Buffalo Soldiers," as applied to black troopers of the 9th and 10th Cavalry Regiments, has been a title of respect.

In October 1918, Corney received orders to proceed to Fort Huachuca for his third tour, this time to command both the post and the 10th U.S. Cavalry. In a glowing article, the *Nogales Daily Herald* hailed Corney's arrival as follows:

> Colonel C. C. Smith is coming to Huachuca. He will relieve Col. George Rodney who will assume command of the 17th Cavalry. Col. Smith is probably one of the best known army officers in the west, and is universally admired by all who know him. He is a strict disciplinarian and an excellent soldier. . . .

For his part, the new assignment satisfied Corney. If he could not get an overseas command, Huachuca was about as nice a place as any and the 10th had an exemplary reputation. In assuming command of Fort Huachuca he followed a group of distinguished predecessors: Adna R. Chaffee, Samuel M. Whiteside, George A. Forsyth, De Rosey C. Cabell, and others of equal stature.

The Regiment, however, was Corney's primary interest. The 10th Cavalry had mustered in at Fort Leavenworth, Kansas, on September 30, 1866. On that auspicious occasion it had exactly one man present for duty, Colonel Benjamin H. Grierson, the Commander. Lieutenant Colonel Charles C. Walcut was carried on the morning report as absent on recruiting duty. Well he might be; the Regiment had no men, no horses, no equipment. By December, the command had two field officers, one captain and sixty-four recruits.

As the weeks passed, enlistees came into Leavenworth, a willing but soldierly pathetic lot consisting of ex-slaves, fieldhands, and house servants. Most were illiterate and, even worse, unable to ride. Grierson faced a monumental task in making soldiers of these men.

In addition, ignorant whites and Southern diehards made life miserable for the early soldiers of the 10th. Frequently they were thrown out of gin mills and beaten in the streets. They were overcharged for just about every commodity bought in civilian stores and frequently did not even know that they were being cheated.

Perhaps the "most unkindest cut of all" was the issue of poor horses to these inexperienced but willing soldiers. While white cavalry units rode the best horses the Army could buy, their black counterparts rode about on spavined old plugs and skates a jump or two ahead of the glue factory. These iniquities, insults and stupidities were not always to endure, but they were sad factors surrounding the early years of the two black cavalry regiments.

When it came time to "lay it on the line," the black soldier did surprisingly well. At the Sabine River Fight north of Fort Hays, F Company of the 10th fought off a band of 300 Indians in a six-hour fight. This battle on August 2, 1867, was the Regiment's first firefight; its representative troop acquitted itself with honor, as others would in many conflicts to come.

In the winter of 1867, the Regiment engaged in hard and bitter fighting against Black Kettle's band of Cheyennes. In one terrible part of that campaign, over 100 horses froze to death in a howling "Norther." In September 1868, G Company inflicted heavy casualties on roving Cheyennes in Kansas. Meanwhile, I and H Companies rescued Lieutenant Colonel George A. Forsyth from an island in the Republican River surrounded by some 750 Indians. Troopers of H Company arrived on the scene first. They found Forsyth and his men crouching in shallow holes scooped out of the sand and living on rotten horse flesh. Every horse and mule of Forsyth's command had been killed and lay there bloated and stinking in the sun.

Before long, the battle-hardened men of the 10th proudly compared their regimental standard with the best of them. Streamers for Buffalo Springs, Sulphur Springs, Saragossa, Pinto Mountains, Sierra Carmel, Tinaja de las Palmas, Rattlesnake Springs and many other lonely, parched, desolate little way stations bespoke the path to glory.

The Regiment came to Arizona in 1885 at the very height of troubles with the Apache tribes. Geronimo, Mangas Colorado, Eskebenedel and others were raiding the ranches and stock farms of southern Arizona and New Mexico and the lonely little villages over the line in Chihuahua and Sonora. Now new names appeared on the rosters of the Regiment: Mizner, Lebo, Baldwin, Morrison, Henry — some of these men Corney would know later in the Philippines. All of them he would know about, and, coming into Huachuca as Commander of the 10th in 1918, he was not unmindful of the proud heritage handed down by these warriors of another time.

One of the truly unique aspects of Fort Huachuca was the use of Indian Scouts. Captain Samuel Marmaduke Whitside did not originate the concept but introduced it to the Huachuca area. The organization had been brought into being by Congress in July 1866, under the provision of an "Act to Increase and Fix the Military Peace Establishment of the United States." These Scouts were regular enlisted men of the U.S. Army, receiving the same pay and allowances as their black counterparts for identical work. They could not be moved about from station to station, however, and their service was limited to the Huachuca area.

In the Apache Campaigns of 1882-84, General George Crook

used the Scouts to great effect. Crook's greatest problem was trying to pronounce the Indian names. He finally introduced a numbering system designating Scout 1, Scout 2, etc. Others solved the dilemma by giving them pseudonyms of colorful character: "Deadshot," "Skippy," "Dandy Jim," "Chow Big," "Peaches," "Charlie Bones," "Shorten Bread."

During Corney's final tour at Fort Huachuca a number of the Apache Scouts worked on the post. Sergeant "Chicken," whose Apache name was Eskehnadestah, had enlisted in July 1893 and served continuously since that time. In 1918, he became a first sergeant. "Chow Big" had joined the Scouts in July 1891 and served continuously after 1902. He was promoted to sergeant in 1918. Other Apache Scouts serving in Corney's command in 1918 included Nonotolth, Deklay, Charlie Bones, Askeldelinney, Chissay and Nos Chuky Grasshopper.

A couple of months prior to Corney's arrival at Huachuca, the Military Intelligence Division (MID) reported suspicious activity across the line in Nogales. Reports described the arrival of many Mexican soldiers with large amounts of arms, ammunition, food and clothing. Europeans, presumably Germans, were observed lecturing the Mexicans in the use of arms and kindred matters. American suspicions were confirmed when a letter from a dissident Mexican arrived in Nogales, Arizona, and was delivered to Lieutenant Colonel Frederick J. Herman, 10th Cavalry officer and acting Sub-District Commander in Nogales.

On August 27, some two weeks after the Military Intelligence Division's report, a firefight involving U.S. and Mexican forces occurred. It might have been avoided but happened as the 35th Infantry, ordered to France, had just begun moving a few companies at a time. The Mexicans (and presumably their German advisers) mistakenly assumed that only a skeleton crew remained on the American side. They engaged a small detachment of the 35th's border guard and firing spread rapidly all along the line. Soon the surprised Mexicans faced Troops A, C and F of the 10th Cavalry in addition to three infantry companies (F, G and H) under Captain R. J. Marshburn. In this fight two American officers and three enlisted men were killed, and two officers and twenty-nine enlisted men wounded. One of them was Lieutenant Colonel Herman.

While at Bliss, Corney learned about German activity in Mexico and was not surprised to hear of this affair. Indeed, he had seen evidence of the problem while serving at Naco in the fall of 1914. On assuming command of the 10th Cavalry at Huachuca, he put his officers on a constant alert for a repetition of the August incident but none occurred.

Nonetheless, the command retained a state of perpetual readiness for any such eventuality. One training item concerned the use of hand grenades while mounted, which according to Corney required "excellent horsemanship and rigid discipline." Defensive grenades could not be used because fragments carried one hundred yards or more. The offensive grenade, a time fuse weapon made of tin or some other soft metal, had an effective radius of seven or eight yards. Thus mounted men could throw one, gallop on and be out of range when the grenade exploded.

Corney used cement dummies at first, then small canvas bags filled with oats or beans. Soon the drill field was filled with charging lines of cavalrymen tossing grenades. In several special exercises live grenades were used; fortunately, no men or animals were hurt.

Shortly after arriving at Huachuca, Corney received a letter from General De Rosey Cabell mentioning a possible promotion to brigadier general. "In order to have a Brigadier in command of the Arizona District, I sent a telegraphic recommendation for your promotion to the adjutant general a few days ago but have heard nothing from it." Nor would he. The March-Pershing feud continued with Corney a casualty.

Smith, however, was too busy to nurse a grudge. He maintained high standards and when he gave orders he expected them to be carried out. One of his subordinates, Lieutenant Colonel John H. Healy, told this story:

> The 10th Cavalry with headquarters at Fort Huachuca was patrolling the Mexican Border in October of 1918. A new CO was assigned, one Colonel C. C. Smith. Colonel Smith was born of the army, from a line of frontier fighters.
>
> There was no indirectness about this new commanding officer, the giant with long wavy black hair, this man who looked like Daniel Webster and thundered as easily.

One noon at Officer's call, he announced that leather equipment, bridles, saddles, gun boots, etc., were not being properly cleaned. Henceforth, when the Regiment returned from drill, on each troop picket line there would be three buckets of water, so that men would be able to clean properly all leather equipment. I knew that buckets were not plentiful in supply, and without waiting for the one o'clock formation, I got my supply sergeant on the phone and told him to get those buckets — and now. It was well I did.

Next morning at recall all troops returned to regimental picket line. I looked across at my friend Capt. Rogers, who had the troop next door. No buckets there. He had sent his sergeant for buckets but there were none; so what of it? He had tried. Some minutes later came Colonel Smith.

"Capt. Rogers, yesterday, I instructed all troop commanders to have three buckets with water on each troop picket line so that leather could be cleaned properly. You have none." Rogers was not phased.

"Colonel, I have no extra buckets in my supply room. I sent to regimental supply, they had none. So I sent to the quartermaster. Again, they had none."

Colonel Smith was not softhearted, nor easily sidetracked. "Capt. Rogers, go to Tombstone, go to Tucson, go to Yuma, go to hell, but get those buckets." The junior officer saluted, "Very well, Sir."

Comedy and tragedy were travelling hand in hand. Rogers walked slowly away. He gathered his wits. A smile played over his face. Old First Sergeant Jordan was coming toward him.

"Sergeant Jordan, yesterday I told you to have three buckets with water on the picket line for stables this morning. And now no buckets."

"Sir, Captain, there ain't no buckets. I sent Sergeant Carter to the regimental supply, to the quartermaster and also he went to the PX. There just ain't no buckets."

"Sgt. Jordan, go to Tombstone, go to Tucson, go to Yuma, go to hell, but get those buckets."

And out of thin air three buckets mysteriously appeared.

Shortly before leaving Huachuca for St. Louis and a new duty assignment, Corney was sent to Fort Apache as a witness for a court-martial. One of his officers, a Southerner, had become angered with a black trooper in his command and insulted him before witnesses. He had been transferred but the damage had been done. Of interest is Corney's letter to Kathleen from Fort Apache on February 17, 1919:

> Don't gossip about what I am here for — just say you don't know. I am comfortable here but my trip was atrocious. These "hotels" are little more than shacks or barns, and poor ones at that. The toilets are 50 to 60 yards away, on snow-covered paths. The rooms are like icehouses, and the beds all too short and "stringy."
>
> It is very cold. Last night at Pine Top the water pitcher in my room froze over, and this morning there was nothing in the fireplace to build a fire with. I ought to get back to Huachuca about March 3rd or 4th. . . .

The offending officer was found guilty, reduced on the promotion list, and fined. Black troopers at Huachuca were not satisfied, but there was no more trouble.

Corney's third tour of duty at Huachuca was brief — not unusual considering the wartime conditions with officers and men moving about to meet changing situations. He always considered Huachuca to be one of the highlights of his career, because he had served there in the "best ranks." He told Corney Jr., years later, that the two best ranks in the army are captain and colonel. "Then you are virtually autonomous, and you command. The ranks of lieutenant, major and lieutenant colonel aren't worth a damn in that respect — you're either on a staff or carrying out someone else's orders."

He liked the Buffalo Soldiers. "They're obedient and they've got guts." The 10th Cavalry served longer at Huachuca than any unit ever stationed there — except the Apache Scouts. The Regiment remained there from 1913 until 1931. An obedient soldier himself, Corney epitomized the famed Regiment's motto as he left for his new assignment: "Ready and Forward."

Colonel Cornelius C. Smith, Commanding Officer, 314th Cavalry, Camp Owen Beirne, Texas, April 1918. (Photo from personal files)

CHAPTER EIGHTEEN

Retirement

A FTER LEAVING HUACHUCA, Corney served for five months in St. Louis on recruiting duty. He found shuffling from one assignment to another distasteful. "My God!" he exclaimed, "in the old Army, a man made a career out of a regiment." He had served for over ten years with the 14th Cavalry and three with the 2nd. His was in no way an isolated case. In the frenzied rush to enlist, train, and ship men to France, the Army moved its key people about like chessmen on a board. Short tours were both a necessity and a rule.

It was in St. Louis that Corney received two letters which he put away to keep. One was from ex-corporal Elihu Evans of C Troop, 314th Cavalry:

> Dear Sir: As it will be a long time before I again visit St. Louis, I wish to ask the Colonel to grant a favor which will indeed be highly appreciated by the writer, namely this: that the Colonel will send me a small picture of himself. The time that I spent in the service under your command shall always remain in my memory as time well spent, and tho' we drilled hard I know

that every one of us was proud of the man we all considered the best cavalry Colonel in the U.S. Respectfully yours.

Sergeant Virgil C. McCall wrote similarly:

Dear Sir: Words are inadequate to express my regret at losing you as our Commanding Officer. I will miss you especially, for it was because of my profound respect for you that brought me back to recruiting service. I wish to thank you again for all of your kind considerations to me, and trust that the blessings of good health and prosperity go forward with you and yours through life. With lifelong remembrance of you, I beg to remain, obediently yours.

Corney's final assignment took him again to Fort Leavenworth where he attended the School of the Line, an advanced tactical course for senior commanders. He remained in Kansas from July . 1919 until April 1920, when on the ninth day of the month he voluntarily retired — thirty years to the day after his enlistment in Missoula. He later regretted this early retirement. An active man, accustomed to order and command, he found civilian life unappealing.

In an effort to recapture some semblance of the military environment, he returned to Tucson to become the Professor of Military Science and Tactics at the University of Arizona from July 1920 until the following February. The position was uninspiring but he made several good friends including Dr. Rufus B. von Kleinsmid, president, and Dean Byron Cummings, an archaeologist. With Cummings, he made several excavation trips into northern Arizona.

In October 1920, Corney saved Dr. von Kleinsmid from possible serious injury from an attack by a bald eagle. Near the main gate of the university, a large aviary contained an interesting collection of birds. One day the two men were inside the huge cage when suddenly the eagle swooped down upon von Kleinsmid from the rear and clawed viciously at his head. In a great welter of lunging, flailing arms, and beating wings, Corney threw the bird off. Von Kleinsmid was lacerated about the head and neck and had to be taken to a hospital.

From Tucson the Smith family moved to San Antonio, Texas,

and remained there from October 1921 until June 1922. Tragedy struck on the day before Christmas. Kathleen was preparing for a bath and stepped too close to the gas stove. In a terrifying whoosh of flame her nightgown caught fire and quickly burned her nearly to death. Her pleas to "Shoot me! Shoot me!" horrified Corney as they waited for the ambulance.

She was in Brook General Hospital for six months, much of the time under hooped sheets. Like most severe burn cases she developed pneumonia and nearly died. With the exception of taking Alice and Corney Jr. to school in Alamo Heights, Corney was at her side throughout the hours of each year-long day.

Finally, in June, Kathleen was discharged from the hospital, a veritable scarecrow of skin and bones. Flames had burned the skin from all parts of her body except her face. She needed rest and recuperation, so the family went to Durango, Mexico, to live with Corney's cousin, Dr. Harry Jackson. In a thick-walled old house on Calle Achilles Cerdán, Kathleen slowly regained her health. Each day she sat on the sunny patio, under lemon trees and cages of parakeets while young Mexican servant girls massaged her body with soothing oils. Her Spanish was as poor as Corney's was good. She normally communicated with the girls either in sign language or just plain "understanding."

Harry Jackson was a physician and skilled surgeon who disliked the fast pace of American life and moved to Mexico. He treated anyone who came to him. His outer office was always filled with hordes of people awaiting treatment; sad-looking women draped in funereal black and taciturn men in white cotton drill. His inner office contained a medical bookcase with a human skull on one of the shelves. House servants passing by quickly became fearful and superstitious in the presence of death. They glanced at the grinning apparition furtively and crossed themselves.

Perhaps Jackson's greatest contribution to local medicine was his scholarly treatise on the virulent scorpion abounding in the area. Durango, known as "La Ciudad de los Alacranes" (The City of Scorpions), lost a number of people (mostly children) yearly from the stings of these poisonous creatures. Jackson's study discovered a variety of scorpions in Durango but maintained the only lethal one was a light-colored long-tailed species which he sent to the Bureau of Entomology in Washington, and had classified as "Centrurus Exilicauda." It seemed most dangerous during its mating season, from about June until mid-August. In 1907, fifty-one people died of scorpion bites; fifty-three the following year. Children bitten by these little monsters perished in convulsions within half an hour.

Despite his primitive, often cruel, surroundings, Jackson was a happy man. An old Spanish custom called "alba," the dawn song, meant that the first person to arise in the household started a song to be taken up by other members of the family until all were singing. This beautiful custom was intended to usher in the day with happiness and love and did just that. Harry's favorite was the old spiritual "Roll, Jordan, Roll!" He often began it, Corney joined in, followed by the servants in the kitchen and in the yard until the household rang with the strains of the stately old song.

By September Kathleen had improved enough for the family to move to Guadalajara. They rented rooms in the house of an Italian artist, Enrique Choistry. In December the family took a train for Manzanillo, the seaport town of the State of Colima. A late arrival caused them to miss their boat and to swelter in the little waterfront village for ten days waiting for the Panama mail steamship S.S. *San Juan.*

On the *San Juan* Corney met General Humberto Paso Díaz, nephew of the President of Nicaragua. Neither could know at the time that five years later General Díaz would be dead, a casualty of revolution, and that six years later Corney would be in Nicaragua as President of the Electoral Commission, Department of Granada. Meanwhile the Smiths journeyed on the *San Juan* to Mazatlán where they stayed for two days in a beautiful old hotel. From Mazatlán they sailed to San Francisco, and from there, they took a train to San Diego.

Corney did a lot of writing in San Diego, and took several trips, one with Dr. Neil M. Judd and the Pueblo Bonito Expedition near Crown Point, New Mexico. Corney found this archaeological trek, supported by the National Geographic Society, intensely interesting. He told Judd about travelling in the same area from 1892 to 1901. He took another trip by auto to Cabo San Lucas in the southern tip of Baja California. Tortuous roads made the 1923 trip horrendous but Corney loved every minute of it.

When the Round-the-World flyers put down on North Island in

San Diego Harbor in 1923, the family went to see them. Great crowds gathered on the base and the airplanes were roped off and placed under guard. Exercising a little muscle, Corney and the children moved near the ropes and Corney called to one of the flyers. He was an army officer who had served under Corney during World War I, and took them inside the cordon and into the hangars, where they climbed into the cockpit of one of the planes. Corney Jr. tried on the aviator's helmet and goggles and wiggled the "joystick" around a little. He was given a map that had gone around the world in the plane but unfortunately lost the memento.

San Diego was an interesting city in the twenties. Corney often loaded the old disc-wheeled Oldsmobile and took Alice and Corney Jr. to the zoo in Balboa Park. All of the neighborhood kids piled in to go along. The children rode on the merry-go-round and reached wildly for the gold ring. Then they went to the zoo where Corney gave lectures on the animals. He seemingly knew more about them than the zoo guides.

From San Diego the Smiths went to Sacramento, living there on Portola Way from January until August 1925. Once Corney took the family on a ride down the Sacramento River on the *River Queen*, a graceful old stern-wheeler plugging her way down the river past the fruit orchards of Elk Grove, Courtland and Rio Vista, and into the larger waters of Benicia, San Pablo and Pinole. The passengers remembered waking up in the morning and going out on deck to see a huge elevated signboard on the Embarcadero, a parrot, saying: "Say Gear-ar-delly" (advertising Ghirardelli chocolate).

In August 1925, the Smiths moved to Hollywood and remained there until September 1930. During this interlude Corney took a fling at the movies. He was introduced to Hollywood directors, Sol Wurtzel and King Baggott. Corney worked as technical director for several Western films and met some interesting people including Bill Hart, Hoot Gibson, Tom Mix, Mary Pickford, Douglas Fairbanks, Johnny Mack Brown and Richard Barthelmess.

In one 1927 picture, he played a part. The picture, *Ransom's Folly*, starred Barthelmess and Dorothy Mackaill and dealt with a harum-scarum young cavalry officer (Barthelmess) who held up a stagecoach with a pair of shears (covered) just for the hell of it. Corney played the part of Ransom's commanding officer, Colonel Ballard. Because Barthelmess was shorter than Corney, the supporting actor had to stand in a hole when photographed with the star.

He could laugh at the photography but not at the way the directors "played with" army customs and regulations. When he objected the director responded, "It doesn't matter for our purposes, Colonel — your way doesn't help the story." Corney asked, "Then why pay me to tell you how it was really done?" "Because the budget calls for a technical director," came the innocuous reply.

Corney worked on pictures that achieved some movie immortality, not because of superlative technical direction, but because these early extravaganzas, *The Covered Wagon, The Scarlet West* and *The Iron Horse*, tried new techniques.

The movie technical work was interesting in a way, but generally unsatisfactory because of its unauthenticity. To use time profitably, Corney wrote articles on military history for such publications as *Winners of the West, Frontier Times*, the *Arizona Historical Review* and the *Brewery Gulch Gazette*. He also wrote for *Touring Topics* and for newspapers, including *Los Angeles Times, Tucson Citizen, Arizona Republican, Tombsone Epitaph* and *Arizona Sentinel*. He became friends with some editors but got into journalistic hassles with columnists and reporters for the Los Angeles papers whose writings on the West were, according to Corney, blatantly false and misrepresentational.

Though busy, Corney nonetheless felt dissatisfied. Verbal duels with historical incompetents were trivial affairs at best. The retired officer sought a new challenge.

CHAPTER NINETEEN

Nicaragua

TIME CONTINUED TO WEIGH HEAVILY on Corney's hands. He wanted some project of real substance. One day a casual glance through the *Hollywood Citizen* presented the opportunity. Several months and numerous letters later he was off to Granada, Nicaragua, as a member of the American Electoral Commission. From beginning to end, he faithfully recorded his Nicaraguan experience:

In 1927, I saw in a newspaper one day that the United States would supervise the presidential election in Nicaragua in the following year, and that Brigadier General Frank R. McCoy had been selected by President Coolidge to head up the Electoral Mission. I knew McCoy well, from Cuba and the Philippines, and on the strength of it wrote to him asking if I might be of service in the operation. He answered right away saying that he would be glad to have me with him.

In May, 1928, I received a telegram from the Adjutant General in Washington inquiring if I would accept service in Nicaragua, and of course I replied in the affirmative. Soon I received orders to pick up the USS *Nitro* in San Francisco for passage to Corinto, Nicaragua.

On board the *Nitro* were half a dozen Marine officers and some 200 enlisted Marines. Also traveling to Nicaragua were several naval officers and Colonel O. E. Hunt, U.S. Army, retired. He had been assigned to the Department of León, a Liberal party stronghold, and I to Granada, a Conservative area. This was the basis of some kidding and joke-making aboard ship.

We left San Francisco on June 22 and made a port call in San Diego a couple of days later. Leaving San Diego on the 29th, we then make a pleasant and leisurely trip of one week and steamed into Corinto on July 6th.

We arrived in Corinto at about six A.M. and were lucky to catch the only train of the day for Managua, which pulled out about an hour later. The journey, which took about six hours, was warm but interesting. We passed through Chinandega, León, and a number of hamlets, at which places vendors hawked fruit, "lonches" (sandwiches) and sweet syrup poured over shaved ice.

Of particular interest was the chain of volcanoes, including El Viejo, Telica, Momotombo and its little brother — Momotombito. These were sending up wisps of smoke, a fascinating but slightly disquieting scene. The route we traveled was steeped in history, making our leisurely sojourn less a passage between points and more an adventure into the past. Only a short distance from Corinto lies Realejo, scene of conquistador landings and pirate raids. Our queer little train hence rolled over territory once traversed by the armor-clad men of Spain and the rollicking buccaneers to reach inland places.

Col. Hunt and I sat on a rickety little observation car at the rear of the train and watched the scene unfold before us — emerald green trees, brilliant patches of flowers, and the noisy bustle of vendors in the stations. These sights and sounds, punctuated by the engine letting off steam at stops and the clicking of steel wheels on the uneven roadbed, kept our interest aroused.

From the train the towns looked attractive enough and one is inclined to accept the scene as a tropical paradise come true. Close inspection, however, awakens one to the reality of an impoverished country brought to its lowly state by the vileness of man. Political upheavals and civil wars have laid the country low, and grinding poverty for the many is the obvious result. Despite this, it is easy to be charmed, for the people are kind and hospitable and the scenery breathtaking.

Arriving in Managua we were met by General McCoy and members of his staff and whisked off to the Lupone Hotel. It was a comfortable place, and Hunt and I remained there for a week, attending daily conferences at the general's office in preparation for duties in our respective districts. In this period we were the recipients of social courtesies from General and Mrs. McCoy and Mr. Charles C. Eberhart, American Minister to Nicaragua, whom I had known in Venezuela twelve years earlier.

On July 10, I was sworn in as President of Departmental Board of Election for the Department (state) of Granada, and left to assume that post four days later. I shall always be grateful to the general for sending me there. Founded in 1523, it is one of the most intriguing and beautiful places in the country.

I was met at Granada by Major Howard W. Stone of the Marine Corps who took me to the Marine Barracks established in the old monastery of San Francisco. . . . Stone took me into the officers' mess and invited me to become a member. I accepted readily. My association with Major Stone and his officers and men was most pleasant; during my entire tour as Departmental Chief I was impressed with Stone's Battalion — the efficiency, soldierly qualities of the command, and the patience and tact with which all hands performed duties with a sometimes volatile people.

On arrival, Major Stone informed me that the elite of the city were gathering that night to celebrate Bastille Day. Some of the residents were of French descent, others had gone to school in Paris, and so the observation of this peculiarly Gallic holiday was not entirely out of place. We attended the function, a truly beautiful affair. The men were all properly attired in evening dress and the ladies radiant in Paris gowns. I was not surprised. Granada was the conservative stronghold with a concentration of wealth and political power. Later, I would visit the houses of the poor and dine on mangoes and rice.

Here I met the native members who would serve on my

board: Dr. Horacio Zavala and General H. Rocha of the Conservative party, and Senor Carlos Lacayo Vivas and Senor E. Arguello, Liberal party. The evening was a success. There were no teetotalers in the crowd, and champagne, whiskey and cognac flowed like water. No one became objectionable and decorum was maintained.

On the following morning I set out with the Marine quartermaster, Lt. Fox to look for quarters and an office. In about an hour we found just the thing — a portion of an enormous old private residence consisting of two huge rooms, modern bathroom, and a large and beautiful patio. The front room would serve as my office, and the rear section for living quarters. Later on, I permitted the patio to be used as a school area for 42 enlisted marines who would act as chairmen at the voting precincts throughout the Department. My landlady, an elderly widow, lived next door and kept my desk supplied with flowers. Also she sent in lemonade for me when I awoke from siesta. Yes — I had adopted the local custom, which to me has always made sense.

An hour or so after moving in office furniture from the Battalion QM supply room, I called upon the Alcalde of Granada who asked if he might be of service in finding me quarters. I replied that my office was open and ready for business. "But you just got here!"

"Yes, Sir, and we're ready for business." In light of the fact that Nicaragua is a charter member of mañana-land, his incredulous look was not surprising.

On July 17, I administered the oath of office to the political members and alternates of the Board, and to my newly arrived assistants, Ensigns R. C. Brixner and M. R. Stone, U.S. Navy. These two were part of a 30-man Navy officer team which had been sent to assist in the Mission due to their high individual standing in Spanish at the Naval Academy. They represented the very finest types of young American manhood, and their services to me and consequently to the Mission were invaluable. I assigned Brixner to the job of Assistant Chairman of the Board, and made Stone my secretary. These were really titles only; both officers did all sorts of work, and both were indispensable.

There are thirteen Departments in the Republic, each with the same Electoral Commission organization as mine. The work is confining and constant but, I can say, always interesting. McCoy says that the eyes of the world, and particularly Latin America, are on the American Mission here and that we must do an exemplary job. Certainly the native politicians watch our every move; to date things have gone quietly.

Why are we in Nicaragua? This may admit of three general answers. First, we are here because the Nicaraguans have asked us to supervise their election. Second, we are here to uphold the principles of the Monroe Doctrine; and third, we are here to protect whatever interest we may have in the possible building of a Nicaraguan Canal. I will not address myself to discussion of the Monroe Doctrine and the Nicaraguan Canal. These are well-known subjects, each with a voluminous literature of its own.

The general statement above may not satisfy our critics at home and abroad, but I can think of nothing that would, save total evacuation, and that would only mean continued turmoil, strife and bloodshed in this beleaguered country. Whatever the philosophical assessments of others, I can only show that the American contribution here has been significant in terms of efficiency, honesty and achievement. Significantly, this is borne out by the utterances of Nicaraguans in public life, from both parties and by the Nicaraguan newspapers.

Corney's position also reflected the political history of Nicaragua which was characterized by the long-lasting and bitter feud between the Liberal and Conservative factions. These opponents emerged from the ceaseless opposition of mestizos, citizens of mixed Indian and Spanish blood, and Indians to the entrenched ruling class. Corney described that the "cleavage between Liberal and Conservative was more than political; it was elemental, consisting of race, status, pride and numerous intangibles separating the factions. In Nicaraguan thought Conservatives were aristocrats, Liberals plebeians."

Tracing the conflict and the consequent instability, Corney wrote:

In 1894 José Santos Zelaya, Liberal, became president and ruled with an iron fist for the next sixteen years. His administration was marked by revolutions at home and by friction with the United States and England. In October 1909 an insurrection broke out in the Atlantic Departments and two U.S. citizens, Groce and Cannon, were executed by government troops, allegedly after being tortured. U.S. warships were sent to Nicaragua and the United States severed relations with Nicaragua.

In the absence of full evidence, Zelaya's responsibility in the matter could not be proved, but the strong stand taken by the U.S. State Department gave encouragement to the revolutionists and caused his ouster in 1909. As I write this, nineteen years later, Zelaya is still an issue in Nicaraguan politics. A Conservative has told me that Zelaya was a scoundrel, criminal and tyrant who should have been hanged. A Liberal says that under Zelaya Nicaragua was prosperous and the people happy.

After Zelaya, the Conservatives came into power and remained there until the election just held. Thus the Liberal party came into power in 1894 by revolution, and again in 1928, but this time by an honest, fair and proper election.

In April 1927, Mr. Coolidge sent the Honorable Henry L. Stimson to Nicaragua to consult with the leaders of both parties concerning an American Electoral Mission in the forthcoming Nicaraguan election. He met first with President Díaz, Conservative, who agreed to the following provisions. There would be an immediate general peace, during which crops might be collected and arms turned over to U.S. military custody. A general amnesty would be declared returning all political persons to their homes. Room for Liberal participation in the Conservative government (if re-elected) would be made. A Nicaraguan constabulary (Guardia Nacional) would be organized and commanded by U.S. Military officers. The 1928 national election would be supervised, in every aspect, by Americans. U.S. Marines would remain in Nicaragua after the election long enough to make the foregoing effective.

Mr. Stimson then met with the Liberal leader, Moncada, at a place called Tipitapa. Moncada agreed with the provisions listed above and with the idea of American supervision.

Consequently an Electoral Mission was sent to Nicaragua in June 1928 and did supervise the election of November 4.

U.S. Marines collected over 9000 rifles from both parties, 296 machine guns, and more than six million rounds of ammunition. With this general disarming the Commission was ready to go to work.

Officers serving in the Mission were selected for a knowledge of civil administration and ability to speak, read and write Spanish. Many had served as observers or supervisors of elections in Cuba, Santo Domingo, Haiti and Panama, and in the Tacna-Arica plebiscite of 1926-27. . . .

Heading the Mission was Major General Frank McCoy, U.S. Army, Chairman of the National Board of Elections. His deputy chief was Col. Francis LeJ. Parker. General McCoy directed the thirteen Departmental Boards from his office in Managua.

It is doubtful that a better man than McCoy could have been chosen for the job. I had known him intimately in the Philippines and during the Great War, and looked upon him as a man of strong character and soldierly qualities. Moreover, he was a diplomat and a gentleman, just the sort to succeed in a delicate mission of this kind. He, as I, had received much of his training under that great American, Leonard Wood. He had been on several diplomatic missions prior to Nicaragua, including one in Armenia and another in Japan.

With all of the Boards, National, Departmental and Directorates (voting booth boards), there were native members equally divided between the Liberal and Conservative parties. General McCoy was served by Dr. Ramon Castillo, Conservative, and Dr. Enoc Aguado, Liberal. I have already named my assistants. Board members were always men of considerable standing in their communities — lawyers, doctors, prominent merchants, and so on.

The Electoral Directorates consisted of one American presidente and one American suplente, or vice-chairman, a native member and alternate from each party, two secretaries, and two watchers or challengers. The presidentes and suplentes were U.S. Marine non-coms or trusted privates. The political members, alternates and secretaries were appointed by the native Departmental Directing Body (Junta Directiva) of each party. The watchers (vigilantes) were appointed directly by the Juntas Directivas of each department. Thus, each voting precinct had fourteen administrators: two Americans, six native Conservatives, six native Liberals.

The work of the Mission consisted of three phases: the division of the country into electoral cantons or precincts, registration of voters, and supervision of the election. We found that existing precincts were so distributed as to make fraudulent voting easy. So we set about re-districting. The new division of cantons was made so that each mesa (booth) might serve not more than 600 voters. Obviously in sparsely settled sections mesas accommodated less than 600. In the cities, a staff of fourteen could handle that many easily, but would break down under the pressure of crushing and perhaps unruly crowds. In the whole Republic there were 432 mesas.

My Department consisted of four Electoral Districts: Jalteva, La Parroquia, San Francisco and Nandaime. Jalteva and La Parroquia each had two electoral cantons, San Francisco four and Nandaime five. In further breakdown, Jalteva and La Parroquia each had four voting booths, San Francisco five and Nandaime eight. Thus, my Department could accommodate 12,600 voters. As it turned out, about 88 per cent of that number cast their ballots on November fourth, a considerably higher percentage than attained in most American general elections.

Registration was next on the agenda, a time-consuming and difficult task calling for extreme patience and vigilance on the part of every member of the Mission. To prepare for registration, schools were established for instruction of Marine enlisted personnel who would go about the country registering (with native board members) and who would supervise voting booths on election day. The schools were set up in the capitals of each Department and were under the direction of the Departmental Chairman.

A crash course in Spanish was taught by native teachers and U.S. Naval ensigns. The course was given in the period July 15-September 15, brief by any standard, but not unreasonable given the fact that almost every Marine in the classrooms had seen previous service in Spanish-speaking countries.

On Sunday, September 23, registration commenced and subsequently took place on the two following Sundays and the two intervening Wednesdays, five days in all. Sundays were selected to enable workers in outlying settlements to gather at registration places, Wednesdays to permit the registration of East Coast longshoremen who were generally occupied in loading steamers on the weekends.

During registration, order was maintained at the booths by the Guardia Nacional, whose members, under electoral regulations, could neither register nor vote. There were no disturbances anywhere.

At a board meeting held on July 18, the question of precincts was discussed, and immediately the political board members found themselves at variance concerning the establishment of voting booths. I had studied maps of the Department and had a general idea as to where the best polling station places might be, but suggested that we all go out and look at these places on the ground. Vivas and Zavala readily agreed.

Two days later we headed for the casarillas (hamlets) of Apayo and Capulín in the Jalteva District. This trip was made on horseback. In about an hour we came to a small hacienda owned by Señor Francisco Graniso, a grower who had been educated at Fordham University in New York. We rested for awhile at Graniso's place and then set off for Lake Apayo with Graniso as our guide. The lake sits in an extinct volcano crater, some 400 feet below the jungled plain on its rim. The lake is perhaps 3½ miles in diameter. We went on down to the lake's edge, passing several trees filled with capa blanca monkeys who chattered nervously at the intrusion.

On leaving Graniso's hacienda we proceeded to hacienda Buena Vista owned by Salvador Jarquín, stayed awhile and went on to lunch at a ranch owned by Pilar Sequeira. Here I ate one of the sweetest pineapples I had ever tasted. These pineapples are different from the Hawaiian variety, being more spherical in shape and having white fruit instead of yellow. To my taste, the Nicaraguan pineapple is the better of the two. After lunch we headed for Capulín and had more pineapple. Notwithstanding the tasty treat, we all decided Capulín, already established as a precinct, should be changed, and so struck it from our lists. I noted that in this area people all lived along the roads, because of the impenetrable nature of the jungle. This precluded any sort of centralized location for a polling place. Now, these roads were dotted with people going to Granada to market, people riding in lumbering oxcarts or on skinny little dispirited horses or burros. Only a few burros — there aren't many in Nicaragua.

On July 24, we made another cantonal inspection trip to El Sitio and Santa Clara in the Electoral District of San Francisco. Ensign Stone accompanied us. The first part of this journey was a short train ride to San Blas on the Granada-Managua railroad. At San Blas we picked up horses, provided by Señor Evaristo Carazo, Alcalde of Granada. We rode to San Rafael and stopped at a sugar refinery owned by Señor Adolfo Benard, the Conservative candidate for president. This was "Carazo Country." In the afternoon we passed four of his cattle ranches: Santa Clarita, Santa Ana, San José and Jesús María. Actually, we rode all day on land owned by Nicaragua's two wealthiest men — Benard, the sugar king; and Carazo, the cattle king.

Our guide was Enrique Chamorro, son-in-law of Carazo. The interesting thing about Chamorro was that he had always been a Conservative, married into one of the wealthiest families in the land, but had recently switched party affiliation and become a Liberal. He said that there are only three good schools in the country — one for law, one for medicine and one for dentistry. He added that the country was primarily agricultural but that no training could be had in that field, and that the government was too reactionary to provide for education in this and other fields. He also said that the government did nothing about "guaro," the "curse of Nicaragua." Guaro is a coarse drink made of sugarcane, and the national tipple of Nicaraguans. Its widespread consumption on election days has habitually reduced voting to a noisy, pistol-toting shambles. "The government gives it out free," said Chamorro. "It's time for a change."

On July 27 and 28 we visited casarillas at Panoloya, La Tapia, La Virgen, Malacataya and Santa Lastenia. To do this we had to take a launch on Lake Nicaragua and then make the remainder of the trip on muleback. The lake was choppy with white caps, and all got seasick except Stone and me. Having been in typhoons on the China and Arafura Seas and in the Carribean this bobbing little trip was like sailing on a millpond.

At La Virgen and Santa Lastenia were cattle ranches of Emiliano Chamorro (cousin of Enrique). At the latter place we were well entertained. The scenery was totally different, but in a very real sense the place reminded me of my boyhood in Arizona — the vaqueros shouting, steers bellowing, the roping, and dust clouds flying. Here we ate some quesillo, much like the quesadillo of the old ranches in Arizona and New Mexico. My reverie of Arizona days was broken by the squawking of a large flock of geese and yellow parrots flying overhead.

We went next to Zapatera Island, a piece of land about eight miles long and four miles wide. We used the same gasoline launch as on the Panolaya excursion, but this time the lake was placid. Between Granada and Zapatera is a group of several hundred small islets, Las Isletas. We threaded our way through these beautiful islets, ranging in size from an acre or two to ten or more acres.

Passing close to one we were startled by the raucous challenge of several large male black monkeys, called "congas" by Nicaraguans. In one tree were thirty or more, old males, young adults, mothers, babies. As we moved close to shore the grimacing simians howled with rage.

On Zapatera Island I met Señor Fernando Mora, a rancher who had found a number of large pre-Columbian stone idols, most of which he had given to the Colegio Centro America run by the Jesuits in Granada. He says they are scattered all over the island, overgrown with creepers and vines, and peering out from dappled bowers of shade.

He says that there are jaguars on the island, large and fierce, and that they swim over from the mainland to raid his cattle pens. Three months ago one got into the corrals one night and killed fourteen calves. He shoots some and poisons the others, and is constantly at war with the "tigers."

On my way back to Granada from a recent trip I found another group of islands, a veritable fairyland, covered with large, beautiful trees and resplendent with brilliant flowers.

Monkeys chattered in the branches overhead, and parrots spread wings of crimson and blue. The aquatic birds were too numerous to count. On one of these islands was a castillo, built by the Spaniards against the encroachments of pirates in the seventeenth century. The old fortress was covered by jungle, and good-sized trees sprouted from places in its walls. . . .

We made one more inspection trip on August 3 and 4, this time going to Nandaime, Diriomo, and Diriá in the Nandaime District. Nandaime was settled by the Spaniards very early because of the cacao trees of excellent quality. To cultivate these they brought in Negro slaves from West Africa, and this accounts for the presence of many Zambos living in the area.

At Amalia we could hear the hoarse voices of Congo monkeys at sunrise and sunset, barking and growling like dogs. From the resonance of the voice one would suppose it issued from a body the size of a Great Dane. These are only ordinary-sized monkeys though.

While at Amalia we visited the famous Valle Menier Cacao plantation established by Emil Justín Menier, the chocolate king of Paris. Monsieur Marragan, the overseer, showed us about the place. In the warehouses were thousands of cacao pods waiting to be shelled. The seeds extracted from the pods are dried, toasted, powdered, then pressed together in pure chocolate cakes. These cakes, refined in the Paris factory, become the world famous Chocolate Menier.

Diriomo and Diriá are two small towns about 500 yards apart. Separate and distinct, they are hotbeds of political rivalry. So bitter is the feeling between residents that shootings are frequent, sometimes resulting in murder. Guaro and cucusa, the two low-grade alcoholic beverages, frequently turn these places into veritable hells. As the inhabitants are "civilized" Indians it is not difficult to imagine what a heated political meeting can turn into. Here I saw a humorous sign advertising guaro. "Alto! un quemon y al camino!" ("Halt! a hot one and on your way!") We passed it up.

Diriomo and Diriá are Ruritania — tucked away in the heart of the country — but they played an important part for the liberation forces during the Walker Filibuster of 1855. Here the allied forces of Central America gathered to concentrate their attack on Granada to drive Walker out. Now, except for an occasional loud phonograph playing in some shack, and the presence of an almost wholly hidden line of telephone poles, one has no feeling of 20th Century life. Here are some of the malodorous stills cooking sugarcane juice for guaro. We could hear these archaic grinders squeaking long before we reached them and, coming upon them, could smell the peculiar sour odor of stale cane juice.

At the conclusion of our field trips we agreed upon the establishment of voting precincts and I forwarded our recommendations to the National Board. General McCoy approved in toto.

Once the voting precincts had been verified, Corney faced the awesome task of ensuring a fair election. A broad electorate and a history of corruption compounded the problem. Corney described his challenge stating:

In Nicaragua, the right to vote is awarded to all male citizens of twenty-one years of age or over, and to males of at least 18 who are married and literate. There is no property qualification. The right to vote is barred to the insane, to minors, to any known to lead habitually violent or criminal lives, to those under indictment for crime, to one who abandons wife and children, to non-citizens, to repeat voters, and to those endeavoring to vote where they have no legal residence. Obviously, women's suffrage has not yet reached Nicaragua, and the ladies can only watch from the sidelines.

Of the classifications listed above, minors, repeaters, men under criminal indictment, and those attempting to register away from their own cantonments give the most trouble. Each case, whether valid or not, was looked upon as a sacred trust, and authorities were compelled to research civil registers, parochial records, and criminal files to determine voter eligibility.

Such searches used valuable time and often caused vitriolic exchanges between the directing agencies of the two political parties. Each acrimonious confrontation had to be settled by Departmental Boards and, in some cases, appeals went to Managua for judgement by General McCoy.

Until the 1928 election the Conservative party had the

advantage, controlling troops, police, local officials and the treasury. Also, it was in a position to censor mail, control the press, use the government monopoly on the issuance of liquor licenses to its ends, and juggle ballots during and after elections.

During registration there were complaints in some of these areas — censorship, unfair treatment in the press, and so on. Each was investigated. Significantly, there were only a handful of complaints in the entire country concerning fraud during the election. These were investigated also. Most proved false; the several which were of substance caused the total vote count to be changed, but in minute numbers making no effect or perceptible change in the final tabulation.

As might be expected, voting tricks certainly played a part in this election. Names were taken from tombstones in local cemeteries and offered for registration. This fell through when the men could not be produced. Men were imported from the neighboring republics, but could not satisfy officials as to local residence. Clergymen, Conservatives with a vengeance, preached vituperatively from pulpits to their taciturn Indian communicants. In the light of the convincing Liberal victory, one wonders how effective church opposition to change really was.

It was of course impossible to eliminate all forms of improper efforts to exert undue pressure upon voters, but strenuous measures were taken to prevent abuse of authority by native civil officials in all categories. Close supervision over the communications system and the liquor trade prevented their improper use. Perhaps most significant of all was the use of the Guardia Nacional in the establishment and maintenance of order — in place of federal Nicaraguan troops and civil police. Thanks to these well-led troops and the complete absence of liquor on election day, a large, spirited and eminently fair election was held. Said one Nicaraguan, "You cannot imagine the difference. Election days used to be full of shooting, with drunks careening through the streets — veritable Donnybrook Fairs!"

At the end of the five-day registration period 150,618 men had been registered to vote, more than had ever been registered for a general election, and 25 per cent more than in 1924. The local press (Conservative) claimed immediately the high number of registrants could not have been effected without "repeaters." Thorough investigation of the charge proved it false. Actually, the large registration was due to measures taken to prevent intimidation and the general belief of people in both parties that the elections would be fair. In contra-distinction to previous elections, this one was really in doubt, right up until November 4th. In previous elections the outcome had been determined far in advance of election day, and voting was simply an exercise.

Sunday, November 4th, was a beautiful day. A heavy vote was forecast and the estimate was correct. Voting went on at the rate of from one to three persons per minute, so that by 4:00 P.M. every eligible voter had voted and then the polls were closed. Of the 150 thousand plus who had registered 132,939 voted, for a whopping 88 percent. Of the total number of votes cast, 76,200 were Liberal and 56,739 Conservative. Thus the Liberal party and its standard bearer, General José María Moncada, went into office with a plurality of 19,461 votes.

Voters' hands were marked with Mercurochrome to prevent plural voting, Some ludicrous incidents developed from the use of the bright red liquid. In León, a man parked his wife and boy across the street from the booth and went in to vote. He emerged with Mercurochrome dripping from his hand. "Oh my God," wailed the distraught wife, "what have they done to you?"

Numerous newspaper editorials indicated that both sides considered the American-supervised elections fair. The Conservative *La Prensa* of Managua noted:

> We must frankly confess victory of our political adversaries. With unrestricted freedom Nicaraguan citizens went to the polls under the eye of American supervision. Conservatives and Liberals alike made use of their right to vote. Liberals obtained victory in this democratic struggle . . . we will not allege fraud. American honesty in the supervision of our election must constitute a testimonial of legitimate pride.

The Liberal organ of Managua, *El Comercio*, commented:

Victory of democracy which shone in Nicaragua Sunday marks an epoch not only in Latin America but even in the land of Washington. . . . This election, free from tears and sorrow, the like of which has never been seen in our country before, places us in the company of advanced nations. Blessed be the United States!

Los Hechos, a religious publication in León, concluded that:

American supervision and the absence of intoxicants contributed to eliminate the disorders so much lamented at previous elections. Americans exercised the most effective control. May the lesson be well learned, so that in the future we may conduct ourselves in the same manner.

The Conservative *El Correo* of Granada asserted:

We have lost, and lost in a fair fight. The American supervision, under General Frank R. McCoy, has been both fair and honorable.

Individual citizens also voiced their praises. Crisante Briceño observed that:

In the 54 years that I have struggled against the Conservative party, I have never, until now, witnessed a free election. I congratulate General McCoy and President Coolidge.

Joaquin Gomez of Granada wrote:

The elections completed, it is to General McCoy and his assistants that I send sincere congratulations for the brilliant success attained. They have acted with judgement, impartiality, and justice. . . . Would that our fatherland might continue to enjoy the benefit of their invaluable assistance in the fields of civic enterprise.

American supervision, however, was not universally applauded. Corney recognized that:

I agree, but there will always be a vocal and self-righteous minority whose opinionated members will look no further than the tips of their noses. It is well and good to advocate the exercise of political freedom by those wishing to practice it. It is something else to turn a deaf ear to peoples who seek removal of tyranny, exploitation and fear. Our great country need never forego its responsibilities in this regard, but there will always be those willing to sell out the rights of the many to a noisy clamoring of the militant few. After all, Nicaraguan politics had been oligarchical for over 300 years. One wonders how long our homegrown sophists are willing to let others suffer for their pet beliefs.

The individual who has become the darling of the radicals at home and abroad is Augusto Sandino. In fairness I must state the he has some followers here too, but it is generally conceded that he is a renegade and a bandit, even by his own people. He had agreed to join with Moncada and espouse the Liberal cause, but soon defected and went off into the hinterland with a band of Honduran mercenaries. His influence here is nothing as spectacular as some U.S. newspapers would lead readers to believe.

These papers, and authors like Nogales — *The Looting of Nicaragua* — write only what is sensational and inflammatory, thus putting forward a compilation of mis-statements and half-truths. I am not talking about presenting the opposite point of view — no one minds that. I am talking about presenting a case based upon emotion, hearsay and gut-feeling only.

The lauding of Sandino, a cutthroat, is lamentable. A photo in Nogales' book shows a street in Chinandega after its destruction by troops. The caption attributes the destruction to American Marines. Marines took no part in the action. It was a purely Nicaraguan affair. Hence do some unprincipled people lie and cheat to press a point of view.

The Nicaraguan press also expressed its opinion of Corney. A reporter from the most strongly conservative newspaper in Granada, *El Correo*, interviewed the election supervisor and gave his appraisal stating:

I confess that I dislike Yankees, and feel that they are the cause of our misfortunes. I felt, therefore, that I would be unwelcome to call on the president of the Electoral Commission here in Granada. On the contrary, I found Col. Smith to be well informed, affable and courteous. He would not engage in polemics with me, but answered questions on our country's future, and on economics, history and Nicaragua's role in Latin American affairs. I asked him if the election would remedy our misfortunes. He said, "Yes, if your people will dedicate themselves to hard work, and keep at it." In sum, although I still dislike Yankees, I was pleased with this man. He is a good Catholic, honorable and simpático. It is a pity he is not in our army and his name Colonel Perez, Garcia or Sandino.

Wrote Corney in his diary: "About Perez or García — I don't know; Sandino I can live without."

With the elections completed, departmental personnel made ready to go home. At the new President's request, U.S. Marines were asked to stay on to help implement new programs and to train Guardia Nacional troops for security against revolutionaries.

The letters of commendation for Corney's role had come as early as August 1928. In one of these General McCoy wrote:

Your services as President of the Departmental Board of one of the two most important departments in the Republic have been of special value. I wish specifically to commend you for the ability you have shown in grasping the essential requirements of the situation, for your energy in making a thorough reconnaissance of your province, and your intimate knowledge of the customs and the language of the people — also for your courteous and impartial attitude which has been made the subject of favorable comment by the President of the Republic and by the political leaders of both parties.

In December McCoy sent another commendatory letter:

The success which attended your efforts has been evident in many ways. There was a complete absence of disorder in your department . . . your harmonious relations with the political members of your board and with the local commanders of both Marines and Guardia, and your cordial relations with civilians have been made the subject of commendatory remarks from many sources.

President Coolidge wired General McCoy: "I feel you must be gratified by the results of your work and I wish to take this occasion to express to the members of your staff the sincere gratitude not only of myself but of the government and people of the United States for a difficult task well done."

On November 22, 1928, Corney and his associate, Colonel O. E. Hunt, sailed for San Pedro, California, on the S.S. *Guatemala.* Both were given free entry passes back into the U.S. by General McCoy, acting on orders for the U.S. Department of State.

Corney's Nicaraguan venture was not fully completed. In January, President Moncada offered him the position of Chairman of the Board of Claims in the Nicaraguan Government. Corney contacted the Adjutant General in Washington asking how acceptance of the position would affect his retired army pay. There followed a flurry of telegrams and letters from the U.S. State Department, Nicaraguan Government, General McCoy, Enrique Chamorro, and others concerning the legal implications of such employment. McCoy's last wire was significant: "Careful and simpatico attention being given here by State Department but JAG decision adverse."

Indeed it was, quoting as its final authority Article 1, Section 9, Paragraph 3 of the Constitution of the United States, the Judge Advocate General wrote:

> No title of nobility shall be granted by the United States, and no person holding any office of profit or trust under them, shall, without the consent of Congress, accept any present, office or title, of any kind whatever, from any King, Prince, or foreign state.

Still, a Congressional Act of May 19, 1926, (44 Stat 565) permitted the hiring of retired U.S. Army, Navy and Marine Corps personnel by foreign governments provided such employment was in the public interest (of the U.S.).

Another flurry of telegrams and then the finale from the Judge Advocate General of the Army on March 26, 1929:

> The matter has been carefully considered, and this office is constrained to adhere to the opinion expressed in the second endorsement of letter of 5 March, 1929, that the Consent of Congress should be regarded as a condition precedent to the acceptance by Colonel Smith of the position of Chairman of the Board of Claims, Republic of Nicaragua.

"Well," said Corney, "that settles it. I'm damned if I'll get the whole United States Congress into the act." There were no regrets.

The Nicaraguan experience had been profitable in many ways. Sadly, it was Corney Smith's last active association with the military. In many ways this service, while brief, was a fitting climax to his military career, encompassing the elements of command, diplomacy and foreign scene.

CHAPTER TWENTY

The Great Army-Apache Controversy

DURING THE THIRTIES a number of writers addressed themselves to stories concerning the role of the Army in the Apache campaigns. Some, generally published in small state historical journals and erudite little magazines dealing with American history, were meticulously researched and well written. Newspapers, on the other hand, published accounts of these half-forgotten incidents with little regard for historical accuracy. Corney found a sloppy or cavalier article bad enough; but when it misrepresented familiar people and places, he was unable to contain himself.

Thus began a series of letters to editors of newspapers and magazines citing errors in their publications. Although he built up a certain following of history buffs and service personnel, Corney's reception by authors and editors was not enthusiastic. Angry editors often ignored or lacerated his material. Yet undaunted, like Don Quixote, he kept charging at the windmills of indifference and inaccuracy. In a letter to the editor of the *Los Angeles Times* Corney wrote in 1931:

It is with some hesitancy that I enter on the task of controverting the writings of some of the "romancers" writing for the *Times* who pervert Southwestern history. I hesitate only because these people are trained writers and have a regular outlet for their pearls of misinformation. If my style is lacking, I have the advantage of knowing personally many of the people your people write about. Moreover, I have in my possession hundreds of documents pertaining to the very cases in issue. This gives me the priceless advantage of authenticity, and where history is concerned, that is a more valuable coin than conjecture.

Why your writers persist in making erroneous statements can be explained only in that they follow faulty leads, or because embroidery makes a better story, and they simply don't give a damn for the truth. In that many of the stories are vicious and caustic where the army is concerned, I suspect the latter. In any case, the end is the same, and the reading public is misled.

Your Mr. Harry Carr is a case in point. In his column, "The Lancer," he will tackle anything, admirable in a way – except for the fact that his information concerning the army is almost always wrong. Still, he is not alone in this vendetta; Mr. Shippey is as culpable, as are others who appear in your pages from time to time. Why? I do not know if you will want to give me space in the *Times*, but whenever these people misrepresent the army with error or innuendo, I shall refute it.

With this letter introducing his interest in the matter, Corney shortly thereafter composed another and mailed it to the editor of the *Los Angeles Times*:

For some time past the *Times* has been conducting a propaganda campaign in laudation of the Apache Indians and condemnation of the U.S. Army. This work comes from the pen of Mr. Harry Carr, who apparently is stimulated by information given to him by Mr. John P. Clum, who at one time was connected with the Indian Service in Arizona. In today's issue of the *Times* comes a garbled story by Mr. Lee Shippey. With all respect to the literary capabilities of your writers, I must disagree with their remarks concerning the Apache campaigns of the 1870's and eighties. . . .

endered 49 years ago this September, these must have been
e scouts!

so the months passed. A long and somewhat acidulous
ge developed over Carr's writings on the American military
nce in the Philippines. Corney, however, was not alone in
d with Harry Carr. On June 4, 1934, the editor of the
er-News in Abilene, Texas, wrote:

I never met or heard of your Mr. Harry Carr, but I have
tion that he must be at least 90 years old. Nobody but a
genarian could possibly accumulate as much misinforma-
as he displayed in his column of May 22 [1934], clippings
hich have been sent to this office by more than one
nant Texan now residing in California. Take for instance,
eference to Larry Chittenden who, according to Carr,
buried in the churchyard at Anson. William Laurence
enden, basking in the summer sunshine of his summer
in Christmas Cove, Maine, will be interested to learn of
mise. . . .

piece scored Carr on half a dozen or more additional
hen ended with the words, "In fairness to West Texas I
u can see your way clear to publish this." The Times did.
y also entered into a controversy with Lee Shippey of the
hippey wrote a column entitled "The Lee Side o' L.A."
equently printed stories on the Southwest. In one of these
ed that the Apache Indians had a company of militia in
aigns of the 1880s. Corney answered: "There was never
company of Apache Scouts, regardless of what Mr.
s."

y, operating on the assumption that "a soft answer turn-
wrath," replied: "I'm convinced that you're a charming
teous gentleman, and that both you and Mr. Clum are so
g that I could easily be convinced by either t'other way."
was not to be put off. "As I have controverted most of
's statements in his printed interview with you, as my
returned, and as you have again written in defense of his
tements, I can scarcely expect anything I write to appear
es. But you know, as I do, that the truth prevails. . . ."

The Great Army-Apache Controversy

There followed a ten-page description on the Apache problem
from Theran's expedition into Chihuahua in 1695 through Geronimo's surrender to Lieutenant Gatewood. Though this treatise, too
long for the usual "Letters to the Editor," was not published, it
stimulated some discussion. Carr was especially stung by it. In a
letter to Clum on October 14, 1931, he wrote: ". . . here is a letter
you might want to answer yourself. We don't want to use it in the
Times. When you get through with it please put it in the enclosed
envelope and send it back to the writer."

Learning that lengthy dissertations were useless, Corney
resorted to specific letters. On May 3, 1932, Carr wrote: "John
Clum was the first agent of the San Carlos Apaches, organized the
first company of Apache Scouts to serve in the United States
Army, and founded the Tombstone Epitaph and the Tucson
Citizen."

Corney answered four days later in a letter to the editor:

Clum did not organize the first company of Apache
Scouts to serve in the United States Army. Clum came as Agent
to San Carlos on February 26, 1874, and remained until
June 22, 1877. They were used in the 1872-73 campaign in the
Tonto Basin area of Arizona and afterwards by General Crook,
who officially acknowledged the excellent work done by
Alchesay, Sergeant Jim, Machol, and others.

Mr. Clum did not found the Tucson Citizen. It was
established by John Wasson on October 15, 1870, who put it
under the management of P.W. Dooner and the editorship of
W.W. Hayward. My grandfather, William Sanders Oury, along
with Sylvester Mowry, bought the Press from Colonel Edward
Cross in Tubac on July 30, 1859, on the day of the famous
Mowry-Cross duel. The paper was then called the Tubac
Arizonian.

From the spring of 1859 to the fall of 1860 it was
edited by J. Haywood Wells, and after he retired a young
Californian named Gelwick took charge. The last issue was
published in May 1861 wherein editor Thomas J. Turner
announced suspension of the paper on account of the approach
of the Civil War. The old printing press lay in my grandfather's
backyard, under cover [on Calle Real between Jackson and

Ochoa], until 1866, when Sidney de Long started the paper going again, first under the editorship of a man named Pierce, then by Shearer, under the name *Weekly Arizonian*. It ran for only about one year, and was not renewed until Wasson took it over in October 1870, chiefly to advocate the cause of Peter Rainesford Brady, Democratic candidate for Congress against Richard C. McCormick.

Clum bought the paper in 1877 and moved it to Florence probably for the purpose of securing official patronage through the land office there. The paper was returned to Tucson in 1879 and reverted to Wasson. He renamed it the *Daily Citizen* and published it until 1880 when he left for Tombstone. By any standard, John Clum was a Johnny-come-lately in connection with the *Tucson Citizen*.

On May 5, 1932, Carr wrote in "The Lancer":

Major Charles T. Cornell was acting Chief of Scouts in 1880 when Clum was Apache Agent in the San Carlos Reservation. . . . Anton Mazzanovitch was the hero of Skeleton Canyon massacre. . . . George K. French was an early army officer friend of Clum's. . . . Clum distinguished himself as a defender of his Indian friends against the depredations of marauding soldiers, and later became a member of the posse which captured Geronimo.

Corney answered in exasperation:

I scarcely know where to begin. It's almost as though Carr is writing this way to bait me. If so, he's doing a creditable job. Cornell was not agent at San Carlos in 1880, "acting" or otherwise. There were two agents then: Adna R. Chaffee, July 19, 1879 to May 31, 1880, and Joseph C. Tiffany, June 1, 1880 to August 31, 1882.

Mazzanovitch, a good friend of mine, was not the "hero" of Skeleton Canyon Massacre — there was no such massacre. George K. French was not only not "an early Arizona Army Officer," he was never a regular army officer at any time.

Soldiers were not marauders; they were fighters against as bloodthirsty a set of savages who ever walked the earth. The annals of Southwestern history are filled with frightful tales of scalping, burning, torturing and killing of white settlers and Mexicans by Apaches.

Clum had absolutely not
Geronimo. Lieutenant Charles B.
induced Geronimo to surrender
Canyon, Sept. 3, 1886. I know Gat
wood, Jr., intimately and have st
him pertaining to that event. Gatev
Street in San Diego, sends me data

On April 10, 1933, Carr penned
regarded by most military experts a
who ever lived, at any period."

Corney responded the same day:

What Mr. Carr says abou
Apaches is purely a gratuitous g
They were brave, stealthy and c
superlative fashion. Still, they we
as, Sioux, Cheyenne or Nez Perc
long-distance marksmen, making
cover at very close range.

In writing about Pancho Villa,
with the 12th U.S. Infantry. Sai
fought the 12th Infantry but di
Cavalry in March, 1916, after the
I would suggest that Mr. Carr rea
Tompkins. It was put out by
Company in Harrisburg and is avail

On August 14, 1935, Carr
commander of the last of the Ap
whom he commands are the last
catch Geronimo. By a treaty ma
job and live in magnificent lei
Mexican border."

Corney answered:

No such treaty was e
Riley is not the last "comm
Provost-Marshal at the post.
Carr speaks of range in age fro

Corney had his partisans as Carr, Shippey, and Clum had theirs. Writing from his position of Curator of History at the Los Angeles Museum in Exposition Park, Arthur Woodward noted in a February 24, 1932, letter to Corney:

It is with great interest that I read your letter in the last copy of the *Arizona Historical Review*. I am glad someone has had the courage to open fire with battle sights on some of the attackers of our military forces in their connection with Indian activities. I have always felt that had our military been given free play, and had the promises of the Army men in the field to conquer Indian tribes been backed up by the politicians, our Indian problems would have been averted. I am convinced that if the records were carefully scrutinized and impartially analysed, they would show that the greater portion of our troubles has been caused by incompetent, civilian political appointees.

I am not a sentimentalist where the Indian is concerned. My work, as an ethnologist, is with him living and dead. I see him as one member of the human race, and in him I see reflected all of the traits of the human race. Consequently, I cannot agree with Mr. Clum when he states that Apaches would not commit murder or rape of a white woman, nor with Mr. Carr when he bursts forth with effusion as to the superiority of the Indian over the white man.

I agree with you that Carr treats his history lightly. I have often chuckled over his flowery statements concerning the Navajo, Apache, and Hopi. He is, however, a good newspaperman. So is Mr. Shippey; as ethnologists or historians — they are both good newspapermen.

In a letter to Corney, the author, Joe Chisholm, wrote:

I have just received and read with deep interest your punch in the nose for yours truly. I have known John P. Clum for about fifty years, since 1881, to be exact. I do not agree with him in the Army-Apache controversy, but he is a likeable soul, over 80, and I would hesitate to say anything which could hurt him.

Carr and Shippey, like I, must accept such information as we find it. I know that Harry makes mistakes, but he is a busy fellow and cannot run everything down. Clum, of course, became a partisan early through some conflicts he had with the military. That's the only way I can judge his attitude of making near-angels out of vicious, torturing Apaches. I have no patience with "armchair historians." I lived through the hell of it in Bisbee, when the men patrolled the streets with guns ready, and the women and children sat cowering in our darkened houses, while the hostiles flashed their signals from peak to peak above us.

This old hogwash about the superiority of the Apache over the U.S. cavalryman was started, I think, by the late Charles F. Lummis. It's a lot of slop. There never was an Apache who could shoot as well as a cavalryman. In fact, I never saw one who was worth a whoop in hell at anything over 200 yards. I'll keep your letter, Colonel, and if I ever have the good luck to sit down with you for a good powwow, I'll explain some of the things you think are wrong.

Sadly, Corney and Chisholm never met, although they continued to correspond. Interestingly, John Clum did call on Corney in Riverside in the winter of 1931. He came unannounced but was welcomed, and the two talked in Corney's den. They were courteous and pleasant, agreeing on some points but disagreeing on the role of the Army in the Apache Campaigns. It was the only time they ever met.

Early in 1933, Owen P. White wrote a story entitled "Talking Boy" which was published in the February 18 issue of *Collier's Weekly*. Corney read it and was horrified. He wrote his historical objections to the editor of the *Brewery Gulch Gazette* who published them in the May 26 issue under the headline: "Retired Army man takes hide off Owen P. White, author of 'Talking Boy'." The article was actually a copy of a lengthy letter Corney had addressed to the editors of *Collier's* who sat on it. In part, the missive stated:

If Owen P. White's story in your February 18 issue is meant for fiction, fine, but if he is attempting to write a true story of Arizona in the seventies and eighties, he misses the mark. Some of White's statements are not only lacking in authenticity — they are ridiculous. He tries to make readers believe Al Sieber hired Tom Horn as a scout and interpreter for the army. Civilian scouts and interpreters never had the right to hire. Hiring was done by army officers in the position of post quartermaster. Scouts had a status compared to civilian wagon-master, teamsters and packers. Regardless of the fact that these men were frequently of superior intelligence and great courage, they never hired (or fired) anyone.

Like so many of today's fiction writers, Mr. White would have it appear that the scouts ran the show, ordering army officers about and making decisions. It was exactly the other way around. Scouts were employees of the army, no more, no less.

The term "Chief of Scouts" as used by White is meaningless. At best, it was but a nominal title, applied from time to time to a senior scout among several. The real Chiefs of Scouts were army officers, men like H. L. Scott (later Chief of Staff of the Army), Adna R. Chaffee, Frank D. Baldwin, Constant Williams, Tony Rucker, Austin Henely, Thomas Cruse, Philo Clark, and last but not least, C. B. Gatewood who prevailed upon Geronimo to surrender to General Miles. These men did more for, and were more respected by, the Indians than Tom Horn or any of his kind.

Mr. White calls tizwin cactus whiskey. Wrong. It's made from corn and is rather a sweetish drink. I've tasted it and it's not bad, comparable to grape juice, whereas Tulpai is more like grape brandy.

Mr. White makes much ado of "Chief" Pedro with whom Horn lived for awhile. Pedro was not a San Carlos Apache (as claimed) and was never of any real importance in the Apache hierarchy — like Natchez, Geronimo, Chato, Ju, Bonito or Sanchez. At best, Pedro was leader of a small band somewhere near Fort Apache.

Also, for Mr. White's information there were eight, not six, branches of the Apache family. They were: Mimbreños, Chiricahuas, Sierra Blancas, Pinaleños, Coyoteros, Tontos, Mogollones and Ojos Calientes.

White says "no sooner had Major Chaffee, the first military agent to arrive in Arizona, gotten himself comfortably seated in his swivel chair than he sent for Tom Horn. . . ." First, Chaffee was not a Major when he was Indian agent, and he was not the first military agent. He was preceded by Lt. Col. George Andrews, 13th Infantry, Lt. Royal E. Whitman, 3rd Cavalry, and Captain W.H. Brown, 14th Infantry.

Second, the inference that Chaffee was a swivel chair soldier and Horn the rugged strategist is odious. Chaffee, who rose from the ranks to become a Lt. General, and among other things commanded the American forces in China during the Boxer Rebellion of 1900, was a man of action with a powerful physique. He was a better frontiersman than Horn could ever hope to be. He was campaigning against the Indians in Texas in 1865, against Lipans and Comanches when Tom Horn was a little boy.

White then regales his readers with a long conversation between Horn, Sieber and Geronimo, the gist of which is that General Willcox should place entire dependence on the two scouts to keep the Indians quiet — since the army was incapable of doing it. Again, Mr. White has the tail wagging the dog. If he will consult Volume Two of *Heitman's Historical Register and Dictionary of the U.S. Army*, he will find that between January 1, 1871, and October 18, 1886, U.S. troops defeated Apaches in Arizona on 126 separate occasions — to say nothing of those victories in New Mexico.

White then says that "Tom Horn was put in command of one force, Sieber of another." Command of what? Scouts were an integral part of army commands; they commanded no one.

White says that Chiricahuas "began to raid towns and ranches in Mexico and proceed to the border where escorts awaited them, under the immunity agreement, and cross the line safely with stolen loot." One wonders where Mr. White studied International Law. How long would Mexico, or any sovereign nation, put up with such shenanigans?

Mr. White charges Captain F.C. Hentig was away at the Cibicu fight, running down renegades. He was not. He was a part of Eugene A. Carr's command and was killed in the fight by renegade scouts. I have in my possession a copy of the diary of General Thomas Cruse, given to me by him, with permission to use it as I see fit. He was a Second Lt., 6th U.S. Cavalry, and a participant in the Cibicu affair. I have known Tommy Cruse for over 50 years and correspond with him regularly. He has told me: "I knew personally and by name, every officer, non-com, enlisted man, packer, Indian scout, horse and mule in that fight, and Tom Horn was not there. He was with the pack train at either Prescott or Verde. From his own description (Horn's) he was the hero of that occasion. General Carr asked his advice and Carter, McCreery, Stanton and the rest of us looked to him to save the day, a colossal lie. I would like to have seen any man living offer any advice to Colonel Carr on that occasion. I hired and fired all packers with the pack train and I know Horn was not a packer in it.

"He did visit the scene of the fight about September 6, when Wotherspoon and Kingsbury were coming to our supposed relief, (we did our own relieving). And he did get first-hand accounts of the fight from a number of soldier-participants. He was, poor fellow, trying to save his own neck to show that a hero of this magnitude ought not to die — he was hung for murder about a month after his book was published."

Excerpts of Cruse's diary have been published in the *Tombstone Epitaph* on June 2, 9, 16, and 23 of 1932. I suggest Mr. White read these excerpts.

White refers to the Cibicu Apaches and a guide named Dead Eye. Cibicu is the name of a creek, about forty miles from Fort Apache; there are no Cibicu Apaches. Perhaps White was thinking of Dick Dead Eye in *Pinafore*. There was a scout named Dead Shot, under the command of Lt. Cruse at Cibicu. He was hanged at Fort Grant on March 3, 1882, for shooting at his own officers during the fight.

White writes: "Captain Hentig was killed and Tom Horn saved the Command." No mean feat for someone who wasn't even there! Also, White's yarn would lead you to believe that Tom Horn had much to do with Geronimo's surrender to Miles. "Tom Horn fixed it," he writes. He had absolutely nothing to do with that. The credit goes entirely to Lieutenant Charles B. Gatewood, 6th U.S. Cavalry. Let Mr. White consult any reputable history of Arizona.

I have before me a letter from Mr. White wherein he attempts somewhat truculently (to another party) to uphold statements made in the *Collier's* article. He says his father was collector of Customs at Arizona in 1881-82, and that the Apaches drove his family out. Well, that being the case, one wonders why he lauds them and lambastes the army.

Corney was not alone in his condemnation of White. On March 4 Lewis Gandy wrote to the editor of *Collier's* from Baldwin, Long Island:

> On February 12, I sent you a letter criticizing the story "Talking Boy." I note that you have passed the buck by sending my letter to the author. As you will see from the enclosed copy of Mr. White's answer, he evidently believes in levitation, since he tosses your present in the air, doubtless with the hope that it will always remain aloft. Permit me once more to deposit the spluttering globule gently in your lap, at the same time calling attention to the fuse, which is now getting very short. . . . May I have the courtesy of a reply?

One week later, Mr. W. J. Ghent wrote to Gandy, and the letter was printed in *Collier's* columns:

> I suppose your criticisms may make some impression on Mr. Chenery, [Editor of *Collier's* magazine], but they will not alter the practice of Owen P. White. He makes good money out of his fantastic distortions of history. I talked with White once when he addressed the Writer's Club in New York City. He had just published *Them Was the Days,* and I had reviewed it amicably but unfavorably in *The Outlook.* Not a single gesture of his portrayal accorded with my recollection, and accordingly I have poked fun at him. When we met he showed no resentment at my criticism . . . and his manner indicated that he was totally unconcerned as to whether or not he had been telling the truth. . . . An attempt to glorify Tom Horn might well turn the stomach of any decent person who has studied that scoundrel's career. . . .

Thoroughly angered with the jibes of Gandy and Ghent, Chenery wrote on March 23, 1933:

> I do not think any public interest will be served in giving space to a consideration of differences between Messrs. Owen P. White and W. J. Ghent concerning Southwest episodes. Both are

honorable gentlemen and if they differ in their historical interpretations they can hire a hall so far as I am concerned. . . .

"Well, that figures," stated Corney in a letter to Ghent. "White can write junk that reaches readers by the thousands, and his detractors 'can hire a hall'! The wrong of it is that authentic pieces go a-begging while error-filled stuff goes to print."

Corney's wife often asked, "Why do you care so much, honey — what difference does it make?" His look was incredulous. "Because it's wrong."

Cornelius C. Smith, Baja California, 1932. (Photo from personal files)

CHAPTER TWENTY — ONE

The Last Five Years

After retiring from the army in 1920, Corney moved his family from place to place searching for that certain spot where he could buy a large old house with several acres and settle down. Although attractive to him in many ways, none of the places, Texas, San Diego, Sacramento, had the appeal he sought.

One day in 1929, several months after returning from Nicaragua, he drove to Riverside, a town with about 20,000 inhabitants some sixty miles east of Los Angeles. Providentially, while lunching in the Mission Inn, he met Jack Stewart. A retired Army officer, Stewart had served under Corney in 1918 on the Mexican border. He was now a realtor and, on hearing of Corney's desire for a country place, said, "Colonel, I have something you may be interested in."

The two men drove three miles to an old California frame house situated behind a small grove of thirty orange trees. To the rear were twelve acres of large, old walnut trees. Built around 1886 with shiplap porch railings, the large house had 5,000 square feet of space, five bedrooms upstairs and one down. The living room was about forty feet long and half as wide. Later, when

Kathleen saw it, she cried, "My Lord! It looks like a skating rink!" For once, though, everyone would have all the room he needed, not only for a separate bedroom, but for work projects and storage. Under the walnut trees were long rows of blackberries, boysenberries and raspberries. The property also contained apple, peach, plum and fig trees. Behind the house was a huge, old barn and a long chicken shed with built-in nests and a concrete deck.

The Smith family drove out to take a look at Corney's "find." With their general approval, he bought the place on the spot. Kathleen had reservations. "It's a little bit far from town," was her plaintive disclaimer. Later she came to love it dearly.

One of the first things Corney did was to fix up his den, a large high-ceilinged room adjoining the "skating rink." In it he hung his Moro knives, spears and inlaid shields, his Apache baskets, several saddles, a brace of rifles and pistols, battle flags, photos of army greats, and a floor-to-ceiling bank of books on one entire wall. In time this room became a mecca for retired army personnel in the area as well as a local showplace. In one corner of the room was Corney's desk where he worked quietly for hours on end, under a green eyeshade which made him look like a croupier at a gaming table. Nonetheless, he penned many articles that were published in western and historical journals, and acid letters to newspaper columnists.

In 1932 Corney Jr. attended prep school in Washington, D.C. Bert Randles, an Annapolis graduate, owned and ran the school. It was staffed with six or eight instructors, one of whom, "Beany" Millard, also conducted a West Point cram school across the street. The work was hard and the hours long. Students studied six days a week, and had study table every night from 7:00 until 10:00 with lights out at 10:30. The daily "homework" assignments forced most of the young men to repair to the "head" (bathroom) to study from 10:30 until around midnight. Corney sent revealing letters to his son in this period:

> My dear boy: You are going at a grueling pace but soon the work will be easy. You are just now really studying and getting into study habits. This is necessary if you are to survive in a tough, competitive society — and think of the reward when you succeed, as you surely will. Keep a stiff upper

lip and play to win. We have faith in you. . . .

My dear boy: Don't worry about my expenditures on your behalf. You are worth it, and when you make good, it will have been money well spent. Just do your best; that's all that Mother and I ask. . . .

My dear boy: Avery says he thinks he can sell your football shoes for you. I told him I'd give him fifty cents if he could. . . . Don't get mad at Mr. Millard for "reading you off." He's only doing his job and his best to make you and the others shape up. One day you will see that. . . .

My dear boy: Here is a letter from Senator Carl Hayden. He has given out his appointments to Arizona boys. He seemed impressed when you called on him in the Senate office building. He says "your son is a fine looking young man." Keep trying. Keep making the rounds, in the Senate, in the House. We're working for you here. . . .

As it turned out, Corney Jr. was unable to get an appointment to West Point but did get an athletic scholarship to the University of Southern California. He received a Marine Corps commission in 1937, after completing its program at the University.

Corney Sr. was a little over six feet in height and erect as an arrow. His piercing eyes were black as coals. His nose was straight and the nostrils flared like those of a horse when he became angry. His hair was blue-black in youth and he always wore it longer in the back than most army men, perhaps a sentimental hangover from the days when frontiersmen wore long hair. One could liken him to Captain Robert May of the Second Dragoons leading his wild charge at Resaca de la Palma with his locks flowing behind. A potential sentimental factor existed here, too, since Corney's grandfather, William Sanders Oury, had been with May at Resaca de la Palma.

In his youth Corney was lean, muscular and trim — the perfect cavalry man. In 1921 General Frank McCoy wrote to Major E.L.N. Glass, 10th Cavalry historian:

I remember the day of my arrival in Cuba. We were ordered to mount up and call upon the colonels and officers of the other cavalry regiments in camp, and I got my first impression of the dash and spirit of the regiment as we went over at a full gallop to call on the Second Cavalry, a fine bold lot, and what is more, they looked the part. There wasn't a fat dud in the outfit. In this lean lot were Col. Guy V. Henry, Pershing, Paxton, Smith, Wint, and Ayres. . . .

Once, in Fort Riley, Kansas, in the summer of 1896 Corney and some of his brother officers attended a circus. They laughed at some of the easy tricks performed by the highly touted riders and one of them stopped before the derisive group and said: "Who among you people can do any better?"

"I think I can," said Corney, whereupon he rode a borrowed horse up and down the tanbark doing the most difficult tricks imaginable. He got a standing ovation from the delighted crowd. In his later years, Corney took on some weight, but he always rode a horse like a centaur, dashing, impressive and in complete control of the animal.

He had his own unique code of ethics and did many memorable things over the years. Once, in San Diego, a wasp became entangled in a spiderweb near the family's living room window. "I'm going to save him!" cried Corney Jr. making a dash for the front door. Corney stopped him and said quietly, "No, leave them alone – that's nature's way. The spider must eat as well as the wasp. When you interfere with nature, you do more harm than good."

Another time he asked Corney Jr. why a certain thing was not done and the latter answered, "Why, I thought Graham was supposed to do that!" Corney replied: "Never take anything for granted – *anything*, always check." That practice saved both boys much misery over the years.

On another occasion Graham was brisk with a door-to-door salesman selling novelties. When he had gone Corney acknowledged, "Graham, it's just as easy to be courteous as it is to be rude. That man is only trying to make a living, and what he's doing isn't easy. You remember that."

In 1931 Graham had taken a job and was suffering the pangs of doubt concerning another he had turned down. Corney reasoned, "It's always well to look before you leap, but once you have made a decision – stick with it. Worrying is not only useless; it's harmful – and you can't turn back the clock."

Once Alice's high school Spanish teacher came to call. A

pacifist, he looked disdainfully at Corney's collection of military mementoes and disapprovingly remarked, "This is wrong, Colonel, all wrong. You ought not to bring up children in a house filled with weapons."

"Mr. List, you have your beliefs and I have mine," answered Corney. "You may rest assured I won't interfere with the conduct of your classes."

Alice was mortified. When the teacher was gone she said, "Oh, papa!"

"What would you have me do, honey, agree with him?" Corney asked. Meekly, she agreed, "No."

Once Riverside Junior College had a three-way track meet with San Bernardino and Chaffey. Corney Jr. was entered in the pole vault, broad jump and javelin. When he came from Ontario (Chaffey), Corney inquired, "How did you do?"

"I got one second, and two thirds, good enough, right?" asked his son.

"No, not good enough. Admirable, but not good enough — never settle for second place, that's a loser's game," came the reply.

The family once watched a Memorial Day parade in Riverside, and each band, marching unit, and drill team had its own American flag. As each passed, people would stand, with men and boys uncovering. A man standing in front of the Smith family did neither. Corney tapped him gently on the shoulder and firmly directed, "Remove your hat, Sir, when the flag passes by."

The man gave him a sullen look but said nothing. When he failed to uncover for the next flag, Corney reached over and flipped his hat to the ground. The man wheeled in anger and looked into flashing, piercing eyes. He turned, picked up his hat and held it in his hand.

Corney Smith lived in an era when law and order were relatively stable behavioral elements. In his own way, he helped to achieve these ends. He firmly believed that citizens owed allegiance to their country and you did your very best, all of the time. You neither lied, stole nor cheated, and you did not curse around women, children or the elderly. You were considerate of people and kind to animals.

Yet Corney was no plaster saint. In male company he could tell a good ribald story and loved to gamble. Unfortunately, he was a terrible poker player, staying on for the draw to hit inside straights, three-card flushes, and the like. He had a temper and lost it frequently. But he was quick to forgive and never held a grudge. He remained adamant in the face of meanness or dishonesty but in the face of contrition was forgiving in the extreme. He could roundly damn a scoundrel, and he could have tears in his eyes at one of Alice's songs. He could chastise the boys in the family and keep their love and respect.

He was forever giving or lending money to those in need and forever writing letters of recommendation for young men seeking work. He was scrupulously honest and direct in his business dealings. He was also naive. Shady businessmen operating within the letter rather than the spirit of the law always amazed him. He was almost always broke, yet his bills were always paid and his family comfortable. In retirement, he constantly thought up some scheme to make money, but his direct, practical, soldierly ways made any such plan inoperable.

He was a scholarly man, writing much of the time and reading the rest. People looking at the books in his library were amazed at the range of his interests. Long pages of annotations and cross-references filled such tomes as Brehm's *The Animals of the World*, Gould's *The Tragedy of the Caesars*, Caesar's *Commentaries*, *The Dialogues of Plato*, and Mahan's *The Influence of Sea Power upon History*. Also annotated were the works of Rousseau, Locke, Hume, Kant, Shakespeare, Hugo, Descartes and Clausewitz. Last, and by no means least, was his abiding interest in the *Holy Bible*. He did not read it now and then but referred to it frequently.

In the summer of 1935 Corney suffered a stroke. He was down for several weeks and then began a slow climb back to health. He was not feeble and did not have to use a cane, but the old spring and zest were gone. His face partially paralyzed, he was reduced to eating things like oatmeal and milk toast which he called "pap." He continued to write, but spent less and less time at his old oak desk in the den. The months passed, and while he got no worse, neither did he improve.

On the evening of Friday, January 10, 1936, Corney Smith quietly died. With him at the last were Kathleen, Alice and Monsignor Peter Lynch of St. Francis de Sales Church in Riverside. A service was held at St. Francis de Sales. The church was filled to capacity. Additional mourners stood in the narthex while others occupied the forecourt and the sidewalk outside. People came from miles around — Hollywood, Los Angeles, San Diego and even from as far away as San Francisco and Washington, D.C.

Corney was laid to rest in Evergreen Cemetery. A firing squad from March Field offered the traditional three volleys and an erect bugler sounded taps flawlessly. Corney would have approved the precision of this sharp ceremonial team.

Letters of condolence poured in from all over the country. Generals John J. Pershing, Malin Craig, G.W. McIver, plus other active and retired officers expressed their sympathy. Pershing wrote: "You can be proud of Corney's record. I recall particularly his splendid services in Mindanao in the early days. Throughout his entire career he served the Army and the nation loyally and efficiently."

Corney's editors conveyed their sorrow and praised his scholarly approach to writing and his honesty. He had lived his life with an enthusiasm and intensity of purpose which had impressed others.

In reading Bulwer-Lytton, Corney had underscored these words: "Nothing is so contagious as enthusiasm; it moves stones, it charms brutes. Enthusiasm is the genius of sincerity, and truth accomplishes no victories without it."

That passage could have been his epitaph.

Bibliography

Any biography derives its strength in large part from the primary source material available to the author. The diaries, reminiscences or letters that the subject bequeaths future generations constitute the essential well from which biographers draw their basic information. Many fine studies remain unwritten or have been abandoned because researchers were not able to unearth that ground spring needed to sustain further effort.

The reconstruction of the career of Cornelius C. Smith, however, has not suffered from a dearth of primary sources. Indeed, the abundance of firsthand information in possession of the author makes the usual bibliographic listing unnecessary. Instead, the following study citing those works of particular importance indicates the scope and depth of Corney Smith's personal papers, which he compiled with the same meticulous dedication that distinguished his military career.

Perhaps the best contributions of this habitual chronicler are the detail and color with which he recalled his tours in the Philippines. In a number of unpublished reminiscences such as "Moro Trickery," "A Monkey-Eating Expedition," "An Expedition into Mindanao, 1904," "The Operations of the Provisional Troop, Fourteenth Cavalry, in the Datu Ali Campaign of 1904-05" and "Amai Detsan of Raman," Smith presents with unusual vividness his campaigns against the Moro tribesmen. These often day-by-day entries provide graphic descriptions of the appearance, customs and savagery of this island people against whom the United States Army waged one of its most tenacious campaigns. Other notations in "The Last Indian War," "Field Notes, Walsenburg," "Reminiscenses of the Border," "Colombian Diary" and "Cloak and Dagger in the Caribbean" provide equally fascinating insights into other phases of his military career. These ten accounts, plus a number of unpublished manuscripts, are the primary sources from which this study was prepared.

As if his diaries were not a sufficient boon to posterity, in his constant efforts to compile an exact record of his exploits, Smith wrote nearly sixteen unpublished manuscripts which elaborated upon or filled in gaps in his other reminiscences. In the usually difficult task of piecing together the subject's early life in the absence of letters or other professional communiques, the author was particularly fortunate to have Smith's "Reminiscences in Tucson" and "Arizona Chronicles." A three-part "Philippine Diary" added a finishing touch to other accounts of those exciting years. Finally, "Scheme for Instruction of a Cavalry Regiment," "The Army in the Southwest," "Mexican Border Troubles, 1912-1914" and "Nicaragua and the Electoral Mission of 1928" provided the basis for chapter material and organization.

A third sort of primary source, not exclusively in the possession of the author, includes telegrams, official records and newspapers. The messages and reports of Corney Smith and his associates provided much of the specific details needed to chronicle the soldier's widespread assignments. Newspapers, especially the *Denver Post,* added descriptive material concerning many of his voyages, stations and duties.

Any author trying to recreate a man and his era cannot confine his research to any single body of papers—regardless of its comprehensiveness. He must refer to numerous articles and books to substantiate certain points, elaborate others and insure a well-balanced study. To mention only a few of these sources would necessitate serious omissions but to cite them all would tax both author and reader. Nonetheless, certain monographs must be noted.

John G. Bourke, *On the Border with Crook* (1892), J. Ross Browne, *Adventures in Apache Country* (1869) and Cornelius C. Smith, Jr., *William Sanders Oury, History-Maker of the Southwest* (1967) highlight the frontier conditions which nurtured young Corney Smith. The Indian troubles leading to a young corporal's winning the Congressional Medal of Honor can be found in Fairfax Downey, *Indian-Fighting Army* (1941), John K. Herr and Edward S. Wallace, *The Story of the U.S. Cavalry, 1775-1942* and Nelson A. Miles, *Personal Recollections,* (1896). To supplement Corney

Smith's writings on the Philippines, see: Garel A. Grunder, *The Philippines and the United States* (1951) and Mrs. Campbell Dauncey, *The Philippines: An Account of their People, Progress and Condition* (1910). In E.L.N. Glass, *The History of the Tenth Cavalry, 1866-1921* (1921), Isaac J. Cox, *Nicaragua and the United States, 1909-1927* (1929) and Cornelius C. Smith, Jr., *Emilio Kosterlitzky: Eagle of Sonora and the Southwest Border,* (1970) information on the soldier's later life unfolds. While these primary and secondary sources provided the substance for the biography, the author remains indebted to the subject for the inspiration that made the search both enjoyable and rewarding.

Index

Index

Index

Index

Wright, E.S., 28
Wurtzel, Sol, 173

Yaguanbo (River), 38
Yates, "Hoss," 28
Yosemite National Park, 105
Ynoch's Market, 79

Yznaga, Carlos, 40

Zamboanga, 52, 55, 57, 92, 93, 110
Zamorro, 141
Zavala, Horacio, 178, 183
Zeckendorff, William, 8
Zelaya, José, 180